THE PEACETIME ARMY, 1900–1941

D0169105

Recent Titles in
Research Guides in Military Studies
Series Adviser: Roger J. Spiller

The Peacetime Army, 1900-1941: A Research Guide
Marvin Fletcher

Special Operations and Elite Units, 1939-1988: A Research Guide
Roger Beaumont

THE PEACETIME ARMY, 1900–1941

A RESEARCH GUIDE

MARVIN FLETCHER

RESEARCH GUIDES IN MILITARY STUDIES, NUMBER 1

GREENWOOD PRESS
NEW YORK • WESTPORT, CONNECTICUT • LONDON

Library of Congress Cataloging-in-Publication Data

Fletcher, Marvin.
    The peacetime army, 1900-1941 : a research guide / Marvin
Fletcher.
      p.   cm. — (Research guides in military studies, ISSN
0899-0166 ; no. 1)
    Bibliography: p.
    Includes index.
    ISBN 0-313-25987-9 (lib. bdg. : alk. paper)
    1. United States. Army—History—20th century—Sources—
Bibliography. I. Title. II. Series.
Z6725.U5F57 1988
[UA25]
016.355′00973—dc19   88-21433

British Library Cataloguing in Publication Data is available.

Library of Congress Catalog Card Number: 88-21433
ISBN: 0-313-25987-9
ISSN: 0899-0166

First published in 1988

Greenwood Press, Inc.
88 Post Road West, Westport, Connecticut 06881

Printed in the United States of America

♾️

The paper used in this book complies with the
Permanent Paper Standard issued by the National
Information Standards Organization (Z39.48-1984).

10 9 8 7 6 5 4 3 2 1

Contents

SERIES FOREWORD

"I hate wars," said the Russian archduke, "they spoil the armies." Comic though the duke's quip is, it nevertheless underscores the investment in time, thought, and treasure that modern nations have made in their standing armies. It emphasizes, too, how the division between war and peace, in modern times increasingly blurred, once separated and clearly demarcated an army's functions. Armies and the soldiers who constituted them were said to be at rest when in garrison between wars, and the government that officiated over their size, composition, and functions saw little use for them once the peace was made. As for society at large, the less seen of soldiers during peacetime, the better.

Those, at least, were the views that predominated in the United States during much of its history, despite a great deal of evidence to the contrary. From the beginning of its career, the American Army's history has been characterized by an ever more complex elaboration of its "peacetime" functions and, consequently, an ever greater degree of integration with a Republic founded upon an innate suspicion of all things military. If national conflict occasionally attenuated the uneasy relationship between state and army in America, declarations of peace and demobilization always signalled a return to the *status quo ante bellum*. Between the wars, the Army slowly articulated its peacetime role in continental expansion and modernization and just as slowly took its place as one of the nation's most important institutions.

On the eve of the twentieth century, as America began its "leap overseas," the Army was destined to become the nation's most important agency of imperial expansion. The emergence of an internationalist role for the Army has been the single most important factor in the evolution of the modern American Army, a factor whose influence extends to every facet of its character as an institution in peace as well as war.

The transformation of the American Army in this century is bounded by the years between the turn of the century and the beginning of the Second World War. This period is the subject of Marvin Fletcher's bibliographic investigations on *The Peacetime Army, 1900-1941*, the first of Greenwood Press' Research Guides in Military Studies. An explosion of scholarship in military studies over the past generation has produced a body of sophisticated work in history, political science, sociology, and many other fields. Military studies now incorporate a much broader and more sophisticated appreciation of armies and their role in society than ever before. Traditional approaches to the study of military affairs, still important, are now illuminated by studies that view military institutions within the larger context of their society. Professor Fletcher's own work on Blacks and the American Military is representative of the more catholic view of military affairs.

The Greenwood Research Guides in Military Studies are designed to subject major topics in this field to bibliographic examination, and to select and arrange scholarly works along lines suggested by the major divisions of the subject itself for the benefit of scholars, students, and research libraries. Each of the Guides is compiled and edited by a scholar already well recognized for his research in the subject under consideration, and consequently each will contain an extensive introductory essay that draws the major outlines of the subject, illuminates and comments upon abiding issues, and suggests profitable lines for future investigation. The result, we hope, will be a bibliographic series that aids and encourages future research in the general field of military studies.

Roger J. Spiller
U.S. Army Command and General Staff College
Fort Leavenworth, Kansas

Preface

This research guide focuses on the United States Army during an era of general peace, but of significant change.

MATERIALS INCLUDED

The basic criteria used in selecting an item for inclusion was that it be in English, not written as a first person account, and published since World War II, although there are exceptions to the latter.

The bibliography includes books; articles from scholarly, professional, and popular journals; and dissertations. If a dissertation was later published as a book, and the material seemed essentially the same, only the book was cited.

If the material included in an item spanned the two chronological periods it was included twice.

MATERIALS EXCLUDED

Items that dealt primarily with the Navy or the development of airpower were not included.

Materials that dealt primarily with the Spanish-American War or World War I were also excluded.

CHRONOLOGICAL LIMITS

The general chronological limits are 1900 to 1941, but there are exceptions. Because the Philippine-American War and the reforms led by Secretary of War Elihu Root began in 1899, some materials from that year are included. In the middle of time period encompassed by this bibliography is World War I. The events of that conflict are ignored, with the exception of the accounts of the American forces in North Russia and Siberia. These expeditions began at the end of the war but continued until 1920. The bibliography ends with the declaration of war against Japan in December 1941. A number of items, however, are included which deal primarily with the period of World War II, but have some material on the interwar period.

ORGANIZATIONAL STRUCTURE

The entries are organized into two chapters and sixteen topics. The first chapter covers the Army from 1900 to 1917, while the second goes from 1919 to 1941.

The topics:

1. General--This includes book-length histories of the Army or articles which survey the period.

2. Biography--Included in this section are accounts of the lives of individuals who served in the Army or the National Guard, or civilians who had a great influence on the military. The emphasis is on an overall view of the individual's career or on a specific event when the emphasis is on an individual. The item must have been written at least several years after the events described.

3. Conflicts--These are accounts of clashes between American troops [either Army or National Guard] and civilians in the United States or overseas. Among the topics included: the Philippine-American War and its aftermath, the 1914 occupation of Veracruz, the Mexican Punitive Expedition and its revolutionary context, the Boxer Rebellion, and the expeditions to Russia and Siberia.

4. Economic Issues--This includes the impact of the Army on the economy, the military-industrial complex, and economic planning by the military.

5. Education--Military education, either at West Point, the Army War College or other military schools, or at civilian institutions, both of a military and non-military nature is encompassed. This includes a discussion of ROTC and its development.

6. Engineers--The focus is on the Corps of Engineers and its activities [flood control, river navigation, harbor improvements, fortifications] on a local and regional level in the United States.

7. Logistics--The process of supplying troops with equipment and the organizations which handled this activity is covered in this section.

8. Management--Among the topics encompassed in this section are: the evolution of the General Staff; relations with the National Guard; and the connection between the military reforms, the progressive era, and managerial changes in the business sector.

9. Manpower--In the pre-World War I section the focus is on the preparedness movement, including who supported it and why, and the arguments over the nature of the reserve system. The interwar section includes material on post-World War I demobilization policies, recruiting, pre-war manpower planning, and the debate over selective service in 1940-41.

10. Miscellaneous--This section includes a variety of items that do not fit into other areas, such as information on Army uniforms, narrative histories of military bases, the military judicial system, accounts of the development of the chaplaincy, regimental histories, and unit lineages.

11. National Guard--This component of the American military grew in importance in this century. The bibliography includes a number of histories of state units as well as accounts of their utilization in domestic disturbances and national emergencies.

12. Overseas--The Army was stationed overseas in the Philippines, Mexico, and the Caribbean in non-conflict situations throughout the period covered by the bibliography. Items deal with civil government, construction of the Panama Canal, development of foreign policy, occupation and government of foreign territory, and relations with foreign nationals.

13. Political Issues--Among the items included: the general climate of opinion regarding the military and war itself, the attitudes of political leaders toward conflicts and the military, the development of pro- and anti-war movements, and Army officers in political situations.

14. Social Issues--The military has had a continuing influence on American society and vice versa. Topics covered include: backgrounds of soldiers and officers, interaction between civilian and military communities, the military and the process of acculturation, race related issues, and the Bonus March.

15. Strategy--During peace the Army has prepared for war. The kind of plans they made reflect their perception of the world and the nature of war. Subjects included in this section: the roles of individual branches of the Army, war plans, maneuvers, inter-service cooperation.

16. Technology--The period covered by this bibliography was an era of tremendous technological innovations, most of which impacted on the military. Materials in this section cover such topics as: the machine gun, the internal combustion engine, the organization and utilization of new weapons by the Army, and the evolution of artillery.

SAMPLE BOOK ENTRY

1   2   3   4

1. Millett, Allan R., and Maslowski, Peter. (1984). *For the Common Defense: A Military History of the United States of America*. New York: The Free Press, 621 pp.   5

6   7

8

About fifty pages of this excellent survey describes the events which followed the end of the Spanish-American War in both the Army and the Navy. A very useful bibliography. Primary and secondary sources.

9

1. Item number
2. Author(s)
3. Year of publication
4. Title of book
5. Place of publication
6. Publisher
7. Number of pages (or specific pages referred to)
8. Annotation
9. Types of sources used

SAMPLE DISSERTATION ENTRIES

1   2   3   4

2. Johnson, Elliott L. (1975). "The Military Experiences of General Hugh A. Drum from 1898-1918." Dissertation, University of Wisconsin-Madison, 36/7-A, pp. 4674-75.   5

                  6   7

8

The author suggests that Drum was a representative of a new kind of Army officer, a staff officer. A significant phase of Drum's career was his time at the Army School of the Line as a student and teacher. This prepared Drum for his duty as Chief of Staff of the First Army in World War I.

1. Item number
2. Author
3. Date degree granted
4. Title of dissertation
5. University granting degree
6. Volume and issue of *Dissertation Abstracts* where abstract is found
7. Pages of abstract
8. Annotation

1   2   3   4
3. Franklin, Ben G. (1943). "The Military Policy of the United States, 1918-
1933: A Study of the Influence of World War I on Army Organization and
Control." Dissertation, University of California, Berkeley. Doctoral
                                        5
Dissertations Accepted by American Universities, 1942-1943, p. 78.
              6   7
     8
     Three aspects of interwar policy are examined: the national guard and its
upgrade to the second line of defense; the general staff and its power,
especially over supply and industrial mobilization; and the problem of
manpower mobilization planning. The author explains how the lessons of
World War I were applied.

1. Item number
2. Author
3. Year of dissertation
4. Title of dissertation
5. University granting degree
6. Source of listing and year
7. Page of listing
8. Annotation

SAMPLE GOVERNMENT DOCUMENT ENTRY

1   2   3   4
4. Moore, Jamie W. (1981). *The Lowcountry Engineers; Military Missions and
Economic Development in the Charleston District, U. S. Army Corps of
Engineers*. Charleston, South Carolina: U. S. Army Corps of Engineers,
                        5   6
Charleston District, 140 pp. SD D103.2:L95.
                      7   8
     9
     A brief history of the Engineers and their activities in this region including
harbor improvements, coastal fortifications, and construction of part of the
Intercoastal Waterway. Primary and secondary sources.
                                        10

1. Item number
2. Author(s)
3. Year of publication
4. Title of book
5. Place of publication
6. Publisher
7. Number of pages (or of specific pages referred to)
8. Superintendent of Documents catalog number
9. Annotation
10. Types of sources used

SAMPLE ARTICLE ENTRY

1   2   3   4
5. Watson, Mark S. (1948). "First Vigorous Steps in Re-Arming, 1938-39."
Military Affairs, 12, 65-78.
       5   6   7

    8
    This article is taken from Watson's book on the Chief of Staff in World
War II. Primary sources.
                9

1. Item number
2. Author(s)
3. Year of publication
4. Title of article
5. Name of journal
6. Volume number
7. Inclusive pagination
8. Annotation
9. Types of sources used

Acknowledgements

This project could not have been accomplished without the assistance of a number of individuals.

I began my bibliographic work at the Ohio University Library. Many librarians at this institution were of great assistance to me in searching out a variety of obscure titles or finding items throughout the country through inter-library loan.

I did further research at a number of collections. Uniformly the librarians were of great assistance and extended me every courtesy. The library of the U. S. Army Military History Institute at Carlisle Barracks, Pennsylvania, and The University of California, Berkeley, especially the Bancroft Library, were also of great help in the first stages of this project.

I would also like to thank the Ohio University Computer Center for the use of their computer facilities to create the index for this project.

I hope that this work is of assistance to students of this fascinating period. Much has already been done, but my study has revealed many topics that still need to be studied or reexamined.

Marvin Fletcher
Athens, Ohio

CHRONOLOGY

1898
25 April - United States declares war on Spain

1 May - Dewey defeats Spanish fleet in Manila

1 July - Battle at El Caney and San Juan, Cuba
25   - Occupation of Puerto Rico is begun

13 August - Manila surrenders to the Army

10 December - Treaty of Paris is signed ending the war

1899
February - Philippine-American War begins

2 March - Congress authorizes volunteers to suppress Philippine-American
          War

April - First radio operations of Army Signal Corps between Fire Island and
        Fire Island Lightship

19 July - Secretary of War Russell Alger resigns under fire

1 August - Elihu Root appointed Secretary of War by President McKinley

December - Elihu Root's first report details problems of the Army

1900
20 June - Boxer revolt begins in Peking

14 August - International force rescues foreign missions in Peking

September - Walter Reed, Army Medical Corps, discovers yellow fever virus
            transmitted by mosquito

1901

23 March - Emilio Aguinaldo, leader of Philippine forces, captured by Frederick Funston

27 November - Army War College created, Tasker H. Bliss, president

1902

20 May - US troops withdrawn from Cuba

4 July - Civil government established in Philippines

1903

21 January - Militia Act passed

14 February - General Staff Corps established

8 August - Commanding General Nelson A. Miles retired; Samuel Young becomes first Chief of Staff

18 November - US and Panama sign treaty creating Canal Zone

1904

1 February - Elihu Root resigns as Secretary of War

4 March - Record & Pension office merged under control of Adjutant General Fred C. Ainsworth

1906

18 April - San Francisco earthquake

13 August - Shooting affray in Brownsville, Texas

16 September - Pershing promoted from captain to brigadier general
29   - US troops sent to Cuba

1907

27 February - Corps of Engineers given task of completing Panama Canal construction

3 March - Appointment of Fred Ainsworth as Adjutant General confirmed by Senate

1910

22 April - Leonard Wood appointed Chief of Staff

1911
7 March - Mobilization of troops on Mexican border; creation of "Maneuver
        Division"

1912
February - Wood vs Ainsworth dispute reaches head with sharp response
        from Adjutant General to Wood's actions

1913
24 February - 2nd Division mobilized along Mexican border

10 October - Panama Canal opened for shipping

1914
20 April - Leonard Wood's term as Chief of Staff ends
        - Massacre of 21 people at Ludlow, Colorado, by Colorado National
          Guard
21   - Navy dispatched to Veracruz, occupation begins shortly thereafter

1 August - War begins in Europe

23 November - Occupation of Veracruz begins to end

December - National Security League created

1915
21 July - President Wilson asks Secretary of War for national defense
        proposals

10 August - Leonard Wood creates military training camp at Plattsburg, New
        York

1916
9 March - Newton D. Baker becomes Secretary of War
        Pancho Villa attacks Columbus, New Mexico
15   - Army Reorganization Act passes Congress
        - Pursuit of Villa begins commanded by John Pershing

9 May - Wilson orders mobilization along the Mexican border

3 June - National Defense Act of 1916 enacted
21   - Clash between Americans and Mexicans at
            Carrizal

1917
5 February - Punitive Expedition comes to an end as American troops return
        across the border

8 April - Congress declares war on Germany

1918
6 July - Decision made to send troops to North Russia and Siberia

1 September - William Graves arrives at Vladivostok as part of American
                forces in Siberia
4   - American troops arrive at Archangel in North Russia

11 November - War stops on the Western Front

1919
15 March - American Legion is formed by AEF veterans in Paris

27 June - American forces leave North Russia

1920
1 April - American forces leave Vladivostok

4 June - Congress passes National Defense Act of 1920

1921
12 March - First War Department Radio Net established with control station
              in Washington, D.C.

1 July - John Pershing becomes Chief of Staff

1923
10 January - Last American troops leave Germany

1928
15 May - Congress passes Flood Control Act

27 August - Fourteen nations sign Kellogg-Briand Treaty outlawing war

1930
21 November - Douglas MacArthur becomes Chief of Staff

1932
28 January - Japanese troops land at Shanghai

28-29 July - Bonus marchers driven out of Washington by Army

1933
31 March - Congress passes the law which creates Civilian Conservation
              Corps

1934
12 April - Nye Committee to investigate munitions trade is established

15 June - National Guard Act passed making the NG part of the Army in
time of war

16 July - Longshoreman's strike in San Francisco

3 December - Supreme Court upholds right of land grant colleges to require
ROTC.

1937
18 May - First Army radar set successfully demonstrated at Fort Monmouth,
New Jersey

1938
10 January - Ludlow war referendum amendment effectively defeated in
Congress

1939
1 September - War begins in Europe as Germany invades Poland
George Marshall becomes Chief of Staff

1940
April - Corps maneuvers in the South

May - Division maneuvers in South
- German invasions of Belgium, Netherlands, France

10 July - Henry Stimson becomes Secretary of War

18 August - US and Canada set up Joint Board of Defense

16 September - First peacetime draft goes into effect

28 October - Benjamin O. Davis appointed Brigadier General

1941
27 January - Staff talks begin between US and Great Britain

26 July - Philippine forces nationalized and MacArthur appointed
commander

18 August - Roosevelt signs bill extending Selective Service

7 December - Japan attacks Pearl Harbor

THE PEACETIME ARMY,
1900–1941

Introduction

The first forty-one years of the twentieth century were predominantly peaceful but not uneventful. Shaken out of its lethargy by the Spanish-American War and its aftermath, the acquisition of the new colonial empire did not allow the Army to fall back into old patterns and practices of behavior in peacetime. It could not go back to the relative isolation of the frontier constabulary. The managerial and technological revolutions which occurred in the industrial sector also had an impact. In the years after World War I change continued, propelled by these forces, the rise of expansionistic dictatorships overseas, and economic problems unleashed by the Depression. The Army that entered World War II in December 1941 was quite different than that which had defeated the Spanish only forty-two years earlier.

The Spanish-American War changed the American Army. The flaws in the structure were exposed and had to be remedied. Although some individuals, such as William T. Sherman, had already made suggestions for changes, they had been ignored. This was no longer possible. The system of command which had been in place since the time of Secretary of War John C. Calhoun had not worked effectively in the recent war. Secretary of War Russell Alger had failed to provide the necessary leadership which the inefficient managerial plan then in effect demanded. The highest ranking military officer, the Commanding General Nelson A. Miles, was more concerned about politics than leadership. The chiefs of the various bureaus, such as the Adjutant General or Quartermaster General, had shown that they were not really prepared for war, at least as it was shaped by Congress and the President. No line officer had any real command experience and few had the skill to coordinate an overseas expedition or occupation force. The revived militia, the National Guard, had been willing to serve, on its own terms, but was not well trained or equipped to perform in combat.

In 1899 President William McKinley appointed Elihu Root, a lawyer, as the new Secretary of War and gave him a mandate to improve the Army. After studying the existing situation and consulting with a number of officers, Root laid out his proposals in his December 1899 report to Congress. During the next four years he began to put into execution a number of those ideas.

One of the first problems that Root tried to resolve was the inefficiencies of the command structure. Other than the Secretary of War, no one was in complete control. The commanding general really commanded no one. The individual bureaus had developed independent fiefdoms. The various combat arms operated without any real direction. Finding that this system was not very effective, impressed with the German model, and supported by the rediscovered writings of Emory Upton, Root put into effect a number of changes. He got Congress to agree to abolish the position of commanding general and replace it with a chief of staff. The exact functions of this position were unclear, however, and would not be defined for quite a while. To assist the chief of staff Root created a staff system and the Army War College. It quickly became apparent that neither the staff nor the bureaus knew whether this new element was to be involved with the daily routine of the service or to be limited to overall decisions and plans for the future. The bureau chiefs, especially the Adjutant General, resisted any intrusion on their turf. The fight simmered until 1912 when Chief of Staff Leonard Wood locked horns with Adjutant General Fred C. Ainsworth in a conflict over paperwork. With the support of Secretary of War Henry Stimson, Wood was successful in exerting his authority over Ainsworth. By World War I it was clear that the chief of staff was the ultimate military authority. What was still unclear was whether the staff should be involved more in the daily routine or in the long-range planning. These managerial changes paralleled those occurring in the business sector as more attention was being given to the efficient operation of an enterprise.

Root also was disturbed about the lack of continuing education for both officers and enlisted men. Building on reforms begun earlier, Root began a wide ranging program. No longer would officers stop their learning with graduation from the Military Academy. Post schools were created and a program of military education was devised for the entire service. As a second level of instruction, Root expanded and revised the program of the existing Infantry and Cavalry School located at Fort Leavenworth, Kansas. Recognizing that his new staff system needed officers with the proper training, he authorized the establishment of the Army Staff College. Under the leadership of John F. Morrison, officers were trained in the art of war and began to find positions in the managerial system Root had established. Root then created the Army War College as the capstone of the education program. Here officers prepared for work as staff planners and assisted the General Staff. Slowly it became clear that success as an officer required attendance at these two institutions.

Another issue that Root faced was the need for a workable reserve system. Two different traditions were available for Root to follow. Many Army officers, embracing the ideas enunciated by Upton, firmly believed that professional soldiers, trained and controlled on the federal level, were the only true basis for a reserve force. They dismissed the militia/national guard as a weak reed. On the other hand, there were a few officers and many civilians who firmly believed that the National Guard must form the real manpower pool for the nation. To them professional soldiers seemed undemocratic and European. Given the performance of the National Guard in the recently concluded war, however, Root realized that the status quo and bickering had to end. He understood that the Uptonian concepts were politically unfeasible and possibly unnecessary in an America distant from European challengers. Working with Congress resulted in the passage of the Militia Act of 1903, which began to change the relationship between the National Guard and the Army. In return for federal funds, the Guard agreed to follow Army patterns in training and equipment and to attend summer encampments and joint maneuvers. Over the next few years further legislation made clearer the commitment of the Guard to serve overseas in times of crisis. The manpower issue was not settled, for many officers clung to the Uptonian approach. In 1915 the staff made suggestions for an expansion of the Army. The key was a Continental Army, a federally raised reserve force, relegating the National Guard to the third line of defense. After an intense political battle, the National Guard was able to retain its second-line status, and the Continental Army concept was rejected. Some officers, such as John McAuley Palmer, began to believe that this was the proper solution to the manpower issue. These officers felt that citizen-soldiers could be rapidly trained and should be accepted as the basis for the reserve. This debate over the nature of the reserve force was not to be settled until after World War I.

The reforms initiated by Elihu Root began to transform the Army into a more modern, effectively organized force which was able to perform a variety of tasks, usually efficiently. One continuing role was that of policeman. Instead of dealing with Native Americans, as they had done before 1898, they were called upon to perform this task in a variety of foreign arenas. Though nominally a period of peace, soldiers still died in combat. The Philippine-American War raged for several years. Even after Frederick Funston managed, in 1901, to capture rebellion leader Emilio Aguinaldo, the revolt simmered on. The military government was replaced by civilian rule, and the police functions were taken up by a variety of Philippine groups, including the Philippine Scouts, organized on the Army model and officered by some US Army personnel. In 1901 American forces were involved in rescuing foreign legations attacked in China during the Boxer Rebellion. After it was over, the Fifteenth Infantry, along with some Marines, remained as a protector of American business interests in China. Army garrisons could also be found elsewhere in the Pacific and the Caribbean.

American relations with Mexico often involved the Army. In addition to their long-standing task of protecting the border against Indian and bandit incursions, American troops twice entered Mexican territory for extended periods. In 1914 American naval forces captured Veracruz, but the Army was placed in charge during the ensuing period of occupation. On a larger scale, an expedition under the command of John J. Pershing went deep into Mexico in an effort to capture Pancho Villa after Villa's raid on the border town of Columbus, New Mexico. When the Punitive Expedition ended in early 1917, its commander had demonstrated great ability, the troops had reached a new level of readiness, and Villa's band was broken up.

In other situations officers were called upon to exercise civil authority. In Cuba they helped reconstruct the war-torn nation during the two periods of occupation. In Panama occupation involved even more. The Army, especially through the Corps of Engineers, was given the task of finishing the canal. To achieve this goal William Gorgas and George W. Goethals had to conquer a variety of physical and medical problems. The Corps of Engineers' work was crowned with success in 1914 when the Panama Canal was opened to traffic. Subsequently the Army garrisoned the Canal Zone.

At home the Corps of Engineers began to expand on the tasks that they had begun to assume in the late nineteenth century. From building military related projects, such as coastal fortifications and harbor defenses, the Army became involved in a variety of civilian projects, such as harbor improvements, river navigation hazard removal, and flood control programs. As the century continued, civilian projects became more significant than military ones.

In a variety of instances the Army and the National Guard served the states as auxiliary police. In a number of labor disputes the National Guard was employed as strike breakers, though not to the extent that they had in the previous century. The most notorious incident occurred in a coal strike in Colorado in 1913. The Colorado National Guard effectively broke the strike when they intervened and killed a number of miners. This use of military power generated tremendous hostility from the working class elements of society. On the other hand, the Army helped to stabilize the situation in earthquake-torn San Francisco and provided a strong measure of discipline, along with the California National Guard, to prevent looting and reestablish some measure of order.

For black soldiers the improvements in the Army, such as expanded education and world travel, continued to make this an attractive career choice, but problems were equally significant. Segregation continued. Their numbers within the Army remained the same while the total force slowly expanded. On several occasions there were conflicts between black soldiers and white civilians. The Army did not try to understand the racial hostility that generated the problems, but reacted strongly to any attempts by blacks to challenge the status quo. The most notorious of these incidents occurred in Brownsville, Texas, in 1906. Black soldiers from the garrison supposedly rampaged through town, fired at a number of civilians, and killed one individual. After a perfunctory investigation, President Theodore Roosevelt ordered the discharge without honor of all the blacks. Despite cries of unfairness from blacks and some whites, Roosevelt stuck firmly to his position. Not until many years later was some partial justice accorded these individuals.

Several key inventions slowly began to have an impact on the Army. The internal combustion engine had its first effect when it was applied to the movement of equipment and supplies. Reluctantly the Army began to use trucks, though their unreliability, especially over rough terrain, made their use problematic. This was illustrated during the 1916 Mexican campaign. The trucks' utility were limited by the inadequate Mexican road system and frequent breakdowns. Other innovations, such as machine guns, were slowly adopted by the Army. Monetary considerations and technological conservatism were significant factors in retarding this process.

Americans, when they thought about the Army at all, were positive about it. The successful completion of the Panama Canal, the crushing of the Filipino resistance, the assistance rendered to the earthquake victims in San Francisco, all provided a good image. For the upper class, they felt that it provided a possible support in times of economic stress, such as during labor disputes. Others felt that it could help Americanize the growing immigrant hordes.

On the other hand there was a growing anti-war movement. Some of its adherents sought world peace, but more were concerned about achieving peace through arbitration treaties. Many influential Americans lent their backing to this crusade. A number of women included world peace in their agenda for reform. After the war started in Europe in 1914, most Americans wanted to remain out of the conflict, but did not support the anti-militarists. On the other hand, only a few supported the efforts of military leaders, such as Leonard Wood, and their civilian supporters, including Grenville Clark, to encourage military training, like that conducted at Plattsburg, New York. Woodrow Wilson won reelection in 1916 on a platform committed to neutrality and a minimal level of preparedness. The pre-war support for pacifism and arbitration treaties seemed to be waning.

When the United States entered World War I in April 1917, the American Army was a much different institution from that which had emerged from the Spanish-American War eighteen years earlier. The managerial revolution had created a structure which could plan and organize for the increase in manpower which the war brought. A number of officers had the skills to do that planning and to command the vast number of men that began to be drafted. The Army and the National Guard had reached a level of preparedness that had never been seen before. On the other hand, all was not perfect. Only a few modest efforts had been made to harness the new technology to warfare. Little thought had been given to industrial preparedness or how to train the vast influx of civilian soldiers. There were deep divisions on how and from where to obtain the manpower needed. Progress had been made, but much still needed to be done, as the ensuing war was to demonstrate.

When the war ended in 1918, the Army looked confidently to the future. They had helped to conquer a mighty enemy. The staff reforms had provided a firm basis for an efficient command structure both in Washington and in France. The graduates of the Command and General Staff school had proven themselves in the field. The Army hoped to build on this basis during the expected post-war restructuring and shrinkage.

The first topic that Congress tackled was the old one of manpower. After previous conflicts, the Army was reduced to its pre-war size. The General Staff decided that this time a large regular Army was still necessary, and drafted plans to retain a large number of soldiers. These proposals were submitted to Congress. A number of Congressmen could not see the necessity for such a large force, given their feeling that there were no immediate threats to the United States and the antipathy to peacetime military expenditures. In addition, many members of Congress felt that the war had proven that citizens could rapidly be trained to become soldiers and that thus there was no need for a large standing army. The supporters of this position found a knowledgeable advocate in John McAuley Palmer, who felt that the war had demonstrated the utility of the citizen-soldier and the futility of clinging to the old Uptonian ideas. He was instrumental in creating the landmark piece of legislation which shaped the post-war Army, the National Defense Act of 1920. The new law authorized a regular Army of 280,000 [about half of what the staff had originally requested]. The reserve was to be made up of the National Guard and an Organized Reserve, both composed of citizen-soldiers. In addition, the law authorized a variety of programs, such as the Reserve Officers Training Corps, to train prospective officers at civilian institutions.

There were other significant provisions in the new law. The legal system of the Army finally began to be modified. Samuel Ansell, a member of the Judge Advocate General's Corps, had criticized the existing system as one which did not provide enough protection for the rights of the soldiers. Despite the opposition of Enoch Crowder, The Judge Advocate General, some changes were made in the Army Regulation's provisions for courts martial. Much remained to be done, and the process would continue after World War II.

The 1920 Act also codified the central role of the staff and established it as the planning center of the Army. Several new branches, on a level with traditionals such as Infantry and Cavalry, were created such as the Chemical Warfare Service and the Finance Department. On the whole, the act merged the Root reforms with the modifications that experience, especially World War I, had made necessary.

In the post-war period the manpower goals established in 1920 proved to be unachievable. Congress did not provide enough money for the Army to recruit the authorized limits: the Army grew smaller and smaller. Not until the period of the Depression would recruiting increase, but the Army still remained small. Not until the latter half of the 1930s did Congress authorize the expansion of the Army. By 1940 it had finally surpassed its 1921 peak.

While the Army shrank in size, it did undertake planning for future conflicts. There were direct discussions with the Navy Department on possible war scenarios. Despite the naval disarmament treaties of 1921 which included a treaty establishing the status quo in the Pacific, the most significant plan was that code named ORANGE, a possible war with Japan. While this plan envisioned a major role for the Navy, the Army was supposed to fight its way across the Pacific to relieve the embattled Philippine garrison. However, little was done to prepare a force capable of carrying out this plan.

Industrial mobilization planning also began in the 1920s. World War I had demonstrated that channeling industrial production was a crucial element in winning a war. The planners envisioned a structure coordinated by a joint civilian-military board similar to the War Industries Board of 1917-1918. This plan was revised and expanded throughout the interwar period. The goal was to provide material for another expeditionary force sent to Europe. The resulting war plan is an illustration of how the different sets of planners failed to coordinate their efforts and how they aimed at improving, but not deviating from, past experiences.

In the interwar period the National Guard gained in esteem. Officers continued to serve on the staff and Army officers were detailed as instructors. However, the Guard had problems meeting its share of the manpower program for the same reasons that the Army itself had. Conditions did not improve during the Depression as states found it hard to supplement decreasing federal allocations. In the 1930s legislation clearly defined the role of the Guard as the major reserve force, able to serve overseas at the order of the President and, as the police force for the state governments, ready to provide stability in situations when the local law enforcement officers were unable to do so. Several times during this period the Guard performed such duties. Probably the most extensive occurred as a result of a longshoremen's strike in San Francisco in 1934. The city was in turmoil, and the California National Guard was sent in to restore calm.

The educational programs of the Army grew in size and stature in the interwar period. The success of the Command and General Staff school graduates in France made it evident that this was a necessary stop on a career path. About three-quarters of all Army generals of the period followed this route. In addition, and as an adjunct to industrial planning, in 1923 the Army established the Army Industrial College. At this school officers learned the essentials of economic mobilization planning and how to utilize the industrial resources in a war situation. Later the program expanded to take in officers from the Navy.

The two different traditional American strategies continued to compete in the minds of the planners and for scarce resources. The Indian War tradition of a small, mobile police force fit in nicely with the small size of the Army and with the mobility made possible by mechanization. On the other hand, the World War I experience as well as manpower, strategic, and industrial planning all envisioned a large, powerful army in which mechanization would add strength and firepower.

The internal combustion engine had played a role in World War I and figured in the planning for the next war. One use was to provide mobility, in terms of trucks and personnel carriers, to strengthen the infantry division. In addition, light tanks were developed by such individuals as Walter Christie, which had speed, but little armor or firepower. This was to be seen in the

Seventh Cavalry Brigade (Mechanized) under the command of Adna R. Chaffee, Jr. At the same time there was only passing interest in the idea of mechanized power through the development of a heavy tank. As a result of these innovations, by World War II the Army had the prototype for a mobile, mechanized division, whose tanks had speed but little firepower. This concentration on speed as opposed to mechanized power would create problems when the Army attempted to carry out the strategic concept of the application of massed power in the effort to defeat Germany.

The racial situation remained much the same in the interwar period. The Army continued its four segregated regiments, though the cavalry units were really relegated to servant roles. The black officer corps fluctuated from a high of three to a low of one. In 1936 Benjamin O. Davis, Jr., graduated from West Point, the first black to do so since Charles Young in 1889. However, his request to enter flying training was denied because blacks were not permitted in that branch. The Army's plans for wartime manpower expansion envisioned blacks in labor but not in combat roles. Increasing black agitation for change only made the Army more defensive. Some of these issues would come to a head as the Army began to expand in 1940.

A significant aspect of this era was the public attitude toward the military. Most Americans abandoned their enthusiasm for war with the end of the conflict in Europe. Soon they became cynical about war and the military. One of the early manifestations of this was in public culture, both on the stage and the new cinema. In 1924 "What Price Glory" scored a great hit with its realistic portrayal of war and the inanities of conflict. Its subsequent movie versions transmitted these ideas to a receptive public. As Europe and Asia drifted toward war in the 1930s, Americans became further convinced that involvement would bring no good result. This feeling was manifested in a resurgence of the anti-war and peace movements, especially on the college campuses. The continuation of compulsory military training at land grant institutions was one focus for this hostility. The Army responded with some attempts to infiltrate the movement. Another forum for this feeling was the investigatory hearings conducted by a Senate committee headed by Gerald Nye. The thesis they espoused, and many accepted, was that the previous war had been brought about by the "merchants of death," capitalists who had an investment in Europe and maneuvered the United States into the war to protect their profits. The Neutrality Acts of 1935, 1936, and 1937 represent attempts by Congress to prevent this sequence of events from occurring again. There was also an attempt to require a referendum before a declaration of war could go into effect. However by the end of the decade popular opinion began to move in the other direction, toward rearmament, but not involvement in Europe.

The rearmament process came at the end of a decade of the Depression which affected the Army in a variety of ways. Most directly, the worsening economic conditions made military service attractive again; recruiters were able to choose from a better quality of enlistees. On the other hand, there was little federal money to be allocated to the services, and little was done in terms of weapons development or manpower expansion. During the depths of the economic catastrophe, in 1932, the Army was involved in an incident in Washington which hurt their reputation for a long time. A number of veterans had gathered in the capitol to lobby for the passage of a bill which would pay them their bonus, one which was not due to be paid until 1945. A few government officials, especially Chief of Staff Douglas MacArthur, believed that these veterans were part of a communist conspiracy to overthrow the existing government. Congress, at the urging of

President Herbert Hoover, did not pass the bill. There was some discontent, which MacArthur seized upon as an excuse to call out some troops to drive the veterans from Washington and burn down their shacks.

Not until the end of the decade did President Franklin Roosevelt begin to think of rearmament. Most of the money he succeeded in obtaining from Congress went to the Navy and the growing Air Force. Not until the war began in Europe did military expansion begin in earnest. In 1940, with the collapse of France, Belgium, Norway, and the Netherlands, the situation became grim. A number of concerned citizens, including Grenville Clark, former preparedness leader, and John McAuley Palmer, proposed the institution of a peacetime draft. One issue in the debate was whether blacks would be drafted in proportion to their percentage in the population. Despite misgivings from the War Department as to what they were going to do with all of the black personnel, Congress included a clause preventing discrimination in the drafting of individuals. This provision, along with the entire Selective Service proposal, passed in September 1940. Shortly thereafter the first draft call was issued.

During the months remaining before the United States entered the war, expansion continued. There were large scale maneuvers involving many thousands of soldiers and much new equipment. Defects soon became apparent, and changes were attempted, especially in light of the European experience of 1940. In September 1941 the Selective Service Act was renewed, but only by a one vote majority in the House of Representatives. Chief of Staff George Marshall made the staff the focus of planning and began discussions with Great Britain. When the United States actually declared war on Japan, it was much better prepared for a conflict than it had been in 1898 or even 1917.

During the preceding forty-one years of peace the Army had been transformed from an inefficient, disorganized poorly armed Indian constabulary to an efficient, organized partially armed force with the potential for rapid expansion and the utilization of industrial resources. The period of peace had seen tremendous changes generated by internal and external forces. The new Army could channel the vast resources of the nation for a period of total war.

RESEARCH IDEAS

Although a great deal of recent research has been done on the peacetime Army, many topics still remain untouched or have only been explored superficially. A perusal of the bibliography will give the reader some idea of what has been accomplished. What follows are suggestions for what could be done in the future.

Scholars have already written biographies of the major leaders of the time, such as Wood, Root, MacArthur, Patton, Marshall, and Pershing, but a variety of other approaches to biography are still open. Collective profiles of different graduating classes of West Point might give some insight into the origins of these fledgling officers and whether these demographics changed during this century. The careers of National Guard leaders are virtually ignored by scholars and offer intriguing possibilities for comparison with the Regular Army. Another unexplored avenue, which could offer some interesting insights into the military as an avenue for social mobility, is research on the backgrounds of enlisted personnel. Similarly, one could investigate the changes in the enlisted force over time, as well as the impact of economic events on the Army. A study of some of the key innovators such as Reed, Gorgas, Goethals, Chaffee, would lend insight into the interrelationship between technology and science and the military.

Most of the major conflicts have been well researched by scholars, with the exception of the North Russia and Siberian expeditions. While there are many histories of the political and diplomatic aspects of these groups, little has been published of a scholarly nature on the military role these expeditions played.

While a great deal of research has been done on conflicts, the relationship between the military and the economy is now being considered. Scholars are investigating the origins of the military-industrial complex as well as the impact of the military on the American economy. Studies on the connections between military posts and nearby communities can provide many interesting insights. Those few that have already been done, such as the one on Fort Robinson, Nebraska, indicate what can be learned here. The ideas that shaped the industrial planning that was done in the 1920s and 1930s are also being investigated, but there is more to be learned. The way in which the military analyzed their experiences in World War I and then translated them into industrial planning and training for industrial mobilization also deserves more attention. A study of the curriculum of the

Army Industrial College and the composition of the student officers in the 1920s and 1930s should also provide interesting insights.

Military education is another topic which merits more research. One facet is the development of military training on college campuses. This would include examination of the type of courses taught, the discussion of whether or not it should be compulsory, and the reactions of students to the programs, especially during the 1930s when there was a broad-based student anti-war movement. More analysis of military education at West Point and the Command & General Staff School is clearly needed. The types of instruction, the subject matter, and the changes that were induced by outside reformers and the experiences of World War I, have heretofore been handled only superficially. Another aspect of this topic that merits further research would be military instruction at the small public and private schools. This is especially true of the black colleges which offered these programs throughout this century. Issues of who would do the instruction, how the local communities reacted to black military training, and what happened to their graduates deserve attention. Education within the Army has received limited recognition from scholars. Little is known about the educational programs after the era of the Root reforms. The content of the post-educational programs for officers and enlisted personnel would give some insight into what the Army thinks is important.

The engineering work of the Army has received a great deal of attention from one perspective, but little from others. The official histories of the various districts and divisions of the Corps of Engineers provide a good account of what they did. However, the politics of the decision-making process, as well as the environmental and economic impact of the programs, are virtually ignored in these official studies. In addition, the relations between the Engineers and Congress, which made them a virtually separate fiefdom, need further research.

Supplying the Army, especially as it spread around the world, became a major task in this century. The impact of technology has not been considered, either in terms of what was supplied or how it was delivered. Trucks proved to be both a help and a hindrance during the Mexican Punitive Expedition. Organizational changes, encouraged by the development of the staff system and managerial reforms in private industry, affected the Quartermaster Corps. Little of this has been researched.

One of the major changes which occurred in the Army at this period was in the area of management. Some attention has been devoted to the early years of this process, such as the contributions of Root and Wood, as well as the impact of managerial changes occurring in civilian society. However, these studies need to be expanded. Certainly the changes continued after World War I, as the staff digested the experiences of the war period. In addition, the educational system continued to produce officers who were trained to be staff personnel. The impact that these two factors had on the system is of interest. Following the careers of staff officers and comparing them to those who were not in this career track would be instructive. The personal histories and demographics of the men who became chiefs of staff need to be studied: Why people were appointed, or not appointed? What career patterns they had followed prior to this appointment? In addition one should investigate whether the managerial reforms percolated to the lower levels of the Army structure.

Histories of particular units and posts have been written, but most writers have ignored the broader contexts. Unit histories can be more than recitations of regimental commanders, awards won, and campaigns fought.

Any organization can be viewed in a broad social context, since in this time period these units were definitely small, fairly isolated groups. It would be of interest to examine the social structure of a regiment in terms of the origins of the enlisted personnel, relations with nearby communities, participation in educational programs, athletic events undertaken, and family structures. Similar questions can be raised when researching the histories of individual facilities. Those that have already been completed show a complex inter-relationship between the surrounding communities and the installation. When the race issue is interjected, it becomes even more interesting.

The Army's judicial system and its relationship with civilian society is a topic which has barely begun to be explored. General Samuel Ansell's efforts to give soldiers more rights did have an impact on the system. It would be informative to do studies of the type of judicial procedures carried out at different posts and study for variables such as race of the defendants, age of those accused, type of crime for which they were charged, and how these are related to punishments received.

Much research has been done on the political role of the National Guard, but little has been done on other aspects of this old institution. Among the topics that might be investigated are: how the National Guard was used in labor disputes, and whether this changed as labor gained more political clout; the recruitment of minorities, and their segregation within the Guard; the development of joint Army-National Guard training camps and their course of instruction; and the backgrounds of officers and enlisted personnel and the changes, if any, over the course of this century. A number of dissertations and a few books are available on this topic, but most of the research has been concentrated in the period before World War I. Well-researched state studies would be valuable additions to the literature.

Garrison duties and military government continued for the Army, and some scholars have investigated this topic. Again we need to expand the scope of the research. Relations with native populations, and the impact of the presence of Americans in China, Hawaii, Alaska, the Philippines, and Puerto Rico, are topics which deserve attention. The role of the military attachés, other than in Russia, has generally been ignored. Their contributions to foreign policy and to intelligence gathering should be explored.

Many of the key political issues involving the Army have been well researched. The anti-war and peace movements and their impact on the Army, especially in the 1930s, are among these. It would also be interesting to consider whether the Army continued to be isolated from the broad currents of American society or was very much affected by them. Analysis of the memoirs of the soldiers and officers of the interwar period might provide some insights on this topic.

There were a number of social issues which also made their mark on the Army, and these should be examined in more depth. Prohibition, attacks on drugs and prostitution, and other such crusades either directly or indirectly impacted on the post lifestyles. Whether or not the Army accepted these reform movements, as they did during the Mexican Punitive Expedition, they could not be avoided. The race issue has received a great deal of attention for the period 1900 to 1917, but the post-war period is relatively untouched. The development of athletics in civilian society had an impact in the military, though little is known of this. Athletic programs did exist at some posts, and regiments competed against other Army and civilian teams. Military officers acted as coaches on civilian teams. These interrelationships deserve research and elucidation.

The development of strategy by the Staff has received some scholarly interest, but there are aspects which remain to be explored. The failures to coordinate between the services has been noted as has the development of industrial planning. It would be instructive to explore the backgrounds of the planners and whether this had some impact on what they conceived should be the national strategy. Similarly, the input that military attachés had on the process might yield some insights into the factors that shaped strategy.

The first forty years of this century were certainly a period of technological innovation. It is also quite clear that many of the new inventions, such as the internal combustion engine, had an impact on the military. The process of choosing new weapons is a topic which has received some attention, but much more could be done. Exploring the relationships between the Army and civilian innovators, such as that with tank inventor Walter Christie, might lead to insights in the area of the development of the military-industrial complex. Strategic considerations in the innovation of technology also merit consideration. The whole process of the adaptation of the motor to the military is fascinating, but relatively undiscovered. Histories of the branches which would explore how they were affected by technology and how they reacted to it would prove most enlightening.

In general, research into the American Army in the first years of this century has produced much fascinating material, but a great deal still needs to be done. Hopefully this work will help scholars see what is already available and the many opportunities that remain for further study.

Bibliography

GENERAL

1. Abrahamson, James L. (1981). *America Arms for A New Century: The Making of a Great Military Power*. New York: The Free Press, 235 pp.
   The military leaders of the turn of the century tried to transform the American military structure into a modern war machine. They attempted reforms in the areas of management, weapons, and education and considered the different missions imposed by the new American empire. Based on secondary and primary sources.

2. Bernardo, C. Joseph, and Bacon, Eugene H. (1961). *American Military Policy: Its Development Since 1775*. 2nd ed. Harrisburg, Pennsylvania: Stackpole Company, 548 pp.
   Somewhat limited survey of American military history. Three chapters on the early 1900s covering the evolution of the general staff, changes in the national guard, and the preparedness movement. Nothing on campaigns in the Philippines, Mexico, or Cuba. Primary and secondary sources.

3. Dupuy, R. Ernest, and Dupuy, Trevor N. (1956). *Military Heritage of America*. New York: McGraw-Hill Book Company, 794 pp.
   Survey of American military history. Very brief section on the Philippine-American War; almost nothing on the reforms or other changes in the Army; battle oriented. Secondary sources.

4. Ganoe, William A. (1924). *The History of the United States Army*. New York: D. Appleton and Co., 609 pp.
   Very dated history of the Army. One chapter deals with the 1899-1917 period, with a great deal of emphasis on combat activities and little on other aspects of changes that were occurring. Bibliography, but no sources cited.

5. Hassler, Warren W., Jr. (1982). *With Shield and Sword: American Military Affairs, Colonial Times to the Present*. Ames, Iowa: Iowa State University Press, 462 pp.
   A twenty-page chapter covers the Root reforms, preparedness, militia renovations, as well as the changes occurring in the Navy. Secondary and primary sources.

6. Herr, John K., and Wallace, Edward S. (1953). *The Story of the U. S. Cavalry, 1775-1942*. Boston: Little, Brown and Company, 275 pp.

A popular history of this branch with about twenty pages on the post-Spanish American War period, concentrating mainly on the Punitive Expedition. Secondary sources.

7. Matloff, Maurice, (ed.). (1969). *American Military History*. Washington, D.C.: Office of the Chief of Military History, United States Army, 701 pp. SD D114.2:M59.

A team written general history of the Army, whose primary audience was ROTC programs. The period from the Spanish-American War to World War I is treated in 15 pages.

8. Millett, Allan R., and Maslowski, Peter. (1984). *For the Common Defense: A Military History of the United States of America*. New York: The Free Press, 621 pp.

About fifty pages of this excellent survey describes the events which followed the end of the Spanish-American War in both the Army and the Navy. A very useful bibliography. Primary and secondary sources.

9. Millis, Walter. (1956). *Arms and Men: A Study in American Military History*. New York: Putnam, 382 pp.

An important analysis of some of the key movements in American military history. In this time period Millis examines the managerial revolution and the mechanization of warfare. Secondary sources.

10. Nenninger, Timothy K. (1986) "The Army Enters the Twentieth Century, 1904-1917." In Kenneth J. Hagan and William R. Roberts, (ed.), *Against All Enemies: Interpretations of American Military History from Colonial Times to the Present*. Westport, Connecticut: Greenwood Press, 219-34.

A description of the changes that occurred in the Army after the Root reforms began to take effect. Among the topics covered are: development of the National Guard, maturation of the General Staff, expansion of the education system. Bibliographic essay. Secondary sources.

11. Spaulding, Oliver L. (1937). *The United States Army in War and Peace*. New York: G.P. Putnam's Sons, 541 pp.

About 30 pages relate the history of the Army in this period; much attention to combat, little to substantive reforms or their impact. Bibliography but no sources cited.

12. Weigley, Russell F. (1962). *Towards an American Army: Military Thought from Washington to Marshall*. New York: Columbia University Press, 297 pp.

Two of the chapters in this key work examine military thinkers from this period. Robert Johnston argued for a small professional, highly mobile army, while Leonard Wood accepted the citizen soldier and sought to train him. Primary and secondary sources.

13. Weigley, Russell F. (1967). *The History of the United States Army*. New York: The Macmillan Company, 688 pp.

A basic military history, with three chapters on events of this period. One deals with the conflicts arising from expansionism; another with the reorganization of the military begun by Elihu Root; a third covers the preparedness movement prior to World War I. Secondary and primary sources.

BIOGRAPHY

14. Anders, Leslie. (1985). *Gentle Knight; The Life and Times of Major General Edwin Forrest Harding*. Kent, Ohio: Kent State University Press, 384 pp.
    Biography of this general officer including his years at West Point between 1906 and 1909 and his first assignments. Personal details add a special dimension to this account. Primary and secondary sources.

15. Ayer, Frederick. (1964). *Before the Colors Fade; A Portrait of a Soldier: George S. Patton, Jr.* Boston: Houghton Mifflin, 266 pp.
    A non-objective discussion of Patton's personality, written by his godson, which makes use of personal recollections. No sources cited.

16. Bayne-Jones, Stanhope. (1967). "Walter Reed (1851-1902)." *Military Medicine, 132*, 391-400.
    A good brief account of Reed's career, with the major emphasis on two episodes, a typhoid epidemic in 1898 and most significantly, Reed's work in Cuba between 1899 and 1902 to determine the source of yellow fever. Primary sources.

17. Bigelow, Donald. (1952). *William Conant Church and the Army and Navy Journal*. New York: Columbia University Press, 266 pp.
    A brief biographical sketch of one of the key military journalists in the late nineteenth and early twentieth century. In addition the author has studied the newspaper and extracted from it some of the key issues, such as Army reform and the creation of a general staff, that it covered in the military in this time period. Primary and secondary sources.

18. Bishop, Joseph B., and Bishop, Farnham. (1930). *Goethals: Genius of the Panama Canal: A Biography*. New York: Harper and Brothers, 493 pp.
    A laudatory biography filled with copious quotations from documents. About half of the work deals with his efforts to build the Panama Canal. Few sources cited.

19. Blumenson, Martin. (1972). *The Patton Papers, Volume I: 1885-1940*. Boston: Houghton Mifflin, 996 pp.
    Incorporating the writings of Patton, Blumenson has detailed many important events in his life. There are chapters on his early years in the cavalry and three on his participation in the Mexican Punitive Expedition. Primary sources.

20. Blumenson, Martin. (1985). *Patton: The Man Behind the Legend, 1885-1945*. New York: William Morrow and Co., 320 pp.
    A relatively brief biography with one chapter dealing with the rise of this officer including his participation in the 1912 Olympics and the 1916 Punitive Expedition. Bibliography of secondary sources cited, but no primary sources listed.

21. Brimlow, George F. (1944). *Cavalryman Out of the West: Life of General William Carey Brown*. Caldwell, Idaho: The Caxton Printers, Ltd., 442 pp.

Biography of an officer who served in the Philippines and who commanded the Tenth Cavalry in the Mexican Punitive Expedition. Very much focused on the subject with little attempt to relate to the Army as a whole. Based on Brown's papers.

22. Clark, Paul W. (1974). "Major General George Owen Squier: Military Scientist." Dissertation, Case Western Reserve University, 35/1-A, p. 358.

A key leader, this officer helped bring the Army and scientists together. He studied ballistics, special uses of voice and data transmission, and training in these areas. In World War I he would serve as Chief Signal Officer.

23. Coffman, Edward M. (1966). *The Hilt of the Sword: The Career of Peyton C. March*. Madison, Wisconsin: University of Wisconsin Press, 346 pp.

Two chapters of this biography are pertinent: March in the Philippine-American War and his activities in the pre-war period including work on the General Staff, observer of the Russo-Japanese War, and with the Adjutant General's office. Primary sources.

24. Coffman, Edward M. (1977). "Batson of the Philippine Scouts." *Parameters, 7, No. 3*, 68-72.

A brief description of the career of the founder of the Philippine Scouts. Primary sources.

25. Crouch, Thomas W. (1969). "The Making of a Soldier: The Career of Frederick Funston, 1865-1902." Dissertation, University of Texas, 31/7-A, p. 3464.

A study of the first part of Funston's career, including the campaigns in the Philippines, where he distinguished himself by capturing the leader of the Insurrection. The author also tries to explain Funston's significance as a professional soldier.

26. Deutrich, Mabel E. (1962). *Struggle for Supremacy: The Career of General Fred C. Ainsworth*. Washington, D.C.: Public Affairs Press, 170 pp.

An account of a man who really created the military record keeping system, developed close ties with Congress, and battled with Leonard Wood for the future of the Army. A scholarly narrative, sympathetic to what Ainsworth was trying to accomplish. Primary sources.

27. Dodds, Gordon B. (1973). *Hiram Martin Chittenden; His Public Career*. Lexington, Kentucky: University Press of Kentucky, 220 pp.

A biography of a member of the Corps of Engineers who built tourist roads in Yellowstone National Park, surveyed the boundaries of Yosemite National Park and planned the Lake Washington Ship Canal in Seattle. Primary sources.

28. Editors of the *Army Times*. (1967). *Warrior: The Story of General George S. Patton*. New York: G. P. Putnam's Sons, 222 pp.

One chapter of this popular biography details Patton's years at West Point and his early Army service including Mexico. The authors concentrate on the personality of this officer. Secondary sources.

29. Emmett, Chris. (1959). *In the Path of Events with Colonel Martin Lalor Crimmins, Soldier, Naturalist, Historian*. Waco, Texas: Jones and Morrison, 343 pp.

An account of an officer, with a great deal of money, who served in the Philippines during and after the Insurrection, spent a tour of duty in Alaska, and was a good friend of President Theodore Roosevelt. Based on materials provided by Crimmins.

30. Fritz, David L. (1979). "Before the 'Howling Wilderness': The Military Career of Jacob Hurd Smith, 1862-1902." *Military Affairs, 43*, 186-90.

Provides some background on Smith, an officer who followed a typical late nineteenth-century career pattern and then, in the early twentieth century, found himself in a command position which was beyond his ability. Primary sources.

31. Frye, William. (1947). *Marshall: Citizen Soldier*. Indianapolis, Indiana: Bobbs-Merrill, 397 pp.

Quite sympathetic biography centering on Marshall the man and his experiences. Several chapters cover his work in the Philippines and at the staff college. No sources cited.

32. Gibson, John M. (1950). *Physician to the World; the Life of General William C. Gorgas*. Durham, North Carolina: Duke University Press, 315 pp.

A biography of this Army doctor including his work in Cuba and Panama against the various forms of tropical fevers. Secondary sources.

33. Gibson, John M. (1958). *Soldier in White; The Life of General George Miller Sternberg*. Durham, North Carolina: Duke University Press, 277 pp.

Sternberg was Surgeon General from 1893 to 1902. In this century he dispatched Walter Reed to Cuba to conduct the experiments which proved the role of the mosquito in the transmission of yellow fever. This anecdotal biography describes his various activities. Primary and secondary sources.

34. Goldhurst, Richard. (1977). *Pipeclay and Drill; John J. Pershing: The Classic American Soldier*. New York: Reader's Digest Press, 343 pp.

A popular biography of Pershing with a number of chapters on the key events of this time period. Contains several stories about the officer, rather than a study of the military institutions. Bibliography but no sources cited.

35. Hagedorn, Hermann. (1931). *Leonard Wood: A Biography*. New York: Harper and Brothers, 2 volumes, 960 pp.

A detailed biography of Wood, including a sizable number of direct quotes from the writings the man. The second volume details his career as governor of Moro Province, as Chief of Staff, and in the preparedness movement. Generally laudatory of Wood. No attempt made to evaluate the man. Primary sources.

36. Hatch, Alden. (1950). *George Patton: General in Spurs*. New York: Julian Messner, 184 pp.

Popular biography focusing on the personality of George Patton, with facts included to display the hero growing up toward a battle leader. "Georgie's" marriage, early career, and Mexican adventures are all related in gushing prose. No sources cited.

37. Hogg, Ian V. (1982). *The Biography of General George S. Patton*. New York: Hamlyn, 160 pp.
   A brief biography, well illustrated. Only a few pages deal with his early life including the Mexican Punitive Expedition. No sources cited.

38. Hunt, Frazier. (1954). *The Untold Story of Douglas MacArthur*. New York: Devin-Adair Co., 533 pp.
   A popular, pro-MacArthur biography. Several chapters relate his pre-World War I experiences. No sources cited.

39. James, D. Clayton. (1970). *The Years of MacArthur, Volume I, 1880-1941*. Boston: Houghton Mifflin Company, 740 pp.
   A fine detailed account of one of the most significant officers of this century. There are several chapters on MacArthur's experiences before World War I, especially his friendship with Leonard Wood and work on the General Staff. Primary and secondary sources.

40. Jessup, Philip C. (1938). *Elihu Root*. New York: Dodd, Mead, 2 volumes.
   Nine chapters of the first volume describe Root as Secretary of War. Among the topics covered: administrative reforms, management of Cuba, government of the Philippines, and control of Puerto Rico. Primary sources.

41. Johnson, Elliott L. (1975). "The Military Experiences of General Hugh A. Drum from 1898-1918." Dissertation, University of Wisconsin-Madison, 36/7-A, pp. 4674-75.
   The author suggests that Drum was a representative of a new kind of Army officer, a staff officer. A significant phase of Drum's career was his time at the Army School of the Line as a student and teacher. This prepared Drum for his duty as Chief of Staff of the First Army in World War I.

42. Johnson, Virginia W. (1962). *The Unregimented General: A Biography of Nelson A. Miles*. Boston: Houghton Mifflin, 401 pp.
   Only a brief section of this biography recounts Miles' service after the Spanish-American War, especially his conflicts with Root and Roosevelt. Primary sources.

43. Lane, Jack C. (1978). *Armed Progressive: General Leonard Wood*. San Rafael, California: Presidio Press, 329 pp.
   A profile of one of the key reformers of this period. In addition to helping to shape the staff, he played a key role in the pacification and governance of Cuba and the Philippines as well as led a movement for preparedness. However he was hindered by his belief that his ideas were right and unwillingness to tolerate those who disagreed. Primary and secondary sources.

44. Langellier, J. Phillip. (1980). "General Frederick Funston: Kansas Volunteer." *Military History of Texas and the Southwest*, 16, 79-106.
   A biographical article, covering Funston's whole career. The author contends that despite his great qualities his career was overshadowed by a variety of individuals such as Roosevelt and Pershing. Primary sources.

45. Leopold, Richard W. (1954). *Elihu Root and the Conservative Tradition.* Boston: Little, Brown, 222 pp.
  One brief chapter describes his term as Secretary of War. No sources cited.

46. Lockmiller, David A. (1955). *Enoch H. Crowder: Soldier, Lawyer, Statesman.* Columbia, Missouri: University of Missouri Studies, 286 pp.
  In the period before World War I Crowder served as a lawyer and staff officer. He was legal adviser to the commander of the second Cuban occupation, and in 1911 became Judge Advocate General, a position he retained into World War I. Primary and secondary sources.

47. Longacre, Edward G. (1975). "General James Harrison Wilson." *Delaware History, 16,* 298-322.
  During his long career, General Wilson was a military governor in Cuba and served with the American forces in China following the defeat of the Boxers in 1900. Primary sources.

48. Manchester, William. (1978). *American Caesar: Douglas MacArthur, 1880-1964.* Boston: Little, Brown, 793 pp.
  A well written account of MacArthur, with one chapter on his pre-war life. Some have questioned Manchester's scholarship. Primary and secondary sources.

49. McAndrews, Eugene V. (1973). "William Ludlow: Engineer, Governor, Soldier." Dissertation, Kansas State University, 36/10-A, pp. 6896-97.
  Though most of his career occurred before the Spanish-American War, afterwards Ludlow was a military governor in Cuba and head of the board that Root created to plan a general staff system. He was involved in some of the conflict that ensued.

50. McCracken, Harold. (1931). *Pershing: The Story of a Great Soldier.* New York: Brewer & Warren Inc., 193 pp.
  A popular and anecdotal history of the officer with several chapters on events in the Philippines during and after the Insurrection and in the Mexican Punitive Expedition. No sources cited.

51. Mellor, William B. (1946). *Patton, Fighting Man.* New York: G. P. Putnam's Sons, 245 pp.
  A popular biography, emphasizing the military personality of Patton, with little attempt at objectivity. No specific sources cited.

52. Millett, Allan R. (1975). *The General: Robert L. Bullard and Officership in the United States Army, 1881-1925.* Westport, Connecticut: Greenwood Press, 499 pp.
  Millett describes Bullard's involvement in a number of important aspects of the Army in this period including warfare in the Philippines, the War College, and border patrols on the Rio Grande during the Punitive Expedition. His career reflects the growing professionalization of the officer corps and is typical of the new general officer career pattern. Primary sources.

53. Morison, Elting E. (1960). *Turmoil and Tradition: A Study of the Life and Times of Henry L. Stimson*. Boston: Houghton Mifflin, 686 pp.
   One chapter of this detailed biography recounts Stimson's two years of service as Secretary of War, especially his role in the Wood-Ainsworth controversy. Primary sources.

54. Mosley, Leonard. (1982). *Marshall, Hero For Our Times*. New York: Hearst Books, 570 pp.
   A biography which mixes personal accounts with information about Marshall as a soldier. Several brief chapters cover his pre-World War I career. Source notes but no footnotes. Primary sources.

55. Napier, John H. (1972). "General Leonard Wood: Nationbuilder." *Military Review, 52, No. 4*, 77-86.
   Because of Wood's leadership abilities and absolute authority, he was able to change Cuba during the three years of Army control. He set into motion efforts to improve the school system, combat yellow fever, and create a reliable form of public administration. Secondary sources.

56. O'Connor, Richard. (1961). *Black Jack Pershing*. Garden City, New York: Doubleday & Company, Inc., 431 pp.
   Four chapters of this popular biography relate to Pershing's life in this period, with one on the Mexican Punitive Expedition. Includes some details of the officer's life, but generally does not provide much information on the Army itself or the context of the events. Chapter notes; primary sources; no specific citations.

57. Palmer, Frederick. (1948). *John J. Pershing, General of the Armies: A Biography*. Harrisburg, Pennsylvania: Military Service Publishing Company, 380 pp.
   A popular biography with three brief chapters on this period and almost nothing on the Mexican expedition. No real depth in the material presented. No sources cited.

58. Payne, Robert. (1951). *The Marshall Story; A Biography of General George C. Marshall*. New York: Prentice-Hall, 344 pp.
   A popular account, which aims to understand the officer, but merely succeeds in retelling stories about him. One chapter on his experiences between 1902 and 1916. No sources cited for material presented.

59. Peake, Louis A. (1977). "West Virginia's Best Known General Since 'Stonewall Jackson': John L. Hines." *West Virginia History, 38*, 226-35.
   A brief biographical sketch of his career, with two pages on events before World War I, including service in the Philippines. Primary sources.

60. Perry, Milton F. and Parke, Barbara W. (1957). *Patton and His Pistols: The Favorite Side Arms of General George S. Patton, Jr.* Harrisburg, Pennsylvania: The Stackpole Company, 138 pp.
   Included in this minor work is a chapter on his first use of pistols in Mexico in 1916. Primary and secondary sources.

61. Petillo, Carol M. (1981). *Douglas MacArthur: The Philippine Years.*
Bloomington, Indiana: Indiana University Press, 301 pp.
Concentrates largely on the post-war period, but two chapters deal with
MacArthur's first experiences in the Islands, serving with his father, and then
his first tour of duty in the islands. In addition, the author tries to understand
and explain MacArthur's personality. Primary and secondary sources.

62. Pier, Arthur S. (1950). *American Apostles to the Philippines.* Boston:
Beacon Press, 156 pp.
A series of short biographies of a number of Americans involved in the
Philippines, including Frederick Funston, Leonard Wood and John Pershing.
No sources cited.

63. Pogue, Forrest C. (1963). *George C. Marshall: Education of a General,
1880-1939.* New York: Viking Press, 421 pp.
A scholarly and excellent account of Marshall the man and soldier. Several
chapters detail his early military career, including duty in the Philippines, and
key work at the Leavenworth school. Primary and secondary sources.

64. Province, Charles M. (1983). *The Unknown Patton.* New York:
Hippocrene Books, 261 pp.
The author has attempted, in a series of short chapters, to explore
different facets of this officer's career. There is a brief and superficial
discussion of his early years, his marriage to Beatrice Ayer and his use of
motor vehicles in Mexico. Bibliography of secondary sources but none
specifically cited.

65. Pruitt, Paul M., Jr. (1983). "New-South Soldier: The Prewar Military
Career of Walter E. Bare, 1902-1917." *Alabama Review, 36,* 18-36.
A brief narrative of the life of a soldier and officer in the Alabama
National Guard. Includes material on training and Mexican border service in
1916. Primary sources.

66. Ranson, Edward. (1966). "Nelson A. Miles as Commanding General,
1895-1903." *Military Affairs, 29,* 179-200.
The last third of this article explores the feuds between Miles and
President Roosevelt and Secretary of War Root. For whatever reason, Miles
was opposed to the creation of a staff system and fought against it. To the
relief of many, he finally retired. Primary sources.

67. Readnour, Harry W. (1971). "General Fitzhugh Lee, 1835-1905: A
Biographical Study." Dissertation, University of Virginia, 32/8-A, p. 4537.
During the last years of his life General Lee was involved in the
occupation of Cuba. He advocated independence for the Cubans, though he
hoped for an eventual union with the United States. He left the Army in 1901
and pursued other activities.

68. Riepma, Siert F. (1938). "Portrait of an Adjutant General: The Career of
Major General Fred C. Ainsworth." *Journal of the American Military History
Foundation, 2,* 26-35.
A description of the contributions of Ainsworth and his rise to power as
Adjutant General. The article focuses on the 1880s and 1890s, but explains
the basis of his great power in the 1900s. No sources cited.

69. Semmes, Harry H. (1955). *Portrait of Patton*. New York: Appleton-Century-Crofts, Inc., 308 pp.
   A biography by an officer who served under Patton. One chapter recounts Patton's pre-war experiences, including Mexico. No sources cited.

70. Smith, Cornelius C., Jr. (1977). *Don't Settle for Second; Life and Times of Cornelius C. Smith*. San Rafael, California: Presidio Press, 229 pp.
   The life story of a career officer who served in a variety of posts in this period including the Philippines, San Francisco, and Hawaii. He was also involved in fighting the Moros and putting down strikes in Colorado. Liberal quotations from materials written by Smith.

71. Smythe, Donald J. (1966). "Pershing's Great Personal Tragedy: A Disastrous Mistake Wiped Out His Family, Leaving a Bitter Memory Throughout Life." *Missouri Historical Review, 60*, 320-35.
   Pershing's wife and three daughters perished in the fire at his home in San Francisco, while only his son was saved. The article describes the fire, its causes, and the impact the event had upon Pershing. Primary sources.

72. Smythe, Donald J. (1969). "John J. Pershing: A Study in Paradox." *Military Review, 49, No. 9*, 66-72.
   An overview by this Pershing biographer. Explores the different traits of the man and the paradoxes that they revealed. Also examines some of his things he was supposedly well known for and what he really did. Primary sources.

73. Smythe, Donald J. (1972). "'You Deal Old Jack Pershing'". *American History Illustrated, 7, No. 6*, 18-25.
   Story of the courtship and marriage of Pershing and Frances Warren. Reveals a very human side to this soldier. No sources cited, but includes personal correspondence.

74. Smythe, Donald J. (1973). *Guerrilla Warrior: The Early Life of John J. Pershing*. New York: Charles Scribner's Sons, 370 pp.
   About half of this excellent biography describes the years between 1900 and 1917. Great attention is paid to the Philippines, since it was here that Pershing displayed his talents as a military leader and civil governor. Another major section is devoted to the Mexican Punitive Expedition which prepared Pershing for his role as commander of the AEF. Primary and secondary sources.

75. Tolman, Newton F. (1968). *The Search for General Miles*. New York: G. P. Putnam's Sons, 252 pp.
   A biography by a man searching to find some information on a individual largely forgotten by most individuals. No real understanding of the Army or the major issues; accepts the positions advocated by his subject; sparse on the post 1898 events of Miles' career. No sources cited.

76. Trussell, John B. (1973). "Frederick Funston: The Man Destiny Just Missed." *Military Review, 53, No. 6*, 59-73.
   A biographical article, including some of the highlights of Funston's short but brilliant career: the capture of Aguinaldo, disaster relief after the 1906 San Francisco earthquake, and the Veracruz occupation. No sources cited.

77. Tuchman, Barbara. (1970). *Stilwell and the American Experience in China, 1911-45*. New York: Macmillan Company, 621 pp.
One chapter discusses Joseph Stilwell's first visit to China in 1911. The book is a history of Americans' relation to China and Asia itself. Primary and secondary sources.

78. Turner, Justin G. (1970). "General Homer Lea." *Manuscripts, 22*, 96-102.
This American served in China before the Revolution and also made numerous predictions, many of them accurate, about future wars among the world powers including the United States. This article is a brief sketch of his life, including details on his writing. No sources cited.

79. Twichell, Heath, Jr. (1974). *Allen: The Biography of an Army Officer, 1859-1930*. New Brunswick, New Jersey: Rutgers University Press, 358 pp.
A biography of an officer who was involved in many significant activities: first head of the Philippine Constabulary, a member of the General Staff under Wood, and a leader of the Thirteenth Cavalry in the Punitive Expedition. Primary and secondary sources.

80. Vandiver, Frank E. (1977). *Black Jack: The Life and Times of John J. Pershing*. College Station, Texas: Texas A&M Press, 2 volumes, 1178 pp.
About half of the first volume and a small section of the second relate Pershing's activities in this period, including campaigns in the Philippines and leadership of the Punitive Expedition. Personal incidents are interlaced with the official activities of his career. Primary sources.

81. Webb, Melody. (1986). "Billy Mitchell and the Alaska Telegraph." *American History Illustrated, 20, No. 9*, 22-25.
In the early part of the century, the Army built a telegraph system in Alaska. William Mitchell was involved in this project, was tested by the distances and weather conditions, and proved to be a good leader. No sources cited.

82. Wellard, James. (1946). *General George S. Patton, Jr.: Man Under Mars*. New York: Dodd, Mead, 277 pp.
One of the first biographies of the general, with a concentration on personal incidents. Several chapters describe his early life with a few brief pages on the Mexican Punitive Expedition. No sources cited.

83. Weyant, Jane C. (1981). "The Life and Career of General William V. Judson, 1865-1923." Dissertation, Georgia State University, 44/6-A, pp. 1898-99.
Though this contains a brief sketch of his whole life, the majority of the work concentrates on his service as Military Attaché to Russia in 1917-1918.

84. Wood, Laura N. (1943). *Walter Reed, Doctor in Uniform*. New York: Julian Messner, 277 pp.
A popular biography of this medical pioneer, it includes several chapters on his efforts against disease in Cuba after the Spanish-American War. There is much information on the person and little on the background of the military occupation or other aspects of the Army. Secondary sources.

CONFLICTS

85. Archer, Jules. (1968). "Woodrow Wilson's Dirty Little War." *Mankind, 1,* 44-55.
A survey, with illustrations, of Wilson's policy toward Mexico including the Veracruz intervention and the Mexican Punitive Expedition. Wilson is portrayed as a democrat who is forced to use the military but is opposed to a major war with Mexico. No sources cited.

86. Atkin, Ronald. (1970). *Revolution! Mexico 1910-20.* New York: The John Day Company, 354 pp.
An analysis which focuses on four different revolutionary leaders including Carranza. The book provides a background for the Punitive Expedition and explains the expedition from the American and Mexican perspective. Primary and secondary sources.

87. Bacevich, Andrew J., Jr. (1982) "Disagreeable Work: Pacifying the Moros, 1903-1906." *Military Review, 62, No. 6,* 49-61.
Leonard Wood had to use force to impose American control over the Moros. The author feels that the campaign was a failure due to Wood's unwillingness to understand the Moslem culture. Primary sources.

88. Barker, Stockbridge H. (1964). "Funston's Folly." *Army, 14, No. 7,* 73-80.
An account of the capture of Aguinaldo by General Funston, describing in detail the subterfuges he used. No sources cited.

89. Bain, David H. (1984). *Sitting in Darkness: Americans in the Philippines.* Boston: Houghton Mifflin Co., 464 pp.
Bain interweaves an account of the lives of Frederick Funston and Emilio Aguinaldo and the Philippine-American War with the modern Philippines and the areas in which that conflict was fought. The author seeks to understand the motivations for the war and its meaning for contemporary America. Primary and secondary sources.

90. Braddy, Haldeen. (1963). "Myths of Pershing's Mexican Campaign." *Southern Folklore Quarterly, 27,* 181-95.
The central focus of the article are the stories and songs of the Punitive Expedition. There is also material on Pancho Villa then and later in life. The author suggests that these items reflect the soldiers' views of the expedition. Primary sources.

91. Braddy, Haldeen. (1965). "Pancho Villa at Columbus: The Raid of 1916 Restudied". *Southwestern Studies, 3, No. 1,* 1-43.
A detailed study of why Pancho Villa raided Columbus and of the raid itself. The author suggests that Villa was only after booty when he planned and executed the raid. Primary sources.

92. Braddy, Haldeen. (1966). *Pershing's Mission in Mexico.* El Paso, Texas: Texas Western Press, 82 pp.
Brief overview of the Punitive Expedition's first few months. Because of the book's brevity and narrow focus, this is not a complete history of the expedition. The author uses Mexican and American non-official sources.

93. Blumenson, Martin. (1977). "Patton in Mexico: The Punitive Expedition." *American History Illustrated, 12, No. 6,* 34-42.

One of the formative periods of Patton's life involved his service as an aide to Pershing in Mexico. This well written account includes the story of Patton's use of automobiles to raid the ranch of a Villa leader. No sources cited.

94. Calhoun, Frederick S. (1983). "The Wilsonian Way of War: American Armed Power from Veracruz to Vladivostok." Dissertation, University of Chicago, 44/7-A, p. 2223.

The author compares the different military interventions and finds several common elements. The Mexican interventions are examples of "Wilson's insistence on civilian control of the military." Though Wilson expanded the use of military power, he found many ways to limit its objectives.

95. Clendenen, Clarence C. (1961). "The Punitive Expedition of 1916: A Re-evaluation." *Arizona and the West, 3,* 311-20.

Many observers feel that the Punitive Expedition failed because it did not capture Villa. The author suggests that the goal was to break up the Villa gang, and in this the expedition succeeded, at least for a while. Secondary sources.

96. Clendenen, Clarence C. (1961). *The United States and Pancho Villa: A Study in Unconventional Diplomacy.* Ithaca, New York: Cornell University Press, 352 pp.

History of relations between the Mexican leader and the US, including a discussion of the raid on Columbus and the subsequent Punitive Expedition. Clendenen tries to explain why Villa clashed with the US and the consequences of this action for him. Primary and secondary sources.

97. Clendenen, Clarence C. (1969). *Blood on the Border: The United States Army and the Mexican Irregulars.* New York: The Macmillan Company, 390 pp.

Beginning in the post-Civil War era, there were a continuing series of border clashes between American forces, Native Americans, and the Mexican Army. The largest of these occurred in 1916-1917 when Pancho Villa raided Columbus, New Mexico, and an American force under the command of General John J. Pershing pursued him into Mexico. This well-written narrative account of these events concentrates on the 1916 Punitive Expedition. Based on primary and secondary sources.

98. Coerver, Don M., and Hall, Linda B. (1985). "The Arizona-Sonora Border and the Mexican Revolution, 1910-1920." *Journal of the West, 24, No. 2,* 75-87.

Conflict in Sonora effected the border areas in a variety of ways. American troops were shot at on some occasions, had to prevent violations of American neutrality at other times, and captured fleeing Mexicans infrequently. Primary sources.

99. Cumberland, Charles C. (1954). "Border Raids in the Lower Rio Grande Valley-1915." *Southwestern Historical Quarterly, 57*, 285-311.

A description of the causes and consequences of 1915 border raids for Texas and the Army. They created difficulties for the Army and set the stage for Villa's similar raid on Columbus the next year. Primary sources.

100. Dupuy, R. Ernest, and Baumer, William H. (1968). *The Little Wars of the United States*. New York: Hawthorne Books, Inc., 226 pp.

Brief general accounts of the post-1900 employment of military force in the Philippines, China, Mexico, and the Caribbean. Generally sympathetic to the American military and their goals. Mainly secondary sources.

101. Fleming, Peter. (1959). *The Siege at Peking*. New York: Harper and Brothers, 273 pp.

The Boxer Rebellion and the Allied Relief Expedition are the subject of this book. Much personal detail is included. Based mainly on secondary sources.

102. Fleming, Thomas J. (1968). "Pershing's Island War." *American Heritage, 19, No. 5*, 32-35, 101-04.

An account of Captain Pershing's campaign on Mindanao in 1901 to pacify the Moros. His successful effort eventually led to his rapid promotion to general. One secondary source cited.

103. Francisco, Luzviminda. (1973). "The First Vietnam: The U. S.-Philippine War of 1899." *Bulletin of Concerned Asian Scholars, 5*, 2-16.

Describes the war for the purpose of convincing Filipinos that American rule was not benign. Argued that the total population supported the war against the invaders and that the Americans conducted a war of terror, including killing many Filipinos, in order to destroy the enemy. Primary sources.

104. Ganley, Eugene F. (1960). "Mountain Chase." *Military Affairs, 24*, 203-210.

An account of a 1901-2 conflict between the US Army and a guerrilla leader, Vincente Lukban, on the island of Samar. Much of the pursuit of the guerrillas over the mountainous terrain was carried out by the Philippine Scouts, newly organized native police force. Eventual success led to its commander receiving a commission in the US Army. Primary sources.

105. Ganley, Eugene F. (1961). "Springfields and Bolos." *Military Review, 41, No. 7*, 47-54.

A description of several fights, in 1902, between a group of Filipinos and a unit of the Philippine Scouts. The Scouts were successful in putting down the revolt with their superior organization and firepower. No sources cited.

106. Gates, John M. (1972). "The Philippines and Vietnam: Another False Analogy." *Asian Studies, 10*, 64-76.

The author explains what he feels is the misuse of the analogies between the atrocities of the two wars. He believes that the parallels are not that great, due to changes in the nature of warfare, and therefore of questionable value. Primary and secondary sources.

107. Gates, John M. (1973). *Schoolbooks and Krags: The United States Army in the Philippines, 1898-1902*. Westport, Connecticut: Greenwood Press Inc., 315 pp.

A description of the Army's campaign against the Filipino insurrectos, with its good and bad points, and the ensuing period of civilian government that the Army helped establish. The author discusses the events that led to the abandonment of the benevolent approach and the introduction of harsher measures. Gates believes that the Army was successful in gaining the support of most Filipinos. Primary and secondary sources.

108. Gates, John M. (1980). "The Pacification of the Philippines, 1898-1902." In Joe C. Dixon, (ed.), *The American Military and the Far East: Proceedings of the Ninth Military History Symposium, United States Air Force Academy, 1-3 October 1980*, Washington, D.C.: United States Air Force Academy, 79-91. SD D301.78:980.

A discussion of the Philippine-American War, as well as the lack of parallels between that conflict and the Vietnam War. No sources cited.

109. Gates, John M. (1984). "War-Related Deaths in the Philippines, 1898-1902." *Pacific Historical Review, 53*, 367-78.

The author attempts to arrive at some figure for the number of dead Filipinos in the conflict. The issue then and later got ensnared in arguments over the validity of the war. No definite conclusion is reached, but Gates hypothesizes that the lower of the figures suggested by different authorities probably are the most accurate. Secondary sources.

110. Gilderhus, Mark T. (1977). *Diplomacy and Revolution: U. S.-Mexican Relations under Wilson and Carranza*. Tucson, Arizona: University of Arizona Press, 159 pp.

Wilson's effort for world order and his desire to encourage democracy ran into conflict with the politics of the Mexican revolution. The chapter on the Punitive Expedition fits it into this framework. Primary sources.

111. Ginsburgh, Robert N. (1964). "Damn the Insurrectos!" *Military Review, 44, No. 1*, 58-70.

An account of the Philippine-American War from the perspective of insurgency and counter-insurgency. The author feels that lessons can be learned from the American experience. No sources cited.

112. Haley, P. Edward. (1970). *Revolution and Intervention: The Diplomacy of Taft and Wilson with Mexico, 1910-1917*. Cambridge, Massachusetts: The MIT Press, 294 pp.

The author places the Punitive Expedition in a context of the continuing American problems with Mexico. One chapter is devoted to the expedition, primarily from a diplomatic perspective. Primary sources.

113. Harris, Charles H., and Sadler, Louis R. (1975). "Pancho Villa and the Columbus Raid: The Missing Documents." *New Mexico Historical Review, 50*, 335-46.

Using some long lost documents from the Columbus raid, the authors suggest that no real motive for the attack can yet be proven. The only one that is possibly suggested by these documents is that Villa wanted revenge against Americans. Primary sources.

114. Harris, Charles H., and Sadler, Louis R. (1978). "The Plan of San Diego and the Mexican-United States War Crisis of 1916: A Reexamination." *Hispanic American Historical Review, 58*, 381-408.

This article places the border clashes of 1915 and 1916 in the context of Mexican politics and Chicano discontent. The author connects the ideas behind the Plan of San Diego with Villa's raid, and examines the issue of German involvement in the Villa attack. Primary sources.

115. Haycock, Ronald G. (1979). "The American Legion in the Canadian Expeditionary Force, 1914-1917: A Study in Failure." *Military Affairs, 43*, 115-19.

In the first years of World War I, the Canadian Minister of Militia and Defence tried to recruit five battalions of Americans to fight in France. The effort was a failure because of a variety of political and diplomatic problems. Primary sources.

116. Hines, Calvin W. (1962). "The Mexican Punitive Expedition of 1916". Master's Thesis, Trinity University.

An account of the events leading up to the intervention in Mexico and of the expedition that followed. Though the expedition was "futile", the author feels that new ideas and technologies were tried and many leaders tested. Primary, including many personal interviews, and secondary sources.

117. Hirschfeld, Burt. (1964). *Fifty-five Days of Terror: The Story of the Boxer Rebellion*. New York: Julian Messner, Inc., 191 pp.

An account, for a juvenile audience, of the Boxer Rebellion. Only a small section describes the American relief expedition and the Army's role. No sources cited.

118. Ileto, Reynaldo C. (1982). "Toward a Local History of the Philippine-American War: The Case of Tiaong, Tayabas (Quezon) Province, 1901-1902." *Journal of History, 20*, 67-79.

This article includes a review of the types of information about the war to be found in American military records and an account of the war in the town of Tiaong. The author suggests that it was not until Bell's reconcentration tactics that the rebellion began to disintegrate. No primary sources specifically cited though mentioned in general.

119. Johnson, Robert B. (1964). "The Punitive Expedition: A Military, Diplomatic, and Political History of Pershing's Chase after Pancho Villa, 1916-1917." Dissertation, University of Southern California, 25/6, p. 3537.

A general account of the American expedition into Mexico in 1916-1917. As the title suggests, the dissertation examines all facets of this episode in American military history.

120. Jornacion, George W. (1973). "The Time of the Eagles: United States Army Officers and the Pacification of the Philippine Moros 1899-1913." Dissertation, University of Maine, 34/12-A, pp. 7662-63.

Using ideas developed during the Indian Wars, the Army tried to keep the peace and encourage economic and educational development. This included campaigns against many of the Moro leaders. Key young officers, such as Pershing and Wood, got important command experience here.

121. Katz, Friedrich. (1978). "Pancho Villa and the Attack on Columbus, New Mexico." *American Historical Review, 83,* 101-30.
A description of the events that led to Villa's raid on Columbus and a presentation of the author's explanation: that Villa believed that Carranza and Wilson had concluded an agreement that would make Mexico a colony of the US. Primary sources.

122. Kennedy, John W. (1978). "Border Troubles, and Camp Stephen D. Little." *Periodical: Council on Abandoned Military Posts, 10, No. 1,* 14-25.
A brief account, with long citations of documents, of the border problems that led to the establishment of this post and continued during its existence. Also includes some information on the troops that garrisoned the post. Primary sources.

123. Kestenbaum, Justin L. (1963). "The Question of Intervention in Mexico, 1913-1917." Dissertation, Northwestern University, 25/1, pp. 434-35.
Intervention in Mexico was constantly under discussion during the administration of Woodrow Wilson. Though most people supported the idea, they objected to military intervention. The author also describes the events that led Wilson to finally agree to the policy that most had opposed before.

124. Kolb, Richard K. (1983). "Campaign in Moroland: A War the World Forgot." *Army, 33, No. 9,* 50-59.
A brief account of the bitter campaigns waged by American troops, as well as Philippine Scouts and Constabulary, against the Moro tribesmen in the Philippine Islands in the first decade of this century. No sources cited.

125. Langley, Lester D. (1985). *The Banana Wars: United States Intervention in the Caribbean, 1898-1934.* Rev. ed. Lexington, Kentucky: University Press of Kentucky, 255 pp.
Included in this work are relatively brief accounts of the two Cuban occupations and the military government of Veracruz. There is a discussion of the attitudes of the occupiers and how these shaped policy. Primary and secondary sources.

126. Linn, Brian M. (1982). "Pacification in Northwestern Luzon: An American Regiment in the Philippine-American War, 1899-1901." *Pilipinas, 3, No. 2,* 14-25.
An account of the experiences of the Thirty-third regiment, United States Volunteer Infantry, in the war. Special emphasis is placed on guerrilla warfare and how the regiment responded to the challenge. The author suggests that they did well and that a regional approach to studying the war would be meritorious. Primary sources.

127. Linn, Brian M. (1985). "The War in Luzon: U. S. Army Regional Counterinsurgency in the Philippine War, 1900-1902." Dissertation, Ohio State University, 46/12-A, p. 3843.
This dissertation focuses on pacification campaigns waged in four districts in Luzon. The author believes that the war was different in different areas, that each commander shaped his efforts to deal with local situations, and that generalizations can not be made about the total campaign. Because of these variations, the pacification effort "proved effective in defeating the guerrilla war."

128. Linn, Brian M. (1987). "Guerrilla Fighter: Frederick Funston in the Philippines, 1900-1901." *Kansas History, 10*, 2-16.

In this significant article Linn clearly describes how Funston, as a provincial commander, destroyed the power of the opposition. He successfully employed a variety of means, including using native auxiliaries and winning over the population, to defeat the Insurgents. Primary sources and secondary sources.

129. Linn, Brian M. (1987). "Provincial Pacification in the Philippines, 1900-1901: The First District Department of Northern Luzon." *Military Affairs, 51*, 62-66.

The American campaign to put down the Philippine Insurrection varied from island to island and province to province. In this article the author describes three different types of efforts ranging from a scorched earth policy to pacification through the local religious leader. Primary sources.

130. Machlin, Milt. (1987). "Sunday Morning Ambush." *Military History, 4, No. 1*, 26-33.

An account of the garrisoning of a town in Samar and the Filipino attack on it in 1901. This led to the killing of a large number of Americans, which in turn led to reprisals by Marines under the command of Jake Smith. Illustrative of the nature of the Philippine-American War. No sources cited.

131. Mason, Herbert M., Jr. (1970). *The Great Pursuit*. New York: Random House, 269 pp.

A general narrative of the Punitive Expedition, focusing on the first few months. The perspective is from the top down on the American side, with little material on the individual soldiers. No specific citations though some use of secondary sources and interviews; material in official records seems to have been ignored.

132. May, Glenn A. (1979). "Filipino Resistance to American Occupation: Batangas, 1899-1902." *Pacific Historical Review, 48*, 531-56.

An account of how different of Filipinos reacted to the American invasion and the way in which General J. Franklin Bell responded. The author suggests there were a number of reasons for the long period of resistance, including good local leadership. Primary sources.

133. May, Glenn A. (1981). "The 'Zones' of Batangas." *Philippine Studies, 29*, 89-103.

General Bell's policy of combating the Philippine guerrillas with zones and the human cost of that policy are the subject of this article. The author suggests that the zones did lead to unhealthy conditions and a high death toll, but whether it destroyed the back of the rebellion is not clear. Primary sources.

134. May, Glenn A. (1983). "Why the United States Won the Philippine-American War, 1899-1902." *Pacific Historical Review, 52*, 353-77.

Using the similarities and differences between the Philippine-American War and Vietnam as a starting point, the author explains why the US won the first war. Among the reasons he suggests are: Aguinaldo's inept leadership, and lack of real support from the populace for the revolt. Secondary sources.

135. May, Glenn A. (1984). "Private Presher and Sergeant Vergara: The Underside of the Philippine-American War." In Peter W. Stanley (ed.), *Reappraising an Empire; New Perspectives on Philippine-American History.* Cambridge, Massachusetts: Harvard University Press, 35-57.

By using two examples, an American and a Filipino soldier, May tries to view the attitudes of individuals towards the war. He suggests that the American soldier was enthusiastic about the war, but that the Filipino had mixed feelings. Primary sources.

136. May, Glenn A. (1984). "Resistance and Collaboration in the Philippine-American War: The Case of Batangas." *Journal of Southeast Asian Studies,* 25, 69-90.

A detailed analysis, based on new materials, on how the Filipinos reacted to the American military and responded to the concentration policy of General Bell. The author suggests that a variety of variables, including ethnicity, economic conditions, and the ability of the American commanders, shaped how the Filipinos reacted to the American invasion. Primary and secondary sources.

137. Meyer, Michael C. (1983). "Felix Sommerfeld and the Columbus Raid of 1916." *Arizona and the West, 25,* 213-28.

Sommerfeld was a German agent and was involved with Pancho Villa in 1915-1916. The question of whether he encouraged Villa to raid Columbus, New Mexico, however, has not been resolved. The author suggests that there is no specific evidence to this point, but that the general circumstances seem to suggest that Sommerfeld did encourage Villa. Primary sources.

138. Miller, Stuart C. (1970). "Our Mylai of 1900: Americans in the Philippine Insurrection." *Trans-action, 7, No. 11,* 19-28.

An attempt to link the Philippine-American War and Vietnam in terms of Army policies toward civilians, anti-war opposition, and atrocities. No sources cited.

139. Miller, Stuart C. (1982). *"Benevolent Assimilation": The American Conquest of the Philippines, 1899-1903.* New Haven, Connecticut: Yale University Press, 340 pp.

A description of the war in the Philippines from the perspective that it was part of the American expansionism of the late nineteenth century. The author examines the war in a broad context, including domestic American attitudes as well as the actions of the Army in the field. He is critical of the racist attitudes of the American public and the Army. Primary and secondary sources.

140. Miller, Stuart C. (1984). "The American Soldier and the Conquest of the Philippines." In Peter W. Stanley, (ed.), *Reappraising an Empire; New Perspectives on Philippine-American History.* Cambridge, Massachusetts: Harvard University Press, 13-34.

In the article the author explores the great enthusiasm the American soldiers had toward the war and the feeling of superiority toward the Filipinos. Primary sources.

141. Munch, Francis J. (1969). "Villa's Columbus Raid: Practical Politics or German Design?" *New Mexico Historical Review, 44*, 189-214.
Munch suggests that the raid was partially encouraged by the Germans, but also the result of conditions in Mexico. Villa's anger against the United States was encouraged by German agents, including Felix Sommerfeld. Primary sources.

142. O'Connor, Richard. (1973). *The Spirit Soldiers; A Historical Narrative of the Boxer Rebellion*. New York: G. P. Putnam's Sons, 379 pp.
Only a small section of this book relates to the relief force and the role of the American troops. Mainly secondary sources.

143. Owen, Norman G. (1979). "Winding Down the War in Albay, 1900-1903." *Pacific Historical Review, 48*, 557-89.
An examination of one Philippine province and how it responded to the American invasion. American tactics succeeded in putting down the revolt, at some cost of life, but made no real changes in the social hierarchy of the society. Primary sources.

144. Pomeroy, William J. (1967). "'Pacification' in the Philippines, 1898-1913." *France-Asie, 21*, 427-46.
A description of the development of American military government in the Islands as well as a discussion of the issue of whether the Americans were benevolent or committed atrocities in their efforts to control the Islands. Primary and secondary sources.

145. Porter, John A. (1933). "The Punitive Expedition." *The Quartermaster Review, 12, No. 4*, 19-30.
A detailed account of the expedition and its logistical aspects, including planning, use of trucks, and its overall impact on the Army. No sources cited.

146. Roberts, Richard C. (1978). "The Utah National Guard on the Mexican Border in 1916." *Utah Historical Quarterly, 46*, 262-81.
Called up because of the problems along the border, the process served as a dress rehearsal for the larger mobilization the following year. Though most of their experiences were limited to training exercises, the Utah NG was involved in several border clashes with Mexican troops. Primary sources.

147. Roth, Russell. (1981). *Muddy Glory: America's 'Indian Wars' in the Philippines, 1899-1935*. West Hanover, Massachusetts: The Christopher Publishing House, 281 pp.
This account covers the major campaigns in 1899-1901, but also includes the conflicts with guerrillas over the next fifteen years. A chapter describes the experiences of black soldiers. The narrative is spiced with a variety of anecdotes. Primary and secondary sources.

148. Roth, Russell F. (1982). "A Soldier Song of An Incident in the Service." *Bulletin of the American Historical Collection, 10, No. 2*, 25-43.
Analysis of a song from the Philippine-American war describing the action of what the author believes was the Twenty-fifth Infantry. Provides an insight into the views of blacks on the conflict as well. Primary sources.

149. Sandos, James A. (1970). "German Involvement in Northern Mexico, 1915-1916: A New Look at the Columbus Raid." *Hispanic American Historical Review, 50,* 70-88.

After examining some evidence, the author suggests that there is a possibility that the Germans instigated Villa to attack Columbus in the hope of bringing the US and Mexico to war. Primary sources.

150. Sandos, James A. (1972). "The Plan of San Diego: War and Diplomacy on the Texas Border, 1915-1916." *Arizona and the West, 14,* 5-24.

In 1915 some Mexicans created a plan to encourage revolt along the border, in the hope of returning the territory to Mexico. It led to clashes, some of which concerned the American Army. The extent of German involvement is difficult to evaluate, but probably minimal. The plan really reflected the hostility between Chicanos and Anglos. Primary sources.

151. Sandos, James A. (1981). "Pancho Villa and American Security: Woodrow Wilson's Mexican Diplomacy Reconsidered." *Journal of Latin American Studies, 13,* 293-311.

Based on a new view of the documents, Sandos suggests that the purpose of the expedition was to scatter Villa's band and this was accomplished, though the cost was quite high. The expedition also had a number of effects on Mexican affairs, though whether they were intended is not clear. Primary sources.

152. Sanford, Wayne L. (1982). "Battle of Bud Dajo: 6 March 1906." *Indiana Military History Journal, 7, No. 2,* 4-20.

An account of a battle against the Moros in the Philippines. The article is both a general narrative and the story of a Indiana soldier. Primary sources.

153. Sarkesian, Sam C. (1984). *America's Forgotten Wars; The Counterrevolutionary Past and Lessons for the Future.* Westport, Connecticut: Greenwood Press, 265 pp.

A study of four conflicts including the Philippine-American War and the Mexican Punitive Expedition in the context of American society and the failures and successes of the counterrevolutionary policy and tactics. Secondary sources.

154. Sawyer, Robert K. (1961). "Viva Villa!" *Military Review, 41, No. 8,* 60-75.

Beginning with an overview of the Army in 1916, the author provides an account of the Punitive Expedition. Included are descriptions of the role of the National Guard, logistical problems, and the scope of training. Sawyer feels the real significance of the Expedition derived from the training the soldiers received, which prepared parts of the Army for World War I. No sources cited.

155. Schott, Joseph L. (1964). *The Ordeal of Samar.* Indianapolis, Indiana: Bobbs-Merrill, 302 pp.

An account of a campaign and resulting court-martial of Marine Major Littleton Waller. He was under the orders of Army officers and tried in an Army court-martial. The case involved the issue of terrorism against Filipinos in an effort to punish insurrectos. No footnotes.

156. Sexton, William T. (1939). *Soldiers in the Sun: An Adventure in Imperialism*. Harrisburg, Pennsylvania: The Military Service Publishing Company, 297 pp.

A history of the Philippine-American War but not of the military government that developed at the same time. Sympathetic to the Army. A large number of documents are cited at length. Based largely on the reports of officers included in the Secretary of War annual reports.

157. Smythe, Donald. (1962). "Pershing and the Disarmament of the Moros." *Pacific Historical Review, 31*, 241-56.

As governor of Moro Province General Pershing decided that in order to ensure order, he had to disarm the Moros. Though many argued that it could not be done without a war, Pershing thought he could accomplish it peacefully. It was a major achievement when he reached his goal. Primary sources.

158. Smythe, Donald J. (1966). "Pershing and Counterinsurgency." *Military Review, 46, No. 9*, 85-92.

Describes an incident in 1913 when a group of Moros on Jolo defied the authority of General Pershing. Employing Philippine Scouts and the US Army, he attacked the Moros with great force and successfully defeated them. No sources cited.

159. Tan, Chester C. (1955). *The Boxer Catastrophe*. New York: Columbia University Press, 276 pp.

An account of the whole Boxer Rebellion and the ensuing conflict with Russia. The allied force is only mentioned briefly. Chinese and Western primary sources.

160. Tate, Michael L. (1975). "Pershing's Punitive Expedition: Pursuer of Bandits or Presidential Panacea?" *The Americas, 32*, 46-71.

The author argues that Wilson's mission for the Punitive Expedition changed from merely pursuing the bandits to staying in force to act as a lever in getting Carranza to revise his economic policy. In the end this failed, as Wilson did not understand the Mexican political situation. Primary sources.

161. Taylor, John R. M. (1906). *The Philippine Insurrection Against the United States; A Compilation of Documents with Notes and Introduction*. Pasay City, Philippines: Eugenio Lopez Foundation, 5 volumes.

Taylor wrote a history of the Insurrection and included a large number of the recently captured documents with the narrative. Though marred by anti-Filipino bias, it is a basic account of the war. This work was never published, possibly for political reasons. This edition is based on the 1906 page proofs.

162. Thomas, Robert S. and Allen, Inez V. (1954). *The Mexican Punitive Expedition under Brigadier General John J. Pershing, United States Army, 1916-1917*. Washington, D.C.: War Histories Division, Office of the Chief of Military History, Department of the Army. Typescript, five chapters plus appendix, individual numbered.

A history of the expedition concentrating on the first months of the pursuit of Villa. Little attention paid to border mobilization, logistics, or post Carrizal activities. Primary and secondary sources.

163. Tompkins, Frank. (1934). *Chasing Villa. The Story Behind the Story of Pershing's Expedition into Mexico*. Harrisburg, Pennsylvania: The Military Service Publishing Company, 270 pp.

An account of the expedition written by a commander of a squadron of the Thirteenth Cavalry. The work includes texts of a number of documents, and describes the expedition from the American perspective. The author believes that the effort was close to its goal when Wilson called it off. No sources cited.

164. Tyler, Ronnie C. (1975). "The Little Punitive Expedition in the Big Bend." *Southwestern Historical Quarterly, 78,* 271-91.

Description of a foray into Mexico in 1916 conducted by the US Army to punish a gang of bandits who had raided two towns in Texas. Much more successful than Pershing's larger expedition of the same time period. Primary sources.

165. Wallace, Andrew. (1964). "The Sabre Retires: Pershing's Cavalry Campaign in Mexico, 1916." *The Smoke Signal, No. 9,* 1-24.

A detailed account of the Punitive Expedition's first months. Good description of Pershing's role and narrative of the efforts to track down Villa. Little on the causes of the campaign, events after the end of the pursuit, or the significance of the effort. Printed primary and secondary sources.

166. Wallis, George A. (1963). "Pancho's Raid Not Forgotten." *Infantry, 53, No. 4,* 9-12.

A brief account of the attack by Villa on Columbus, New Mexico, and the response of the Thirteenth Cavalry, stationed in the town. No sources cited.

167. Weinert, Richard P. (1966). "The Balangiga Massacre." *American History Illustrated, 1, No. 5,* 5-11, 37-40.

Description of the events on the island of Samar leading up to and including the worst massacre of American troops during the Philippine-American War. No sources cited.

168. Weinert, Richard P. (1966). "The Battle of Tientsin." *American History Illustrated, 1, No. 7,* 4-13, 52-55.

An account of one battle in the relief expedition in China in 1901 which included American Marines and the Ninth Infantry. No sources cited.

169. Weinert, Richard P. (1968). "The Capture of Peking." *American History Illustrated, 2, No. 9,* 20-31.

A narrative of the relief expedition, including the American troops commanded by General Chaffee. It was the first coalition warfare that the US had participated in. No sources cited.

170. Welch, Richard E. (1974). "American Atrocities in the Philippines: The Indictment and the Response." *Pacific Historical Review, 43,* 233-55.

Discussion of the charges of atrocities levied against American soldiers in the Philippine-American War and the reaction of the American public to them. The author suggests that racism conditioned the lack of any real concern in what the Army did to the Filipinos. Primary sources.

171. Welch, Richard E. (1979). *Response to Imperialism: The United States and the Philippine-American War, 1899-1902.* Chapel Hill, North Carolina: University of North Carolina Press, 215 pp.

The war in the Philippines and the impact it had on different groups in American society is the central focus of this book. One chapter recounts the debates over the military "atrocities". Printed primary sources.

172. Wharfield, Harold B. (1965). *10th Cavalry & Border Fights.* El Cajon, California: n.p., 114 pp.

An anecdotal account of some incidents in the history of the black regiment. Included are chapters on the Carrizal incident, Mexican border service, and the Punitive Expedition itself. No sources cited.

173. Wharfield, Harold B. (1968). "The Affair at Carrizal; Pershing's Punitive Expedition." *Montana, 18, No. 4,* 24-39.

Describes the background of the Punitive Expedition, and what may have motivated Pershing to send a patrol out to Carrizal. The author suggests Pershing may have wanted to create an international incident which might lead to war with Mexico. No sources cited.

174. Whittaker, William G. (1976). "Samuel Gompers, Labor, and the Mexican-American Crisis of 1916: The Carrizal Incident." *Labor History, 17,* 551-67.

Gompers engaged in a series of negotiations with Mexican labor leaders for solidarity between the two groups. During the Carrizal crisis this avenue helped prevent war between the two nations. Primary sources.

175. White, E. Bruce. (1975). "The Muddied Waters of Columbus, New Mexico." *The Americas, 32,* 72-92.

The article centers on Villa, the situation in 1916, and why the raid occurred. The author has brought together a number of the different viewpoints including the issue of German involvement. Primary and secondary sources.

176. Williams, John H. (1985). "'A Nasty Little War': The Winable Filipino Insurrection." *Retired Officer, 41, No. 8,* 30-34.

A brief account of the Philippine-American War, domestic reaction, and the reasons for the US victory. No sources cited.

177. Williams, Vernon L. (1982). "Lieutenant George S. Patton, Jr. and the American Army: On the Texas Frontier in Mexico, 1915-1916." *Military History of Texas and the Southwest, 17,* 1-87.

A detailed narrative of the activities of Patton on the Mexican border prior to and after Villa's raid. A chapter describes his patrols in Texas in 1915; another details the organization of the Punitive Expedition and Patton's participation in it. There is also an account of Patton's headline making shoot-out with some Mexicans. Primary sources.

178. Wolff, Leon. (1961). *Little Brown Brother; How the United States Purchased and Pacified the Philippine Islands at the Century's Turn.* Garden City, New York: Doubleday and Company, Inc., 383 pp.

A popular account of the campaigns of the Philippine-American War up to the time of the accession of Taft as governor. Little coverage of the domestic opposition to the war, nor of the issue of atrocities. Secondary sources.

179. Wolff, Leon. (1962). "Black Jack's Mexican Goose Chase." *American Heritage, 13, No. 4,* 22-27, 100-06.

A description of Pershing and Villa, and a brief account of the expedition itself. No sources cited.

180. Young, Karl. (1966). "A Fight That Could Have Meant War." *The American West, 3, No. 2,* 16-23, 90.

An account of the clash at Carrizal written from the perspective of Lemuel Spilsbury, the Mormon scout who participated in the fight. It is also an attempt to explain why the clash occurred. General list of sources.

ECONOMIC ISSUES

181. Cuff, Robert D. (1972). "The Cooperative Impulse and War: The Origins of the Council of National Defense and Advisory Commission." In Jerry Israel, (ed.), *Building the Organizational Society.* New York: The Free Press, 233-46.

The essay describes how private institutions developed the initiative and the talent for the administrative response to the economic problems of warfare. Howard Coffin and his organization worked closely with the Preparedness Committee. When war approached, the federal government used their expertise. Primary and secondary sources.

182. Molander, Earl A. (1976). "Historical Antecedents of Military-Industrial Criticism." *Military Affairs, 40,* 59-63.

The author presents evidence that from the beginning of this century some individuals criticized what they felt were too close ties between the military and the industrial sector. In the pre-World War I era the idea of a military-industrial complex was not articulated but there was some criticism of industry. Primary sources.

EDUCATION

183. Ambrose, Stephen E. (1966). *Duty, Honor, Country: A History of West Point.* Baltimore, Maryland: Johns Hopkins Press, 357 pp.

This is a detailed history of the academy, centering around the role of key individuals. A section of one chapter describes the educational stagnation which developed and the attempts by a few individuals to reform the institution, while others tried to destroy it. Primary sources.

184. Ball, Harry P. (1983). *Of Responsible Command: A History of the U. S. Army War College*. Carlisle Barracks, Pennsylvania: Alumni Association of the U. S. Army War College, 534 pp.

A detailed history of the War College, with several chapters on the pre-World War I period. Includes the events that led up to the creation of the institution, Root's conception of what the college should be, the differing ideas the heads of the college had as to its role, the course of study, and the contributions of the college to the General Staff. Primary sources.

185. Davies, Richard G. (1984). "Of Arms and the Boy: A History of Culver Military Academy, 1894-1945." Dissertation, Indiana University, 45/5-A, p. 1313.

After tracing the origins of military schools, the author focuses on Culver Academy. In this period the school sought to shape adolescent boys through the use of military training.

186. Dupuy, Richard E. (1951). *Men of West Point; The First 150 Years of the United States Military Academy*. New York: Sloane, 486 pp.

This general history of some of the Academy graduates has part of a chapter on the early years of this century including material on the Philippines. In addition there is a discussion of educational improvement at the school. Brief chapter notes.

187. Fleming, Thomas J. (1969). *West Point: The Men and Times of the United States Military Academy*. New York: William Morrow & Company, Inc., 402 pp.

An anecdotal history of the Academy and its graduates. For the pre-war period there are stories about Patton, MacArthur, and Goethals, as well as information about attempts at educational reform. Secondary and primary sources.

188. Forman, Sidney. (1950). *West Point: A History of the United States Military Academy*. New York: Columbia University Press, 255 pp.

Two brief chapters of this general history describe the period between 1900 and 1917. It includes material on the curriculum and the instructors. Some primary, mainly secondary sources.

189. Kraus, John D. (1978). "The Civilian Military Colleges in the Twentieth Century: Factors Influencing Their Survival." Dissertation, University of Iowa, 39/8-A, pp. 4760-61.

A study of schools with a military environment but having no direct connection with the federal government. They incorporated a military system into their educational structure for a variety of reasons. Three survive and remain healthy from the eleven the Army recognized in 1903.

190. Lyons, Gene M., and Masland, John W. (1959). "The Origins of the ROTC." *Military Affairs, 23,* 1-12.

The focus of this article is on the development of reserve officer education prior to 1916. The author notes the roles of Henry Stimson and Leonard Wood in the creation of these programs. Primary sources.

191. Lyons, Gene M., and Masland, John W. (1959). *Education and Military Leadership: A Study of the ROTC*. Princeton, New Jersey: Princeton University Press, 283 pp.

A brief section of this book explains the pre-World War I development of what became ROTC. Primary and secondary sources.

192. Masland, John W., and Radway, Laurence I. (1957). *Soldiers and Scholars: Military Educational and National Policy*. Princeton, New Jersey: Princeton University Press, 530 pp.

A general study of military education, especially post-graduate training. One chapter examines the development of such programs prior to World War II. Few sources cited.

193. Nenninger, Timothy K. (1978). *The Leavenworth Schools and the Old Army: Education, Professionalism, and the Officer Corps of the United States Army, 1881-1918*. Westport, Connecticut: Greenwood Press, 173 pp.

An account of the development of the school system in the United States Army. Though it began under General William Sherman in the late 19th century, the system greatly expanded under the leadership of Secretary of War Elihu Root and General J. Franklin Bell. The author also discusses the impact of the staff officers on World War I. Mainly based on primary sources.

194. Nye, Roger H. (1968). "The United States Military Academy in an Era of Educational Reform, 1900-1925." Dissertation, Columbia University, 29/3-A, p. 856.

Reform in the military and in American education after 1900 raised questions about the quality of education at the Military Academy. Though some changes were made, they were mainly in the form of improvements in the current system. Little was done to change the curriculum; they "perfected the traditional nineteenth century college."

195. Pappas, George S. (1967). *Prudens Futuri: The U. S. Army War College, 1901-1967*. Carlisle, Pennsylvania: The Alumni Association of the US Army War College, 338 pp.

A somewhat brief history of the college, with several chapters devoted to the formative 1900-1917 period, including the development of the curriculum. The chapter on the creation of the college contains long quotations from documents. Primary sources.

196. Raines, Edgar F. (1976). "Major General J. Franklin Bell and Military Reform: The Chief of Staff Years, 1906-1910." Dissertation, University of Wisconsin-Madison, 38/1-A, p. 442.

This study focuses on the impact of General Bell upon the attempts to modernize the Army. Proposals from military managers ran into opposition from the bureaus. The author further considers the impact of the industrial revolution on the Army. The dissertation also includes a consideration of the officer corps, in terms of its ideology and influence as a pressure group.

197. Reardon, Carol A. (1987). "The Study of Military History and the Growth of Professionalism in the U. S. Army Before World War I." Dissertation, University of Kentucky, 48/4-A, pp. 1005-06.

The study of military history in the early part of this century is an indicator of the development of professionalism within the Army. History was used for training purposes, often based on texts written by soldiers for soldiers. There also developed a split between civilians and soldiers writing military history.

198. Rulon, Philip R. (1979). "The Campus Cadets: A History of Collegiate Military Training, 1891-1951." *Chronicles of Oklahoma, 57,* 67-90.

An article on the development and impact of military training at Oklahoma State University. A brief section concerns the period before World War I. Primary and secondary sources.

199. Vollmar, William J. (1976). "The Issue of Compulsory Military Training at The Ohio State University, 1913-1973." Dissertation, Ohio State University, 37/2-A, pp. 1182-83.

In this early period four men from Ohio State developed and drafted legislation for the program that would become ROTC. It became a feature of undergraduate education at the school.

200. Wainwright, John D. (1974). "Root versus Bliss: The Shaping of the Army War College." *Parameters, 4, No. 2,* 52-65.

An account of how what Root intended when he founded the War College (for it to be a college dedicated to the study of war) was changed by Bliss (a college to assist the General Staff). Primary and secondary sources.

ENGINEERS

201. _____. (1985). *The Federal Engineer, Damsites to Missile Sites; A History of the Omaha District, U. S. Army Corps of Engineers.* Washington, D.C.: U. S. Army Corps of Engineers, Omaha District, 279 pp. SD D103.2:F31.

An introduction to the navigation and flooding problems of the upper Missouri River basin. The majority of the work of the Engineers to deal with these problems did not begin until after World War I. Primary and secondary sources.

202. _____. (1986). *The History of the US Army Corps of Engineers.* Washington, D.C.: Government Printing Office, 132 pp. SD D103.43:360-1-21.

A brief history of the military and civil operations of the Corps of Engineers. No sources cited but a bibliography included.

203. Alperin, Lynn M. (1977). *Custodians of the Coast; History of the United States Army Engineers at Galveston.* Galveston, Texas: U. S. Army Corps of Engineers, 318 pp. SD D103.2:C96.

Description of the role of the Engineers in developing the Texas coastal region through harbor development projects at Galveston, Houston, and other sites, and the building of a section of the Intercoastal Waterway. Primary and secondary sources.

204. Branyan, Robert L. (1974). *Taming the Mighty Missouri; A History of the Kansas City District, Corps of Engineers, 1907-1971*. Kansas City, Missouri: U. S. Army Corps of Engineers, Kansas City District, 128 pp. SD D103.2:M69o/2.

Describes a variety of Engineer activities including flood control and navigation improvements. Mainly secondary sources with some interviews included.

205. Buker, George E. (1981). *Sun, Sand and Water; A History of the Jacksonville District, U. S. Army Corps of Engineers, 1821-1975*. Jacksonville, Florida: U. S. Army Corps of Engineers, Jacksonville District, 288 pp. SD D103.2:Su7.

The projects covered in this work include: flood control, Intercoastal Waterway construction and maintenance, and harbor dredging and expansion. Primary and secondary sources.

206. Chambers, John W., II. (1980). *The North Atlantic Engineers: A History of the North Atlantic Division and Its Predecessors in the U. S. Army Corps of Engineers, 1775-1975*. New York: U. S. Army Corps of Engineers, North Atlantic Division, 167 pp.

A brief history of the development of the Engineers in the East. Includes material on civil projects, such as raising the *U.S.S. Maine*, and military projects, such as coastal fortifications. Mainly secondary sources.

207. Clay, Floyd M., and Williams, Bobby Joe. (1986). *A Century on the Mississippi; A History of the Memphis District, U. S. Army Corps of Engineers, 1876-1981*. Washington, D.C.: U. S. Army Corps of Engineers, Memphis District, 357 pp. SD D103.2:M69/10.

About fifteen pages describes the efforts of the Engineers in the period before World War I to deal with the flooding of the Mississippi and the maintenance of a navigation channel. Primary and secondary sources.

208. Claybourn, John G. (1931). *Dredging on The Panama Canal*. Panama: n.p., 95 pp.

A detailed account, with numerous photographs, of this particular phase of the Army's work on the canal. No sources cited.

209. Cowdrey, Albert E. (1977). *Land's End; A History of the New Orleans District, U. S. Army Corps of Engineers, and Its Lifelong Battle with the Lower Mississippi and Other Rivers Wending Their Way to the Sea*. New Orleans, Louisiana: U. S. Army Corps of Engineers, New Orleans District, 118 pp. SD D103.2:L23.

Among the projects described during this time period are efforts to control the flooding of the Mississippi and river navigation improvements. Primary and secondary sources.

210. Cowdrey, Albert E. (1980). *A City For The Nation; The Army Engineers and the Building of Washington, D.C., 1790-1967*. Washington, D.C.: Historical Division, Office of Administrative Services, Office of the Chief of Engineers, 77 pp.
Description of the role of the Engineers in the construction of many of the important public buildings of this time period including the Army War College and the Government Printing Office. In addition there is material on other projects, such as bridges, which the Engineers contributed to. Primary and secondary sources.

211. Crump, Irving. (1954). *Our Army Engineers*. New York: Dodd, Mead and Company, 274 pp.
A popular account, without footnotes or bibliography, of events in the history of the Engineers. Among those included are the raising of the *U.S.S. Maine* and the building of the Panama Canal. There is also material on navigation and flood control projects.

212. Davis, Virgil. (1977). *A History of the Mobile District, United States Army Corps of Engineers, 1815 to 1971*. Mobile, Alabama: U. S. Corps of Engineers, South Atlantic Division, Mobile District, 109 pp. SD 103.2:M71/815-971.
Description of the regional projects engaged in by the Corps of Engineers, including flood control on the Chattahoochee River and harbor fortifications in Mobile. Primary and secondary sources.

213. Dobney, Fredrick J. (1978). *River Engineers on the Middle Mississippi; A History of the St. Louis District, U. S. Army Corps of Engineers*. Washington, D.C.: U. S. Army Corps of Engineers, St. Louis District, 177 pp. SD D103.2:M69i.
A brief description of the efforts of the Engineers in the St. Louis area to control the river and make it usable for navigation. Secondary sources.

214. Drescher, Nuala M. (1982). *Engineers for the Public Good: A History of the Buffalo District, U. S. Army Corps of Engineers*. Buffalo, New York: U. S. Army Corps of Engineers, Buffalo District, 328 pp. SD D103.2:En3/4.
Different kinds of projects were engaged in by these Engineers including harbor facilities, lighthouses, and power houses on the Niagara River. Primary and secondary sources.

215. Eastwood, Harland, Sr. (1983). *Fort Whitman on Puget Sound 1911-1945*. Lopez, Washington: Twin Anchors Co., 85 pp.
Brief typewritten manuscript on the construction, by the Corps of Engingeers, of this coastal defense post in the Puget Sound area. Includes photographs of the installations. Primary sources.

216. Ficken, Robert E. (1976). "Seattle's 'Ditch': The Corps of Engineers and the Lake Washington Ship Canal." *Pacific Northwest Quarterly*, 77, 11-20.
A discussion of the origins and construction by the Engineers of a ship canal in the Seattle area, whose locks were second only in size to those in Panama. It is an example of the type of work the Engineers were doing in the era before World War I. Primary sources.

217. Granger, Mary L. (1968). *History of the Savannah District, 1829-1968.* Savannah, Georgia: U. S. Army Corps of Engineers, Savannah District, 114 pp.

A brief account of the programs supervised by the Engineers, including harbor improvements and river navigation in the Savannah area. Also includes some mention of coastal fortifications constructed by the Corps. No sources listed.

218. Green, Sherman. (1969). *History of the Seattle District, 1896-1968.* Seattle, Washington: U. S. Army Corps of Engineers, Seattle District, chapters individually numbered.

A poorly written history of the Engineers in Seattle. Only a brief mention of their work on the Lake Washington Ship Canal and in river and harbor work. No sources cited.

219. Hagwood, Joseph J., Jr. (1981). *Engineers at the Golden Gate; A History of the San Francisco District, U. S. Army Corps of Engineers, 1866-1980.* San Francisco, California: U. S. Army Corps of Engineers, San Francisco District, 452 pp. SD D103.2:G56/866-980.

An account of the activities of the Corps of Engineers in Northern California including water systems, navigation, and port development. This includes bridges in Oakland, fortifications in the entrance to San Francisco Bay, and debris collection in the Bay. Primary and secondary sources.

220. Hartzer, Ronald B. (1984). *To Great and Useful Purpose; A History of the Wilmington District, U. S. Army Corps of Engineers.* Washington, D.C.: n.p., 172 pp. SD D103.2:W68.

The Engineers in this district in North Carolina constructed part of the Intercoastal Waterway, dredged harbors, tried to stop beach erosion, and dealt with flood damage. Primary and secondary sources.

221. Hoften, Ellen van. (1970). *History of the Honolulu Engineer District, 1905-1965.* Honolulu, Hawaii: U. S. Army Corps of Engineers, 133 pp.

Brief chapter on the formation of the district and the construction of harbor defenses. Printed primary and secondary sources.

222. Johnson, Leland R. (1975). *The Falls City Engineers; A History of the Louisville District, Corps of Engineers, United States Army.* Washington, D.C.: U. S. Army Corps of Engineers, Louisville District, 347 pp. SD D103.2:F19.

One of the major projects in this time period was the canalization of the Ohio River. In addition the Corps began to work on flood control projects. Primary and secondary sources.

223. Johnson, Leland R. (1977). *Men, Mountains, and Rivers; An Illustrated History of the Huntington District, U. S. Army Corps of Engineers, 1754-1974.* Washington, D.C.: U. S. Army Corps of Engineers, Huntington District, 322 pp. SD D103.2:H 92/754-974.

A description of the activities of the Engineers in part of the Ohio Valley, with projects in Ohio and West Virginia, and an account of the development of the system of navigational locks on the Ohio River. Mainly secondary sources.

224. Johnson, Leland R. (1978). *Engineers on the Twin Rivers; A History of the Nashville District, Corps of Engineers, United States Army*. Washington, D.C.: U. S. Army Corps of Engineers, Nashville District, 329 pp. SD D103.2:T92.

An official history of the Engineers and their work on the Tennessee and Cumberland Rivers, including flood control and navigation projects. Primary and secondary sources.

225. Johnson, Leland R. (1985). *The Davis Island Lock and Dam, 1870-1922*. Washington, D.C.: U. S. Army Corps of Engineers, Pittsburgh District, 170 pp. SD D103.2:D29/870-922.

An early concrete dam on the Ohio near Pittsburgh is the focus of this history. It provided the first step toward the canalization of the Ohio River. The book also discusses the impact of the dam on Pittsburgh and waterway construction. Primary and secondary sources.

226. Kanarek, Harold. (1978). *The Mid-Atlantic Engineers: A History of the Baltimore District, U. S. Army Corps of Engineers, 1774-1974*. Baltimore, Maryland: U. S. Army Corps of Engineers, Baltimore District, 196 pp. SD D103.2:B21/774-974.

In the first part of this century the major work of this group of Engineers was river and harbor navigation. Secondary were harbor fortifications and military construction. Primary and secondary sources.

227. Klawonn, Marion J. (1977). *Cradle of the Corps; A History of the New York District, U. S. Army Corps of Engineers, 1775-1975*. New York: U. S. Army Corps of Engineers, New York District, 310 pp. SD D103.2:N42y/775-975.

This official history describes the work of the Engineers including maintenance of New York harbor and the raising of the *U.S.S. Maine*. Primary sources used but not cited.

228. Larson, John W. (1980). *Those Army Engineers; A History of the Chicago District, U. S. Army Corps of Engineers*. Washington, D.C.: U. S. Army Corps of Engineers, Chicago District, 307 pp. SD D103.2:C43/4.

A variety of projects were undertaken by the Engineers in the area including including developing Chicago and other harbors, dredging ship canals on several rivers, and improving navigation on the Illinois River. Some primary and secondary sources cited.

229. Larson, John W. (1981). *Essayons; A History of the Detroit District, U. S. Army Corps of Engineers*. Detroit, Michigan: U. S. Army Corps of Engineers, Detroit District, 215 pp. SD D103.2:Es7.

Two major concerns of the Engineers in this district that are described in this offically sponsored history were the channels connecting the Great Lakes, such as the locks at Sault Ste. Marie, and harbors from Mackinac Island to Toledo. Primary sources.

230. Merritt, Raymond H. (1980). *Creativity, Conflict and Controversy: A History of the St. Paul District, U. S. Army Corps of Engineers*. Washington, D.C.: Government Printing Office, 461 pp. SD D103.2:Sa2p.

The major task of the Engineers in this period, as recounted in this history, was to keep navigation flowing on the Upper Mississippi. Primary sources.

231. Moore, Jamie W. (1981). *The Lowcountry Engineers; Military Missions and Economic Development in the Charleston District, U. S. Army Corps of Engineers.* Charleston, South Carolina: U. S. Army Corps of Engineers, Charleston District, 140 pp. SD D103.2:L95.

A brief history of the Engineers and their activities in this region including harbor improvements, coastal fortifications, and construction of part of the Intercoastal Waterway. Primary and secondary sources.

232. O'Brien, Bob R. (1967). "The Roads of Yellowstone: 1870-1915." *Montana, 17, No. 2,* 30-39.

The major road system in the park was built by the Corps of Engineers in the 1890s and the early part of this century. It has largely endured to this day. Primary sources.

233. Parkman, Aubrey. (1978). *Army Engineers in New England; The Military and Civil Work of The Corps of Engineers in New England, 1775-1975.* Waltham, Massachusetts: U. S. Army Corps of Engineers, New England Division, 319 pp. SD D103.2:N42e/2/775-975.

A description of the variety of activities performed by the Engineers in New England including building the Cape Cod Canal and constructing harbor defenses. Primary sources.

234. Reuss, Martin. (1985). "Andrew A. Humphreys and the Development of Hydraulic Engineering: Politics and Technology in the Army Corps of Engineers, 1850-1950." *Technology and Culture, 26,* 1-33.

An analysis of the development and continuation of the Engineer's approach to harnessing the Mississippi, levees. It continued to be their policy until the 1930s floods challenged its validity. Primary sources.

235. Richmond, Henry R., III. (1970). *The History of the Portland District, Corps of Engineers, 1871-1969.* Portland, Oregon: U.S. Army Corps of Engineers, Portland District, 273 pp.

A brief account of the various activities of this group of Engineers. Includes material on coastal harbors, river navigation on the Columbia, and harbor defenses. No sources cited.

236. Scheufle, Roy W. (1969). *The History of the North Pacific Division, U. S. Army Corps of Engineers, 1888 to 1965.* Portland, Oregon: U. S. Army Corps of Engineers, North Pacific Division, 53 pp.

A brief section on the pre-war period in this official history. Projects were typical of the Corps, including harbor improvements. Biographical sketches of Division Commanders. Published primary and secondary sources.

237. Small, Charles S. (1980). *Rails to Doomsday: The U. S. Army's Corregidor and Manila Bay Railroads.* Greenwich, Connecticut: Published by the Author, 78 pp.

An account of the construction of a series of short railroads used initially for construction and then for passenger transportation on these islands. Numerous photographs and diagrams. Primary sources.

238. Small, Charles S. (1982). *Military Railroads on the Panama Canal Zone.* Cos Cob, Connecticut: Railroad Monographs, 64 pp.

When the Canal opened a series of fortifications were constructed to guard both entrances. These were served by a series of short railroad lines, described in great detail in this well illustrated brief work. Primary sources.

239. Snyder, Frank E. and Guss, Brian H. (1974). *The District: A History of the Philadelphia District, U. S. Army Corps of Engineers, 1866-1971.* Philadelphia, Pennsylvania: U. S. Army Corps of Engineers, Philadelphia District, 263 pp. SD D104.2:P53.

A variety of projects undertaken by the Corps of Engineers in this area are described including lighthouse building, harbor dredging, canal building, and harbor fortification construction. Numerous illustrations. Secondary sources.

240. Thompson, Erwin N. (1985). *Pacific Ocean Engineers; History of the U. S. Army Corps of Engineers in the Pacific, 1905-1980.* Washington, D.C.: U. S. Army Corps of Engineers, Pacific Ocean Division, 460 pp. SD D103.2:En3/7/905-80.

Included in this official work are accounts of fortification construction in Hawaii and harbor improvement in Honolulu. Primary and secondary sources cited.

241. Turhollow, Anthony F. (1975). *A History of the Los Angeles District, U. S. Army Corps of Engineers, 1898-1965.* Los Angeles: U. S. Army Corps of Engineers, Los Angeles District, 440 pp. SD D103.2:L89A/898-965.

An account of the Los Angeles district, concentrating mainly on projects in water resources. This included harbor projects in San Diego and Los Angeles, and flood control throughout the region. Primary and secondary sources.

242. Tweet, Roald. (1984). *A History of The Rock Island District, U. S. Army Corps of Engineers, 1866-1983.* Washington, D.C.: U. S. Army Corps of Engineers, Rock Island District, 441 pp. SD D103.2:R59/4.

Several chapters describe projects of this era including widening the upper Mississippi navigation channel, building locks, and constructing the Illinois and Mississippi Canal. Primary sources.

LOGISTICS

243. Beaver, Daniel R. (1977). "The Problem of American Military Supply, 1890-1920." In Benjamin F. Cooling, (ed.), *War, Business, and American Society: Historical Perspectives on the Military-Industrial Complex.* Port Washington, New York: Kennikat Press, 73-92.

This essay describes the evolution of the supply apparatus within the Army after the Spanish-American War. The author considers the input received from the industrial sector of the economy and its role in shaping the military institutions. The majority of the article deals with the impact of World War I on the system during and after the war. Based mainly on primary sources.

244. Huston, James A. (1966). *The Sinews of War: Army Logistics, 1775-1953.* Washington, D.C.: Office of the Chief of Military History, United States Army, 789 pp. SD D114.2.W19.

This official history contains a chapter which describes logistics in the pre-war period. Included is information on organization reform, technological changes and overseas expeditions. Secondary and primary sources.

245. Millard, George A. (1980). "US Army Logistics During the Mexican Punitive Expedition of 1916." *Military Review, 60, No. 10,* 58-68.

A description of the supply operations of the Punitive Expedition, including terrain problems, types of vehicles used, difficulties with obtaining forage, and logistical limits on operations. The author suggests the real impact would be felt the following year when the lessons learned were applied in France. Secondary sources.

246. Risch, Erna. (1962). *Quartermaster Support of the Army: A History of the Corps 1775-1939.* Washington, D.C.: Quartermaster Historian's Office, Office of the Quartermaster General, 796 pp. SD D106.8/3:Q2/775-939.

One chapter of this official survey recounts the evolution of the Corps as a result of the Root reforms and the problems that occurred with technological innovations such as motor vehicles. Primary sources.

MANAGEMENT

247. Addington, Larry H. (1976). "The U. S. Coast Artillery and the Problem of Artillery Organization, 1907-1954." *Military Affairs, 40,* 1-6.

From its beginning, the new division of Coast Artillery had to work out its position relative to the other branches and the new Chief of Staff. This articles explains this process as well as the effort to define its mission. Primary and secondary sources.

248. Eyck, F. Gunther. (1971). "Secretary Stimson and the Army Reforms, 1911-1913." *Parameters, 1, No. 1,* 19-28.

As described by Eyck, Secretary of War Stimson continued Root's efforts to improve the Army. He helped Wood defeat Ainsworth, worked to build up an efficient reserve force, and tried to create the organizational structure for a mobile Army. No sources cited.

249. Hammond, Keith. (1983). "From Imperial Eagle to Chicken Colonel: Aspects of Transition." *Army Quarterly and Defence Journal, 113,* 451-62.

A brief and somewhat cynical view of some of factors that led Root to adopt a General Staff system in 1903, including the relationship with the German model. Secondary sources.

250. Hammond, Paul Y. (1961). *Organizing for Defense: The American Military Establishment in the Twentieth Century.* Princeton, New Jersey: Princeton University Press, 403 pp.

An account of the evolution of the structure of the armed forces. One chapter sketches the Root reforms and development of the position of Secretary of War and Chief of Staff. Primary sources.

251. Hewes, James E., Jr. (1974). "The United States Army General Staff, 1900-1917." *Military Affairs, 38,* 67-72.

A brief account of the development of the general staff. The author argues that managerial changes in this period were similar to those in industry, and were resisted by those already in power. Additional sidelights are provided by Edward M. Coffman. No sources cited.

252. Hewes, James E., Jr. (1975). *From Root to McNamara: Army Organization and Administration, 1900-1963.* Washington, D.C.: Center of Military History, United States Army, 452 pp. SD D114.17:Or3/900-63.

A chapter in this book from the Office of the Chief of Military History covers the Army from 1900 to 1940. Included in that is a section on the Root reforms and its impact in the years prior to World War I. Primary and secondary sources.

253. Hittle, James D. (1949). *The Military Staff: Its History and Development.* Harrisburg, Pennsylvania: Military Service Publishing Company, 286 pp.

Hittle has written a general survey of the development of the staff system with one relatively brief chapter devoted to the United States. Secondary sources.

254. Karsten, Peter. (1972). "Armed Progressives: The Military Reorganizes for the American Century". In Jerry Israel, (ed.), *Building the Organizational Society.* New York: The Free Press, 197-232.

Karsten discusses both the Army and the Navy reform movements. In the section on the Army, there is material on the development of the staff and the relations with the National Guard. Primary and secondary sources.

255. Nelson, Otto L. (1946). *National Security and the General Staff.* Washington, D.C.: Infantry Journal Press, 608 pp.

A detailed, and somewhat pedestrian, history of the General Staff. Three chapters describe the origins of the staff, its early years, the battle between Wood and Ainsworth, and the consequences. Numerous documents are cited at length. Published primary and secondary sources.

256. Pohl, James W. (1967). "The General Staff and American Military Policy: The Formative Period, 1898-1917." Dissertation, University of Texas-Austin, 28/10-A, p. 4100

Though Root was able to convince Congress to create a general staff in 1903, the organization had no clearly defined mission. Under Leonard Wood and his successors some progress was made, but disputes over reserve policy weakened the power of the Staff. By 1916, however, the Staff had become a permanent organization. The author views this development in terms of civil-military relations.

257. Powe, Marc B. (1975). "A Great Debate: The American General Staff (1903-16)." *Military Review, 55, No. 4,* 71-89.

Beginning with an introduction on the creation of the staff, the author sketches how different individuals viewed the staff and how its role evolved in the period prior to World War I. The roles of Elihu Root, Major William Carter, and Leonard Wood in creating a staff system are analyzed. Mainly secondary sources.

258. Roberts, William R. (1980). "Loyalty and Expertise: The Transformation of the Nineteenth-Century American General Staff and the Creation of the Modern Military Establishment." Dissertation, Johns Hopkins University, 40/9-A, p. 5158.

Despite what many have claimed, the author feels that the origins of the 1903 reforms can best be viewed as a continuation of the struggle between staff and line which originated in the nineteenth century. Success was achieved when Root joined the staff supporters. The dissertation also examines the parallel experiences, and their differences, in the Navy.

259. Semsch, Philip L. (1963). "Elihu Root and the General Staff." *Military Affairs, 27,* 16-27.

An account of the creation of the General Staff and the role that Elihu Root played in the process. Semsch explains the political and military hurdles Root had to overcome. Primary and secondary sources.

260. Weigley, Russell F. (1963). "The Military Thought of John M. Schofield." *Military Affairs, 23,* 77-84.

Despite having served in the Civil War, Schofield was not wedded to the organizational structures of that conflict. He objected to viewing war as glorious, but felt that if it must be fought, the command structure needed to be revised. An advocate of a staff system, he helped convince Congress in 1902 that this change should be made. Primary sources.

261. Weigley, Russell F. (1968). "The Elihu Root Reforms and the Progressive Era." In William Geffen, (ed.), *Command and Commanders in Modern Warfare; The Proceedings of the Second Military History Symposium, U. S. Air Force Academy, 2-3 May 1968.* Washington, D.C.: Office of Air Force History, Headquarters USAF and United States Air Force Academy, 11-27. SD D301.78:968.

Weigley places the Root reforms in the context of their time and equates the General Staff to regulatory agencies also established by the Progressives. Comments by Louis Morton are included.

262. Zais, Barrie E. (1981). "The Struggle for a 20th Century Army: Investigation and Reform of the United States Army After the Spanish-American War, 1898-1903." Dissertation, Duke University, 42/4-A, p. 1748.

Viewing the Root reforms as the culmination of a long struggle, the author explains what was done and why. The reforms brought about organizational changes which had been long advocated. The author also suggests how the Spanish-American War created a unique situation which also contributed to the success of the reform effort.

MANPOWER

263. Burdett, Thomas F. (1974). "Mobilizations of 1911 and 1913: Their Role in the Development of the Modern Army." *Military Review, 54, No. 7,* 65-74.

Under the leadership of Leonard Wood, the Army in 1911 and 1913 conducted large scale mobilizations. Wood used these occasions to test the staff system and then to develop large unit maneuvers. Deficiencies appeared and efforts were made to correct them. Secondary sources.

264. Clifford, John G. (1971). "Leonard Wood, Samuel Gompers, and the Plattsburg Training Camps." *New York History, 52*, 169-89.
    A series of letters introduced by the author. There is a description of the attitudes of Gompers toward preparedness and the impact that these views had on Wood's program. Primary sources.

265. Clifford, John G. (1972). *The Citizen Soldiers: The Plattsburg Training Camp Movement, 1913-1920*. Lexington, Kentucky: The University Press of Kentucky, 326 pp.
    Leonard Wood and Grenville Clark led the movement to train civilians for military service. This movement had its origins in both the progressivism of the day and the ideas of some military reformers. The goal was to prepare citizen soldiers for a conflict which the leaders felt was coming. Primary and secondary sources.

266. Crossland, Richard B. and Currie, James T. (1984). *Twice the Citizen: A History of the United States Army Reserve, 1903-1983*. Washington, D.C.: Office of the Chief, Army Reserve, 325 pp. SD D101.22:140-14.
    Several chapters discuss the origins of the reserve in this period, beginning with the 1908 legislation which created the Medical Reserve. The authors also include the debates over the reserve force and the 1916 legislation which shaped it. Printed primary and secondary sources.

267. Edwards, John C. (1976). "Playing the Patriot Game: The Story of the American Defense Society, 1915-1932." *Studies in History and Society, 1*, 54-72.
    This organization tried to be apolitical in its efforts to raise support for preparedness in 1915-1916. Its efforts were hindered by political and financial squabbles within its membership. The author believes the Society was part of the upperclass effort for preparedness. Primary sources.

268. Edwards, John C. (1982). *Patriots in Pinstripe: Men of the National Security League*. Washington, D.C.: University Press of America, 236 pp.
    A study of the ideas of the leaders and members of the National Security League (1915-1942), an organization which advocated preparedness. Most of the leaders were upperclass Americans concerned about our lack of preparedness, but the rank and file were a cross section of America. Post-war divisions killed the organization. Primary sources.

269. Finnegan, John P. (1974). *Against the Specter of the Dragon: The Campaign for American Military Preparedness, 1914-1917*. Westport, Connecticut: Greenwood Press, 253 pp.
    The attempt by a number of individuals to make America strong forms the focus of Finnegan's study. The author describes the different civilian and military elements that pushed the preparedness campaign, the reaction of Wilson and the Congress, and the relationship between the campaign and the war in Europe. Mainly primary sources.

270. Herring, George C., Jr. (1964). "James Hay and the Preparedness Controversy, 1915-1916." *Journal of Southern History, 30*, 383-404.
   Hay, as head of the House Military Affairs Committee, played a crucial role in the passage of the 1916 National Defense Act. Though initially opposed to many of the ideas contained in the Army's proposal, he decided that the times needed some legislation. Rejecting the Continental Army concept, he helped put through the final legislation which gave a larger role to the National Guard. Primary sources.

271. House, Jonathan M. (1982). "John McAuley Palmer and the Reserve Components." *Parameters, 12, No. 3*, 11-18.
   The position of Palmer on the utilization of citizen soldiers, as described in this article, was significant in the pre-war manpower debates. Early in the century he began to advocate utilizing citizen soldiers and this helped shape the 1916 National Defense Act. Primary and secondary sources.

272. Kreidberg, Marvin A., and Henry, Merton G. (1955). *History of Military Mobilization in the United States Army, 1775-1945*. Washington, D.C.: Office of the Chief of Military History, Department of the Army, 721 pp.
   One chapter of this classic work describes the formation of the General Staff and how it began to plan for manpower utilization in a possible future war. Also discussed are the various manpower plans and the roles envisioned for the National Guard. Published primary and secondary sources.

273. Mooney, Chase C., and Layman, Martha E. (1952). "Some Phases of the Compulsory Military Training Movement, 1914-1920." *Mississippi Valley Historical Review, 38*, 633-56.
   An account of the development of this program, from the prospective of Leonard Wood, the War Department, and Congress, prior to our entry into World War I. Primary sources.

274. Pearlman, Michael. (1979). "Leonard Wood, William Muldoon and the Medical Profession: Public Health and Universal Military Training." *New England Quarterly, 52*, 326-44.
   Some of the medical profession supported the concept of UMT because they felt it would help society as a form of public health. William Muldoon, a medical friend of Wood, was a leader in this effort. Primary sources.

275. Pearlman, Michael. (1984). *To Make Democracy Safe for America: Patricians and Preparedness in the Progressive Era*. Urbana, Illinois: University of Illinois Press, 297 pp.
   The preparedness movement was seen by some upper class leaders as a way of reforming American society. They also hoped that military training and any possible war would act as a catharsis for the social problems in a society with a disparate population, especially the immigrants and the poor. Based on primary and some secondary sources.

276. Reynolds, Mary T. (1939). "The General Staff as a Propaganda Agency, 1908-1914." *Public Opinion Quarterly, 3*, 391-408.
   The article focuses on Leonard Wood. The author suggests that the Staff made an effort through a variety of forums to influence Americans to adopt the idea of preparedness. These included annual reports, field maneuvers, and speeches. Primary sources.

277. Steinson, Barbara J. (1977). "Female Activism in World War I: The American Women's Peace, Suffrage, Preparedness, and Relief Movements, 1914-1919." Dissertation, University of Michigan, 38/3-A, pp. 1606-07.
A number of women were involved in the peace movement after 1914 and had key roles in it. Others participated in the preparedness movement, though not as many nor with much influence. On the other hand, the male leaders pointed out their support in contrast to the women's peace movement. In addition the preparedness movement included some women's service camps.

278. Steinson, Barbara J. (1981). "Sisters and Soldiers: American Women and the National Service Schools, 1916-1917." *The Historian, 43*, 225-39.
An adjunct to the preparedness movement, these schools for women were supported by President Wilson and (half-heartedly) by General Wood. The four that were held had no major impact on preparedness but they did indicate the interest of women in the issue. They also had a consciousness raising impact on those that attended. Primary sources.

279. Tinsley, William W. (1939). "The American Preparedness Movement, 1913-1916." Dissertation, Stanford University, Doctoral Dissertations Accepted by American Universities, 1940, p. 92.
An early account of the movement to convince the American public to prepare for war, centering on organizations such as the National Security League, military leaders like Leoanrd Wood, and on the debates in Congress. Printed primary and secondary sources.

280. Ward, Robert D. (1960). "The Origin and Activities of the National Security League, 1914-1919." *Mississippi Valley Historical Review, 47*, 51-65.
Description of a very influential organization which advocated preparedness, especially universal military training. Also describes its upper-class leaders. Primary sources.

281. Ward, Robert D. (1971). "A Note on General Leonard Wood's Experimental Companies." *Military Affairs, 35*, 92-93.
A brief article which describes an effort by General Wood to demonstrate that recruits could become competent soldiers within a year, if they had the benefit of intensive training. Wood's companies were part of the debate over the basis of preparedness. Primary sources.

MISCELLANEOUS

282. _____. (1976). *The Army Lawyer: A History of the Judge Advocate General's Office, 1775-1975*. Washington, D.C.: U. S. Army, Judge Advocate General's Corps, 278 pp.
Brief history of the Corps and of the leadership. Some material on the Brownsville affray and 1916 revision of the Articles of War. Printed primary and secondary sources.

283. Alexander, Thomas G., and Arrington, Leonard J. (1964). "The Utah Military Frontier, 1872-1912: Forts Cameron, Thornburgh, and Duchesne." *Utah Historical Quarterly, 32*, 330-54.

A survey of three different posts. Only Duchesne still existed in this century, and a brief part of the article covers this topic. Primary sources.

284. Arrington, Leonard J., and Alexander, Thomas G. (1965). "The U. S. Army Overlooks Salt Lake Valley: Fort Douglas, 1862-1965." *Utah Historical Quarterly, 33*, 326-50.

A general history of the post with brief references to the period after the Spanish-American War. Primary sources.

285. Avins, Alfred. (1956). "State Court Review of National Guard Courts-Martial and Military Board Decisions, 1836-1954." *Cornell Law Quarterly, 41*, 457-71.

The key decision in this area was made in New York in 1901. The principle enunciated was that courts could review decisions of state militia tribunals. This precedent has been followed by most other states. Primary sources.

286. Bayne-Jones, Stanhope. (1968). *The Evolution of Preventive Medicine in the United States Army, 1607-1939*. Washington, D.C.: Office of the Surgeon General, Department of the Army, 255 pp. SD D104.2:P92.

One chapter describes the development of tropical preventive medicine after the Spanish-American War. Included is information on Cuba and the building of the Panama Canal. There is also a discussion of the preparedness movement and disease prevention. Secondary sources.

287. Bidwell, Bruce W. (1986). *History of the Military Intelligence Division, Department of the Army General Staff: 1775-1941*. Frederick, Maryland: University Publications of America, 625 pp.

A detailed history of one section of the General Staff. In the pre-war period it was hampered by conflicts between the Staff and the Adjutant General, but engaged in a variety of intelligence gathering operations, especially after 1914. Primary sources.

288. Bower, Stephen E. (1984). *A History of Fort Benjamin Harrison, 1903-1982*. Washington, D.C.: Command History Office, U. S. Army Soldier Support Center, Fort Benjamin Harrison, Indiana, 179 pp. SD D101.2:f77 b/2.

A brief chapter covers this period, including the stationing of several infantry regiments at the post. Primary sources.

289. Briscoe, Edward E. (1959). "Pershing's Chinese Refugees in Texas." *Southwestern Historical Quarterly, 62*, 467-88.

Upon Pershing's return from Mexico in 1917, he brought with him a number of Chinese. They were detained under military control for several years and finally became citizens in 1921. Primary sources.

290. Brower, Philip P. (1963). "The U. S. Army's Seizure and Administration of Enemy Records up to World War II." *American Archivist, 26*, 191-207.

Description of the evolution of archival policy. A part covers the guidelines that developed during and after the Spanish-American War and Philippine-American War, as reflected in the work of John Taylor. Primary sources.

291. Bruun, Michael C. (1979). "U. S. Army Service Dress Rank Chevrons -- 1905 to 1926." *Military Collector & Historian, 31*, 65-73.
A description and detailed list of the insignia worn on dress coats to indicate branch and rank. Primary sources.

292. Bruun, Michael C. (1981). "The Evolution of the Olive Drab Service Coat, 1902-1916." *Military Collector & Historian, 33*, 148-58.
An account of the factors that led to changes in the service coat and what those changes were. Primary sources.

293. Buecker. Thomas R. (1984). "Fort Niobrara, 1880-1906: Guardian of the Rosebud Sioux." *Nebraska History, 65*, 301-26.
The post was established as one of several riming the Sioux reservation. The article includes a description of the post itself and the activities, on and off duty, of the white and black troops that garrisoned it. Primary sources.

294. Cetina, Judith G. (1977). "A History of Veterans' Homes in the United States, 1811-1930." Dissertation, Case Western Reserve University, 38/5-A, pp. 2994-95.
Though begun in the pre-war era, care for old soldiers evolved in the early part of this century into care for elderly people. The author suggests that this program was the first recognition by the government of the need to care for the elderly.

295. Chappell, Gordon. (1967). "Summer Helmets of the U. S. Army, 1875-1910." *Annals of Wyoming, 39*, 37-64.
Only a small part of this article deals with the helmets used after 1900. Primary sources.

296. Clark, Michael J. (1979). "A History of the Twenty-Fourth United States Infantry Regiment in Utah, 1896-1900." Dissertation, University of Utah, 40/5-A, p. 2818.
A brief section of this short dissertation deals with events that occurred in 1900.

297. Clary, David A. (1987). *The Inspectors General of the United States Army, 1777-1903*. Washington, D.C.: Office of the Inspector General and Center of Military History, United States Army, 465 pp. SD D114.2:In7.
The last two chapters of this work deal with the post-Spanish American War investigations, such as the Dodge Commission, and the impact of Root. There is an extended discussion of the movement toward a general staff, the reaction of the Inspector General, and the retention of the office in the new staff system. Primary and secondary sources.

298. Emerson, William. (1977). "U. S. Army Enlisted Cap Insignia, 1905-1918." *Military Collector & Historian, 29*, 22-29, 38-39.
The article is a description of the branch and unit insignias worn by enlisted men early in this century. Emerson has included a detailed table describing the insignia, its user and the dates of use. Primary sources.

299. Emerson, William. (1977). "US Army Enlisted Campaign Hat Insignia, 1890-1907." *Military Collector & Historian, 29*, 158-62.
A description of the insignias worn by enlisted men on campaign hats used during field service. There is a detailed chart of the insignias. Primary sources.

300. Farrell, John T. (1954). "An Abandoned Approach to Philippine History: John R. M. Taylor and the Philippine Insurrection Records." *Catholic Historical Review, 39*, 385-407.
In 1902 the Army commissioned Captain Taylor to collect documents and then write a history of the Philippine-American War. The manuscript was never published because Taft thought it would injure relations with the Filipinos who supported the American government. Primary sources.

301. Foster, Gaines M. (1983). *The Demands of Humanity: Army Medical Disaster Relief*. Washington, D.C.: Center of Military History, United States Army, 188 pp. SD D114.17:H88.
A brief history of the activities of the Army Medical Department in disaster relief. Includes some pages on the San Francisco earthquake and efforts to deal with epidemics abroad, such as in Panama. Primary and secondary sources.

302. Fratcher, William F. (1959). "History of the Judge Advocate General's Corps, United States Army." *Military Law Review, 4*, 89-122.
An overview of this branch, with only a few pages on the pre-war period. Primary sources.

303. Gilmore, Russell. (1976). "'The New Courages': Rifles and Soldier Individualism, 1876-1918." *Military Affairs, 41*, 97-102.
A discussion of different views on the use of individual firepower--either emphasizing individual discipline or in groups. This dispute became part of the controversy over reform of the staff and the creation of the National Guard. Primary sources.

304. Glass, Edward L. N. (comp. and ed.). (1921). *The History of the Tenth Cavalry, 1866-1921*. n.p., 140 pp.
A general history of the regiment with details on activities, an account of the unit's participation in the Punitive Expedition, and information on the officers. Extracts from regimental returns are included.

305. Graham, John F. (1964). "The 1912 Cavalry Saddle and Equipment." *Military Collector & Historian, 16*, 33-41.
A description, with illustrations, of the cavalry saddle adopted after a long process of testing. The author also details the saber, equipment storage pouches and entrenching tool included as part of the equipment. Primary sources.

306. Halsted, Bruce. (1968). "The 1912 Cavalry Equipment." *Military Collector & Historian, 20*, 74-84.
A further expansion of the information provided in the article by Graham [#305]. Halsted included detailed drawings of the saddle and associated equipment. Primary sources.

307. Hampton, H. Duane. (1971). *How the U. S. Cavalry Saved Our National Parks*. Bloomington, Indiana: University of Indiana Press, 246 pp.

While most of the book deals with events before 1900, the last chapters cover the period between the Spanish-American War and the formation of the National Park Service in 1916. During this time Army units continued to patrol the parks. Primary sources.

308. Hardeman, Nicholas P. (1979). "Brick Stronghold of the Border: Fort Assinniboine, 1879-1911." *Montana, 29 No. 2*, 54-67.

A description of the building and activities of this typical western post. Only a sort section recounts the activities of the garrison after 1898. Primary sources.

309. Hibbard, Charles G. (1980). "Fort Douglas 1862-1916: Pivotal Link on the Western Frontier." Dissertation, University of Utah, 41/11-A, p. 4812.

This history of this frontier post, near Salt Lake City, Utah, also reflects the changing roles of the Army. Though most of the dissertation describes with the fort in the nineteenth century, there is an account of the regiments who garrisoned it after the Spanish-American War.

310. Honeywell, Roy J. (1958). *Chaplains of the United States Army*. Washington, D.C.: Office of the Chief of Chaplains, Department of the Army, 376 pp. SD 101.2:C36/3.

An offical history with one chapter covering the pre-war period. The work describes the role of Chaplains in the Philippine-American War and the legislation which affected their status. Secondary sources.

311. Hunt, George A. (1931). *The History of the Twenty-Seventh Infantry*. Honolulu, Hawaii: Honolulu Star-Bulletin, 204 pp.

An account of the regiment, with some material, arranged in chronological order, on the pre-war years as well as documents illustrating the history.

312. Jacobus, Melancthon W. (1977). "The Martial Spirit 1866-1912." *Connecticut Historical Society Bulletin, 42*, 33-39.

A series of twelve photographs form the centerpiece of this brief article; the caption of each photograph conveys some information about the military life in the state, including the Connecticut National Guard. This illustrates the popular enthusiasm for the military. No sources cited.

313. Kennedy, John C. (1963). *The Great Earthquake and Fire: San Francisco, 1906*. New York: William Morrow & Co., 276 pp.

A chronological narrative of the events including the roles that the Army and National Guard performed in fire control and as police. General bibliography but no sources cited.

314. Lane, Jack C. (1973). "The Military Profession's Search for Identity." *Marine Corps Gazette, 57, No. 6*, 36-42.

The author argues that the military is greatly effected by events in society and examines the late nineteenth and early twentieth centuries to prove his point. Reforms came about in parallel with the new management techniques in the private sector and were influenced by them. No sources cited.

315. Langellier, J. Phillip. (1982). "From Blue Kersey to Khaki Drill: The Field Uniform of the U. S. Army, 1898-1901." *Military Collector & Historian, 34*, 148-58.

The impact of the Spanish-American War and the Philippine-American War on the field uniform of the Army is described in this article. Langellier indicates how these conflicts forced changes in the traditional design of the uniform. Primary and secondary sources.

316. Lewis, Emanuel R. (1970). *Seacoast Fortifications of the United States: An Introductory History*. Washington, D.C.: Smithsonian Institution Press, 145 pp.

A brief history of coastal fortifications. One chapter details the building program in the early part of this century which resulted from the recommendations of the Taft Board. Numerous photographs supplement the text. Primary and secondary sources.

317. Lewis, George G., and Mewha, John. (1955). *History of Prisoner of War Utilization by the United States Army, 1776-1945*. Washington, D.C.: Department of the Army, 278 pp. SD D101.22:20-213.

One chapter describes the development of laws involving prisoners, such as the Hague Conventions, and also the 1916 agreement between the services governing control of prisoners. Primary sources.

318. McKenna, Charles D. (1981). "The Forgotten Reform: Field Maneuvers in the Development of the United States Army, 1902-1920." Dissertation, Duke University, 42/6-A, p. 2821.

The author feels that historians have neglected one aspect of the Root reforms, field maneuvers. The dissertation traces the development of the concept, the forces that influenced progress, and the impact that the maneuvers had on the whole system of reforms. The author feels that by 1920 field maneuvers "had become an integral part of the structure of training in the U. S. Army."

319. McKenney, Janice E. (1985). *Army Lineage Series: Air Defense Artillery*. Washington, D.C.: Center of Military History, United States Army, 429 pp. SD D114.11:Ai7.

An account of the lineage of these units, many of which began as artillery or coast artillery in the nineteenth century. A bibliography is included with some unit lineages.

320. Mahon, John K., and Danysh, Romana. (1972). *Army Lineage Series: Infantry, Part I: Regular Army*. Washington, D.C.: Office of the Chief of Military History, United States Army, 938 pp. SD D114.11:In3/pt.1.

Though mainly an account of the lineage of Army infantry units, there is an introductory section which traces the history of the organization of this arm. A brief part of the introduction describes the early twentieth century.

321. Minott, Rodney G. (1962). *Peerless Patriots; Organized Veterans and the Spirit of Americanism*. Washington, D.C.: Public Affairs Press, 152 pp.

A chapter details the creation of the United Spanish American War Veterans and their relation to subsequent veterans organizations. Primary sources.

322. Patterson, Richard. (1975). "Funston and the Fire." *American History Illustrated, 10, No. 8*, 34-45.

The actions of the Army in the aftermath of the 1906 San Francisco earthquake, under the leadership of General Frederick Funston, are described in this article. Patterson investigates the complaint that Funston exceeded his authority. One source cited.

323. Phillips, William G. (1970). "The Evolution of the Pocket-type Rifle Cartridge Belt in the United States Service." *Military Collector & Historian, 22*, 1-10.

A description of one part of the 1903 and 1910 Infantry uniform, how it evolved, and why. The article includes a list of the various modifications to the belt. Primary sources.

324. Powe, Marc B. (1975). "American Military Intelligence Comes of Age: A Sketch of a Man and His Times." *Military Review, 55, No. 12*, 17-30.

A study of Ralph Van Deman and his efforts to help develop the intelligence gathering activities of the Military Information Division. Van Deman laid the groundwork for the intelligence operations of World War I. Mainly secondary sources.

325. Powe, Marc B. (1975). *The Emergence of the War Department Intelligence Agency: 1885-1918*. Manhattan, Kansas: Military Affairs, 146 pp.

Published copy of an MA thesis. The MID did well in the Spanish-American War and continued under the new General Staff. Powe also describes why the agency disappeared in 1910 and reappeared on the eve of the war. Primary and secondary sources.

326. Rila, Carter. (1969). "The Development of U. S. Army Infantry Field Equipment, 1903-1956." *Military Collector & Historian, 21*, 35-43.

A description, including photographs, of the 1903 and 1910 equipment, why it was originally adopted, and how it evolved. The author contends that the 1910 design remained the basis of infantry gear for the next forty years. Primary sources.

327. Sanow, Gilbert A., II, and Bruun, Michael C. (1983). "Uniforms for America's Tropical Empire: The Evolution of the Khaki Coat for U. S. Army Enlisted Men, 1898-1913." *Military Collector & Historian, 35*, 50-59, 98-103.

This article describes the changes in the uniform of the enlisted men. Many of modifications came about as a result of the campaigns in Cuba and Puerto Rico and the need for tropical weather clothing in the Philippines. Primary sources.

328. Sawicki, James A. (1981). *Infantry Regiments of the US Army*. Dumfries, Virginia: Wyvern Publications, Inc., 682 pp.

General history of the branch along with coats of arms, regimental lineages and the divisional structure which existed in World War I and II. No sources cited.

329. Sawicki, James A. (1985). *Cavalry Regiments of the US Army*. Dumfries, Virginia: Wyvern Publications, Inc., 415 pp.

General history of the branch along with coats of arms and regimental lineages. No sources cited.

330. Sherman, Edward F. (1970). "The Civilianization of Military Law." *Maine Law Review, 22,* 3-103.

A section of this significant article describes the court-martial structure as it existed in the pre-war Army. There was a clear difference between civilian legal procedures and protections and the administrative nature of the military proceedings. Primary and secondary sources.

331. Smith, Cornelius C., Jr. (1981). *Fort Huachuca: The Story of a Frontier Post.* Washington, D.C.: n.p., 417 pp. SD D101.2:F77hu.

A chapter of this work includes material on the Mexican Punitive Expedition and its impact on this isolated post. Primary sources.

332. Solomon, Terry V. (1970). *Sound Defender: History of Fort Lawton.* Fort Lawton, Washington: Fort Lawton, 8 pp.

A very brief and inadequate history of this post in Seattle. It contains a description of the creation of the fort and the first units that were stationed there. No sources cited.

333. Spector, Ronald. (1972). "'You're Not Going to Send Soldiers Over There Are You!': The American Search for An Alternative to the Western Front 1916-1917." *Military Affairs, 36,* 1-4.

Though most Americans had not thought about sending an expeditionary force to Europe in 1916, the Military Attaché to Greece had given considerable study to the idea. His view was that the US should contribute to the war effort by invading the Balkans. Though the idea was considered by the War Department in early 1917, it was ultimately rejected.

334. Steffen, Randy. (1973). *United States Military Saddles, 1812-1943.* Norman, Oklahoma: University of Oklahoma Press, 158 pp.

This definitive study includes descriptions, with copious illustrations, of the military saddles used by the cavalry and artillery in this period. Includes material on McClellan and Model 1912 saddles. No sources cited.

335. Steffen, Randy. (1978). *The Horse Soldier, 1776-1943, Volume III: The Last of the Indian Wars, the Spanish-American War, the Brink of the Great War, 1881-1916.* Norman, Oklahoma: University of Oklahoma Press, 268 pp.

Detailed account, with numerous illustrations, of the uniforms, medals, and rifles of this time period. A basic source for those interested in this aspect of military history. Primary sources.

336. Stockton, Jack P., III. (1962). "Mary Walker, Her Medal of Honor, and the Army Reorganization Bill of 1916." *Military Collector & Historian, 14,* 76-78.

Dr. Walker was the only woman to receive the medal, given for her service in the Civil War. In 1916 the Army reevaluated the awards and ordered a number returned, including hers, but she refused. Primary and secondary sources.

337. Stout, Joseph A. (1986). "United States Army Remount Depots: The Oklahoma Experience, 1908-1947." *Military Affairs, 50,* 121-26.

A brief article on the Army's program to provide replacement animals, especially for the cavalry. It also details the role of veterinary officers in the remount program. Primary and secondary sources.

338. Stover, Earl F. (1977). *Up From Handymen: The United States Army Chaplaincy, 1865-1920*. Washington, D.C.: Office of the Chief of Chaplains, Department of the Army, 302 pp. SD D101.2:C36/5/v.3.

One chapter in this study describes the difficulties facing chaplains in the early twentieth century: reform movements, lack of support from organized religion, minimal acceptance by their military colleagues. Primary and secondary sources.

339. Stubbs, Mary L., and Connor, Stanley R. (1969). *Army Lineage Series: Armor-Cavalry, Part I: Regular Army and Army Reserve*. Washington, D.C.: Office of the Chief of Military History, United States Army, 477 pp. SD D114.11:Ar5/pt.1.

The lineage book begins with a history of the organization of armor and cavalry; nine pages are devoted to this time period. The unit lineages also include bibliographies.

340. Stubbs, Mary L., and Connor, Stanley R. (1972). *Army Lineage Series: Armor-Cavalry, Part II: Army National Guard*. Washington, D.C.: Office of the Chief of Military History, United States Army, 297 pp. SD D114.11:Ar5/pt. 2.

There is a brief history of the cavalry including twelve pages that describes this period. In addition the lineages contain individual bibliographies.

341. Thomas, Gordon, and Witts, Max M. (1971). *The San Francisco Earthquake*. New York: Stein and Day, 316 pp.

An account of the disaster focusing on individuals. Some sections relate how the Army provided order and helped stop the fires. Primary and secondary sources.

342. Williams, Rowan A. (1980). "Reporting From Petrograd, 1914-1915." *East European Quarterly, 14*, 335-44.

The experiences of Sherman Miles, American Military Attaché, during the first two years of the war on the Eastern Front. He observed the Russian units and reported on their successes and failures, providing an insight into the European war. Primary sources.

NATIONAL GUARD

343. Adams, Graham, Jr. (1966). *The Age of Industrial Violence, 1910-1915; The Activities and Findings of the United States Commission on Industrial Relations*. New York: Columbia University Press, 316 pp.

Among the acts of violence investigated, and described, was the one that occurred at Ludlow, Colorado, involving the Colorado NG. Primary sources.

344. Bailey, Kenneth R. (1976). "A Search for Identity: The West Virginia National Guard, 1877-1921." Dissertation, Ohio State University, 37/11-A, p. 7265.

Testing hypotheses about the use of the Guard and its supporters, Bailey examined the history of the West Virginia NG. Up to 1912, the Guard was not seen as strikebreakers. As a result of strike duty between 1912 and 1921, the business community now gave the Guard its unqualified support.

345. Bailey, Kenneth R. (1980). "'Grim Visaged Men' and the West Virginia National Guard in the 1912-13 Paint and Cabin Creek Strike." *West Virginia History, 41*, 111-25.

Bailey describes how the state used the West Virginia NG to break a UMW strike. This action cost the state a lot of money and ruined the reputation of the National Guard for a long time to come. Primary sources.

346. Barr, Alwyn. (1978). "The Black Militia of the New South: Texas as a Case Study." *Journal of Negro History, 63*, 209-19.

Black militia units in the South survived the end of Reconstruction and continued in existence into the twentieth century. They were disbanded when the militias were reorganized as a result of the Dick Act. This article relates the history of the black unit in Texas and why it was dissolved. Primary sources.

347. Barry, Herbert. (1939). *Squadron A: A History of Its First Fifty Years, 1889-1939*. New York: Association of Ex-members of Squadron A, Inc., 390 pp.

Much of the book details the activities (i.e., strike duty, summer maneuver camps, and Mexican border service) of this part of the New York National Guard. No sources cited.

348. Bittle, George C. (1965). "In Defense of Florida: The Organized Florida Militia from 1821 to 1920." Dissertation, Florida State University, 26/10, pp. 5990-91.

A small section of the dissertation describes the failure of the Spanish-American War and the Dick Act to have any impact on the state militia. The author also feels that the Florida Guard was "relative efficient" and prepared for the First World War.

349. Black, Lowell D. (1976). "The Negro Volunteer Militia Units of the Ohio National Guard, 1870-1954: The Struggle for Military Recognition and Equality in the State of Ohio." Dissertation, Ohio State University, 37/5-A, p. 3122.

This dissertation presents the story of how blacks served in the Ohio Guard and their efforts to establish a firm footing in the organizational structure. The author also examines the position in society of the black officers and how this influenced their role in the Guard.

350. Cantor, Louis. (1963). "The Creation of the Modern National Guard: The Dick Militia Act of 1903." Dissertation, Duke University, 24/5, pp. 1992-93.

After several introductory chapters, the author concentrates on the events in 1903 which led to the first modern National Guard legislation. He is interested in why this change took place and the reason it occurred in the way that it did. He also discusses the impact of the federal appropriations on the Guard after 1903.

351. Cantor, Louis. (1969). "Elihu Root and the National Guard: Friend or Foe?" *Military Affairs, 33,* 361-73.

Based on his dissertation research, Cantor explored the issue of whether Emory Upton so influenced Elihu Root that his proposals for National Guard reform were hostile to the continuation of that institution. The author argues that Root understood Upton but also was aware of the political realities. The result was a compromise which created the modern Guard with its elements of national and state control. Primary sources.

352. Clendenen, Clarence C. (1969). "Super Police: The National Guard as a Law-Enforcement Agency in the Twentieth Century." In Robin Higham, (ed.), *Bayonets in the Streets: The Use of Troops in Civil Disturbances.* Lawrence, Kansas: University Press of Kansas, 85-112.

A brief account of the use of the National Guard in a variety of strike related duties such as in the Lawrence, Massachusetts, textile strike and the Ludlow, Colorado, coal strike. Secondary sources.

353. Colby, Elbridge. (1959). "Elihu Root and the National Guard." *Military Affairs, 23,* 20-34.

Using a variety of sources, including the words and actions of Root, Colby assesses whether Root really felt that the National Guard was a useful reserve force. He concludes that Root followed the ideas of Upton and had little confidence in the abilities of the National Guardsmen. Primary sources.

354. Colby, Elbridge. (1977). *National Guard of the United States: A Half Century of Progress.* Manhattan, Kansas: Military Affairs/Aerospace Historian, chapters individually paged.

A typescript, with five chapters on the period before World War I, including material on the Dick Act, the 1916 National Defense Act and the 1916 border mobilization. Primary and secondary sources including state reports.

355. Cooper, Jerry, and Smith, Glen. (1986). *Citizens as Soldiers: A History of the North Dakota National Guard.* Fargo, North Dakota: North Dakota Institute for Regional Studies, 447 pp.

A well written and detailed history of this state's National Guard. One chapter describes the impact of the Dick Act on reorganizing and improving the Guard, while another recounts the Mexican border service of this unit. Primary sources.

356. Cropp, Richard. (1962). *"The Coyotes": A History of the South Dakota National Guard.* Mitchell, South Dakota: South Dakota Board of Military Affairs and the National Guard Officers Association, 220 pp.

A general history of the South Dakota NG with two chapters on this time period. There is a description of organizational structure, training procedures, and Mexican border patrols. Bibliography with mainly secondary sources.

357. Derthick, Martha. (1965). *The National Guard in Politics*. Cambridge, Massachusetts: Harvard University Press, 202 pp.

One chapter describes the birth of the National Guard lobby and its early actions: the Dick Act (1903) and the National Defense Act of 1916. The lobby was successful in beating back the Army's attempts to control the Guard. Primary sources.

358. Diamond, B. I., and Baylen, J. O. (1984). "The Demise of the Georgia Guard Colored, 1868-1914." *Phylon, 45*, 311-13.

The authors detail the effort of the Georgia Adjutant General to remove the black component of the Georgia NG. Though they were dwindling due to attrition, one Adjutant General tried to speed the process up, but failed. Primary sources.

359. Dupuy, R. Ernest. (1971). *The National Guard, A Compact History*. New York: Hawthorne Books, Inc., 194 pp.

A brief nine page chapter describes the Dick Act and its ramifications as well as changes in the types of National Guard units as new technology appeared. Secondary sources.

360. Edwards, John C. (1976). "Georgia Guardsmen and the Politics of Survival, 1915-1916." *Georgia Historical Quarterly, 60*, 344-55.

Campaigns by the Georgia NG for continued independence and by the National Security League for preparedness joined briefly in 1915-1916. Each was a partial winner. Primary sources.

361. Finnegan, John P. (1964). "Preparedness in Wisconsin: The National Guard and the Mexican Border Incident." *Wisconsin Magazine of History, 47*, 199-213.

An account of both the preparedness movement in Wisconsin and its impact on the Wisconsin NG. The call-up in 1916 demonstrated the weakness of the Guard and encouraged a movement toward universal military training. Primary sources.

362. Fowles, Brian D. (1982). "A History of the Kansas National Guard, 1854-1975." Dissertation, Kansas State University, 43/12-A, p. 4011.

Created in the late nineteenth century, the Kansas NG was poorly organized and trained. After 1903 the government mandated more training, but agricultural problems restricted the ability of the state to accomplish these goals. World War I exposed some of these problems.

363. Gillette, Mary M. (1986). "'A Small War in a Beer-Drinking Country': The South Dakota National Guard on the Mexican Border." *South Dakota History, 16*, 35-66.

A detailed account of this state's unit on the Mexican Border in 1916-17. The experience gave the South Dakota NG a chance to bring its standard of training up to a high level. It also enabled the men to participate in Army life in a generally congenial environment. Primary and secondary sources.

364. Gordon, Martin K. (1983). *Imprint on the Nation: Stories Reflecting the National Guard's Impact on a Changing Nation*. Manhattan, Kansas: Sunflower University Press, 98 pp.

A series of one page articles, plus bibliographies, on events involving the National Guard. There is an article on Charles Lindbergh as a Guardsman and one on the California Guard in the aftermath of the 1906 San Francisco earthquake and fire. Secondary sources.

365. Hill, Jim D. (1964). *The Minute Man in Peace and War: A History of the National Guard*. Harrisburg, Pennsylvania: Stackpole Co., 585 pp.

An anti-Uptonian history of the militia and National Guard. Several chapters detail the victory of the Dick Act and the defense against Lindley Garrison's Continental Army plan. No specific citations, but bibliographic notes at the end of each chapter; mainly secondary sources.

366. Holmes, Joseph J. (1971). "The National Guard of Pennsylvania: Policeman of Industry, 1865-1905." Dissertation, University of Connecticut, 32/2-A, p. 884.

From a group of volunteers to a businessman dominated organization, the Pennsylvania NG evolved in the nineteenth century. After 1905, for a variety of reasons, the Pennsylvania National Guard worked hard, and successfully, to stress its new role, that of an official part of the Regular Army.

367. Houston, Donald E. (1975). "The Oklahoma National Guard on the Mexican Border, 1916." *Chronicles of Oklahoma, 53*, 447-62.

The focus of this article is on the mobilization and activities of the Oklahoma force during the call-up which resulted from Villa's raid and Pershing's Punitive Expedition. This process exposed some problems, such as a lack of equipment and training. Primary sources.

368. Hudson, James J. (1952). "The California National Guard, 1903-1940." Dissertation, University of California, Berkeley, Doctoral Dissertations Accepted by American Universities, 1953, p. 228.

Beginning with an overview of the development of the Guard, the author of this pioneering dissertation describes the use of the Guard in natural disasters, such as the 1906 San Francisco earthquake and fire, and its use in civil disturbances, such as the labor disturbances in Siskiyou County in 1909.

369. Hudson, James J. (1976). "The California National Guard in the San Francisco Earthquake and Fire of 1906." *California History Quarterly, 55*, 137-49.

Almost the entire California NG was called out to serve in San Francisco after the earthquake. They remained there for six weeks, preserving order and helping to stop the fires. Some individuals wanted them to remain longer, while others desired their prompt removal. The author feels they did a good job. Primary sources.

370. Johnson, Charles, Jr. (1976). "Black Soldiers in the National Guard, 1877-1949." Dissertation, Howard University, 37/7-A, p. 4531.

Focusing on the organizations which made up the 93rd Division, the author examines the attitudes towards blacks in the National Guard and the problems this created for those trying to serve their state. Includes interviews with personnel.

371. Lens, Sidney. (1973). *The Labor Wars: From the Molly Maguires to the Sitdowns*. Garden City, New York: Doubleday, 366 pp.

Contained in the narrative are accounts of incidents involving National Guardsmen including the Ludlow, Colorado, Massacre. Secondary sources.

372. Littlefield, Daniel F., Jr., and Underhill, Lonnie E. (1978). "The 'Crazy Snake Uprising' of 1909: A Red, Black or White Affair?" *Arizona and the West, 20*, 307-24.

In 1909 there were a series of attacks by Oklahoma whites against a group of Snake Indians and blacks. The situation became so bad that the Oklahoma National Guard had to be called out to restore order. The authors suggest that the hostility was really directed at the blacks, rather than the Indians. Primary sources.

373. Mahon, John K. (1983). *History of the Militia and the National Guard*. New York: Macmillan, 374 pp.

A scholarly account of the growth of the National Guard. One chapter details the battles between the National Guard Association and the War Department, in the arena of Congress, over the size, mission, and control of the state units. In addition there is material on the use of the NG by the states in labor disputes. Primary and secondary sources.

374. Marsh, John L. (1980). "Colonel Fred: The Handsomest Man in the Pennsylvania National Guard." *Pennsylvania Heritage, 6, No. 3*, 10-14.

Biographical sketch of an officer who took his military duty quite seriously but grew out of touch with his men. Though much of the article describes events that occurred in the nineteenth century, the climax comes in this century when the officer was defeated for re-election as a guard leader. No sources cited.

375. McClellan, Grove. (1969). "The Seventy-Fourth New York Infantry on the Mexican Border:IV." *Niagara Frontier, 16*, 55-60.

An account of one unit which moved to the border in 1916 and what it did there. No specific sources cited though primary sources quoted in article.

376. McGovern, George S., and Guttridge, Leonard F. (1972). *The Great Coalfield War*. Boston: Houghton Mifflin, 383 pp.

A detailed account of the coal strike and the ensuing fighting, including that involving the Colorado National Guard. Also includes information on the investigations of the massacre. Primary sources.

377 McLatchy, Patrick H. (1973). "The Development of the National Guard of Washington as an Instrument of Social Control, 1854-1916." Dissertation, University of Washington, 34/5-A, pp. 2524-25.

Begun as a loose volunteer organization, the Washington National Guard evolved into a police force. After 1900, however, it was transformed again, now into a military organization. This process was facilitated by the absence of strike duty.

378. Milner, Elmer R. (1979). "An Agonizing Evolution: A History of the Texas National Guard, 1900-1945." Dissertation, North Texas State University, 40/3-A, pp. 1651-52.

A relatively brief history of the Texas National Guard. Building on a long volunteer tradition in Texas, the National Guard slowly grew in this century. Some units served on the border in 1916 and then were mobilized for service in World War I.

379. Nankivell, John N. (1935). *History of the Military Organizations of the State of Colorado, 1860-1935*. Denver, Colorado: W. H. Kistler Stationery Co., 531 pp.

A detailed history of the Guard by an officer assigned to it. Several chapters recount the duty of the Guard in breaking up strikes, especially in 1913-1914, and on the Mexican Border in 1916-1917. The author is anti-union in sentiment. Documents included in the text itself.

380. Newton, Craig A. (1969). "Vermonters in Texas: A Reassessment of National Guard Duty on the Mexican Border in 1916." *Vermont History, 37*, 30-38.

Based on the diary of a guardsman, the author suggests that a number of benefits arose from service on the border. Among these are a positive view toward military service and an acceptance of military discipline. Primary sources.

381. Osur, Alan M. (1982). "The Role of the Colorado National Guard in Civil Disturbances." *Military Affairs, 46*, 19-24.

A description of the use of the Colorado National Guard in breaking strikes by silver miners. Their role in maintaining law and order made the labor unions unhappy, and pleased the corporate interests. Their performance in the 1913-1914 strikes, including the shooting at Ludlow, is also explored. Primary and secondary sources.

382. Purcell, Allan R. (1981). "The History of the Texas Militia, 1835-1903." Dissertation, University of Texas-Austin, 42/7-A, p. 3275.

The focus of this dissertation is the nineteenth century, but a small section describes the end of the militia in 1903. With its transformation into the National Guard in that year, it brought to a close "an institution which failed to meet the challenges of the Texas frontier."

383. Riker, William H. (1962). *Soldiers of the States: The Role of the National Guard in American Democracy*. Washington, D.C.: Public Affairs Press, 129 pp.

A brief work on the development of the National Guard with two chapters covering the events leading up to the 1903 Dick Act and subsequent developments. The National Guard's desire for federal money led to more Army control over the Guard, and a major debate over the federal role. The author uses this relationship to illustrate federalism in action. Published primary sources.

384. Roberts, Richard C. (1973). "History of the Utah National Guard, 1894-1954." Dissertation, University of Utah, 34/4-A, p. 1838.

The author presents the history of the Utah NG as a case study of National Guard development. It played a variety of roles: source of soldiers for combat, preserver of order, and strike breaker. The Guard came more and more under federal control as more money was provided.

385. Sammond, Frederic. (1964). "The Wisconsin National Guard: A Footnote to Its History." *Wisconsin Magazine of History, 48,* 127-30.

A rejoinder, by a participant, to Finnegan's criticism [#361] of the Guard in Texas and its lack of preparedness.

386. Sterkx, H. E. (1971). "Unlikely Conquistadors: Alabamians and the Mexican Border Crisis of 1916." *Alabama Review, 24,* 163-81.

The article describes the attitudes of the citizens about the border crisis and the activities of the Alabama NG in training camp and on the border itself. Primary sources.

387. Stone, Richard G., Jr. (1977). *A Brittle Sword: The Kentucky Militia, 1776-1912.* Lexington, Kentucky: The University Press of Kentucky, 122 pp.

The last chapter recounts the conversion of the militia to the National Guard and the effect that this had, including increased training. Also relates the impact politics had on the Guard. Bibliographic list, but no sources specifically cited.

388. Suggs, George G., Jr. (1972). *Colorado's War on Militant Unionism: James H. Peabody and the Western Federation of Miners.* Detroit, Michigan: Wayne State University Press, 242 pp.

Included in this work is an account of the role of the Colorado NG in strikebreaking in a number of incidents in the first decade. The governor used the troops to occupy the mine areas and the union camps. Primary and secondary sources.

389. Suggs, George G., Jr. (1973). "The Colorado Coal Miners' Strike, 1903-1904: A Prelude to Ludlow?" *Journal of the West, 12,* 36-52.

The article describes the use of the Colorado NG to break a strike by the UMW. Though the mine owners' goal was achieved, the role of the NG was not decisive. Primary sources.

390. Sunseri, Alvin R. (1972). "The Ludlow Massacre: A Study in the Misemployment of the National Guard." *American Chronicle, 1,* 21-28.

An account of the 1913 strike where the Colorado NG was used to stop violence between miners and owners but instead caused even more killings. The author suggests that the incident demonstrates many weaknesses in the NG system as it then existed. No sources listed.

391. Todd, Frederick P. (1941). "Our National Guard: A Introduction to Its History." *Military Affairs, 5,* 152-70.

A survey of the history of the Guard, with sections on the impact of the Dick Act and the National Defense Act of 1916. Primary sources.

392. Weiner, Frederick B. (1940). "The Militia Clause of the Constitution." *Harvard Law Review, 54,* 181-220.
A review of the legislation and court decisions involving the relations between the national government and the National Guard. Includes material on the Dick Act, the Mexican border crisis mobilization, and the National Defense Act of 1916. Primary sources.

393. Westover, John G. (1948). "The Evolution of the Missouri Militia, 1804-1919." Dissertation, University of Missouri, 9/1, pp. 123-24.
While the militia was not well accepted, the conversion to the National Guard led to their support by the public. Their duties in this century have included restoring order, helping the public in disasters and acting as a reserve force for federal action.

394. White, Earl B. (1977). "Might is Right: Unionism and Goldfield, Nevada, 1904 to 1908." *Journal of the West, 16, No. 3,* 75-84.
A brief section of this article explains how the Army was called into this labor dispute and what they did when they arrived. Primary sources.

395. Wolfe, Margaret R. (1973). "The Border Service of the Tennessee National Guard, 1916-1917: A Study in Romantic Inclinations, Military Realities, and Predictable Disillusionment." *Tennessee Historical Quarterly, 32,* 374-88.
An account of the expectations and realities of border service in Texas in 1916. Though it began with great enthusiasm, the everyday tedium of training and no combat soon diminished the interest of the Guardsmen. No sources listed.

OVERSEAS

396. Bacevich, Andrew J., Jr. (1983). "American Military Diplomacy, 1898-1949: The Role of Frank Ross McCoy." Dissertation, Princeton University, 43/7-A, p. 2423.
The author contends that Army officers were not isolated from roles in carrying out foreign policy and uses General McCoy as an example. In this period he was involved in the American occupation of Cuba and as Military Attaché during the Mexican revolution.

397. Berbusse, Edward J. (1966). *The United States in Puerto Rico, 1898-1900.* Chapel Hill, North Carolina: University of North Carolina Press, 274 pp.
One chapter in this work describes the military government of 1899-1900, including the economic and political problems faced by the Army. Primary and secondary sources.

398. Bertoff, Rowland T. (1953). "Taft and MacArthur, 1900-1901: A Study in Civil-Military Relations." *World Politics, 5,* 196-213.
These two individuals debated over the timetable for civilian rule in the Philippines and the role that the Army should play in governing the Islands. The discussion also brought out the flaws in the existing governmental structure of shared power between military and civilians. Primary sources.

399. Cameron, Ian [psd. Donald G. Payne]. (1971). *The Impossible Dream: The Building of the Panama Canal.* London: Hodder and Stoughton, 284 pp.

A detailed study, with two/thirds of the work devoted to the American builders. The author has described the public health issues, organization of the construction program, and the work of the Corps of Engineers. Bibliography of secondary sources but no notes.

400. Challener, Richard D. (1973). *Admirals, Generals, and American Foreign Policy, 1898-1914.* Princeton, New Jersey: Princeton University Press, 433 pp.

A study of the relationship between the military and the foreign policy makers. The author suggests that it was a static situation, shaped by bureaucratic inertia and presidential aspirations. Little thought was given to the policy consequences of military actions. Primary sources.

401. Coats, George Y. (1968). "The Philippine Constabulary, 1901-1917." Dissertation, Ohio State University, 29/10-A, p. 3554.

American officers created and led this native police force after the American take-over of the Philippine Islands. Though its initial duties involved pacification, most of its activities were as a "semi-military national police force."

402. Cruz, Romeo V. (1974). *America's Colonial Desk and the Philippines, 1898-1934.* Quezon City, Philippines: University of the Philippines Press, 247 pp.

This is an account of the Bureau of Insular Affairs, War Department, and its relationship with the Philippines. It was the chief agency for American actions concerning the Islands. The author argues that the Bureau really protected the interests of the US while it claimed that it was trying to help the Philippines. Primary sources.

403. DuVal, Miles P., Jr. (1947). *And the Mountains Will Move; The Story of the Building of the Panama Canal.* Stanford, California: Stanford University Press, 374 pp.

A history of the Canal with several chapters on the role of the Army and Goethals in the completion of the project. Primary and secondary sources.

404. Fitchen, Edward D. (1972). "Alexis E. Frye and Cuban Education, 1898-1902." *Revista Interamericana, 2,* 123-49.

During the occupation of Cuba, the Army brought in an outstanding educator, Frye, and had him try to revive and revamp the existing school system. With American money, he was able to improve education. He was esteemed by the Cubans for his efforts. Primary sources.

405. Flint, Roy K. (1980). "The United States Army on the Pacific Frontier, 1899-1939." In Joe C. Dixon, (ed.), *The American Military and the Far East: Proceedings of the Ninth Military History Symposium, United States Air Force Academy, 1-3 October 1980.* Washington, D.C.: United States Air Force Academy, 139-59. SD D301.78:980.

The paper examines the garrisoning of US positions in Hawaii, the Philippines and China after 1900 and the impact that this had upon the Army. Among the changes: development of a shipping system, duty as governors, and drill in isolation from the majority of the Army. Some of these paralleled the old frontier experiences, others did not. No sources cited.

406. Foner, Philip S. (1972). *The Spanish-Cuban-American War and the Birth of American Imperialism, 1895-1902*. New York: Monthly Review Press, 716 pp.
Two chapters of this work describe the military occupation and its goals. The author feels that it did improve conditions in Cuba, ignored the Cuban revolutionaries, and opened the way for American capitalists. Primary sources.

407. Forster, Merlin H. (1977). "U. S. Intervention in Mexico: The 1914 Occupation of Veracruz." *Military Review, 57, No. 8*, 88-96.
An account of the joint Army-Marine occupation of Veracruz, under the command of General Frederick Funston. The author describes some of the problems that the occupation authorities had in trying to run a government. Mainly secondary sources.

408. Fritz, David L. (1977). "The Philippine Question: American Civil/Military Policy in the Philippines, 1898-1905." Dissertation, University of Texas-Austin, 38/7-A, pp. 4324-25.
The dissertation presents several themes: the relationship between civilian and military administrators; the debates between imperialists and their opponents; and the terrible health conditions in the Islands and the resulting death toll.

409. Gillette, Howard, Jr. (1973). "The Military Occupation of Cuba, 1899-1902: Workshop for American Progressivism." *American Quarterly, 25*, 410-25.
Leonard Wood, as military governor, carried out an activist policy, which foreshadowed the programs that the Progressives would advocate within the decade. These included programs in municipal governmental reform and sanitation. Primary sources.

410. Gowing, Peter G. (1968). "Mandate in Moroland: The American Government of Muslim Filipinos, 1899-1920." Dissertation, Syracuse University, 29-6/A, pp. 1843-44.
A description of the American government's attempt, through military and quasi-military rule, to integrate the Moros into the life of the Philippine Islands. The Army also tried to develop principles of self-government, but failed to realize the impact of destroying many of the Muslims' institutions and then turning over control to Christian Filipinos.

411. Healy, David F. (1963). *The United States in Cuba, 1898-1902: Generals, Politicians, and the Search for Policy*. Madison, Wisconsin: University of Wisconsin Press, 260 pp.
American conduct in Cuba, which served as a model for later Latin American policy, was strongly influenced by the people in charge of the occupation, such as Leonard Wood, and by Elihu Root. The occupiers protected American political and economic interests and kept alive the possibility of future military intervention. Primary sources.

412. Hitchman, James H. (1971). *Leonard Wood and Cuban Independence.* The Hague, Netherlands: Martinus Nihjoff, 238 pp.

A study of the occupation of Cuba and the goals that the Army hoped to achieve, including the encouragement of democratic institutions in Cuba. The author suggests that the military government may have been terminated too quickly and that the end results were different than the American government had hoped to accomplish.

413. Hitchman, James H. (1975). "Unfinished Business: Public Works in Cuba, 1898-1902." *The Americas, 31,* 335-59.

The military government in Cuba began an extensive series of public works projects, as part of the American attempt to build a stable base for a democracy. Many of the projects were constructed by the Corps of Engineers. Primary sources.

414. Hunt, Michael H. (1979). "The Forgotten Occupation: Peking, 1900-1901." *Pacific Historical Review, 48,* 501-30.

A discussion of the Army's occupation service in the wake of the Boxer Rebellion, a task for which they had no preparation and no real knowledge. There were few problems, largely because the Chinese cooperated with the Americans. Primary sources.

415. Johnson, Thomas L. (1984). "Policing the Philippine Republic, 1901-1917." *Military Police, 11, No. 2,* 19-20.

A brief overview of the American role in the establishment and operation of the Philippine Constabulary. The article reads as if it was written directly from official sources. No sources cited.

416. Kyre, Martin, and Kyre, Joan. (1968). *Military Occupation and National Security.* Washington, D.C.: Public Affairs Press, 198 pp.

A general study of the principles, leadership, and administration of military occupation, mainly using twentieth century examples. The authors try to derive general principles from the historical examples. Secondary sources.

417. Lane, Jack C. (1972). "Instrument for Empire: The American Military Government in Cuba, 1899-1902." *Science & Society, 36,* 314-30.

The military government in Cuba, according to the author, helped prepare the Cubans for independence, ostensibly, but really placed Cuba within the new American empire. Primary and secondary sources.

418. Lee, William S. (1958). *The Strength to Move a Mountain.* New York: G. P. Putnam's Sons, 318 pp.

An account of the building of the Panama Canal, including detailed sections on the role of the Corps of Engineers in overcoming the massive engineering problems. The narrative focuses on personalities as well as general problems. Chapter notes; some primary sources.

419. Lockmiller, David A. (1938). *Magoon in Cuba: A History of the Second Intervention, 1906-1909.* Chapel Hill, North Carolina: University of North Carolina Press, 252 pp.

During the second intervention Magoon and the Army tried to rebuild the infrastructure of Cuban society, such as public works and sewer systems, and also deal with sanitation problems. In addition they helped rewrite the law codes. The author feels that Magoon did a creditable job, though his conciliatory nature hurt his reputation. Primary sources, mainly printed.

420. Mack, Gerstle. (1944). *The Land Divided; A History of The Panama Canal and Other Isthmian Canal Projects.* New York: Alfred A. Knopf, 650 pp.

Only a few chapters of this detailed work describe the construction project itself and the role of the Army. Published primary and secondary sources.

421. McCullough, David. (1977). *The Path Between the Seas: The Creation of the Panama Canal, 1870-1914.* New York: Simon and Schuster, 698 pp.

A third of this quite readable book portrays the efforts of the Army to build the Panama Canal. This includes the campaign led by Colonel Gorgas to control disease and the work of George W. Goethals to supervise the construction. Mainly secondary sources.

422. Millett, Allan R. (1967). "The General Staff and the Cuban Intervention of 1906." *Military Affairs, 31,* 113-19.

One issue in the creation of the staff system in 1903 was what role the organization should take in the supervision of military operations. The first real test of this occurred in 1906 in Cuba. The end result was generally satisfactory though many officers expressed complaints stemming from not enough staff involvement. Primary sources.

423. Millett, Allan R. (1968). *The Politics of Intervention: The Military Occupation of Cuba, 1906-1909.* Columbus, Ohio: Ohio State University Press, 306 pp.

An account of the occupation, including a discussion on how the Army got involved in making policy, and how they tried to reform Cuban society. The author also describes the differences between military and civilian leaders on policy, especially its goals. Primary and secondary sources.

424. Minger, Ralph E. (1961). "Taft, MacArthur, and the Establishment of Civil Government in the Philippines." *Ohio Historical Quarterly, 70,* 308-32.

Depiction of the conflict between the head of the Second Philippine Commission and the military governor of the Islands on the issue of the future of the Philippines. MacArthur viewed the territory in its strategic perspective, while Taft was mainly concerned about relations with the US. Primary sources.

425. Mulrooney, Virginia F. (1975). "No Victor, No Vanquished: United States Military Government in the Philippine Islands, 1898-1901." Dissertation, University of California-Los Angeles, 36/6-A, p. 3935.

For three years the Army was in charge of the Islands and established various levels of government. This was superseded by civilian control and the Army became an enforcement arm of this new government. The military government ceased to exist before its success or failure could be judged.

426. Perez, Louis A., Jr. (1972). "Supervision of a Protectorate: The United States and the Cuban Army, 1898-1908." *Hispanic American Historical Review, 52*, 250-71.
  This article is a description of the creation and training, by Americans, of a military force in Cuba. The goal was to establish a military capable of defending the country and protecting American interests. Primary sources.

427. Perez, Louis A., Jr. (1986). "The Pursuit of Pacification: Banditry and the United States' Occupation of Cuba, 1889-1902." *Journal of Latin American Studies, 18,*, 313-32.
  Banditry became a major problem for the American occupation forces. Their solution was to get Cubans to patrol the areas of unrest, and eventually to take the law into their own hands. The end result was further disruption of the economic and political climate of Cuba. Primary sources.

428. Pomeroy, Earl S. (1944). "The American Colonial Office." *Mississippi Valley Historical Review, 30*, 521-32.
  An overview of the bureaucracy created to deal with colonial possessions including the Bureau of Insular Affairs in the War Department. Primary sources.

429. Quirk, Robert E. (1962). *An Affair of Honor: Woodrow Wilson and the Occupation of Veracruz.* Louisville, Kentucky: Published for the Mississippi Valley Historical Association by University of Kentucky Press, 184 pp.
  A general history of the 1914 occupation with one chapter on what the Army did to the city, including improving the water supply and establishing a system of garbage collection. Primary sources.

430. Rakestraw, Lawrence. (1967). "George Patrick Ahern and the Philippine Bureau of Forestry, 1900-1914." *Pacific Northwest Quarterly, 58*, 142-50.
  This army officer created a forestry bureau in the Philippines and pioneered techniques of land management and conservation, ahead of those being used at the time in the US. In turn his work had influence in the United States and elsewhere. Primary sources.

431. Smith, Richard W. (1968). "Philippine Constabulary." *Military Review, 48, No. 5*, 73-80.
  Organized and initially officered by Americans, this force was quite useful in helping to put down the remains of the revolt. Subsequently the organization became a regular police force. No sources cited.

432. Sweetman, Jack. (1968). *The Landing at Veracruz: 1914; The First Complete Chronicle of a Strange Encounter in April, 1914, When the United States Navy Captured and Occupied the City of Veracruz, Mexico.* Annapolis, Maryland: United States Naval Institute, 221 pp.
  While the major emphasis of this work is on the Navy and its efforts to take over the city, parts of two chapters deal with the occupation of the city, a process in which the Army was heavily involved. There is a discussion of the health measures imposed by the Army. Primary and secondary sources.

433. Thompson, Wayne W. (1975). "Governors of the Moro Province: Wood, Bliss, and Pershing in the Southern Philippines, 1903-1913." Dissertation, University of California-San Diego, 36/4-A, p. 2384.

This dissertation examines the policies of these three officers when they were military governors. The author suggests that they were strongly influenced by their needs to curry favor in Washington.

434. Thompson, Winfred L. (1987). "The Introduction of American Law in the Philippines and Porto Rico, 1898-1905." Dissertation, University of Chicago, 48/5-A, p. 1300.

One of the problems faced by the occupation authorities in Cuba as well as the Philippines and Puerto Rico was to determine the status of the new territories and the rights of the individuals there. The dissertation deals with the efforts by the military and civilian authorities to resolve these problems, as well as the relationship between Spanish and Anglo-American legal practices.

435. Woolard, James R. (1975). "The Philippine Scouts: The Development of America's Colonial Army." Dissertation, Ohio State University, 36/8-A, p. 5479.

The Scouts were an official branch of the US Army, commanded by the head of the Philippine Division. By the 1920s it had become the backbone of the American forces in the Islands. The author also views problems of civil-military relations between the Scouts and others such as the Constabulary.

POLITICAL ISSUES

436. Axeen, David L. (1969). "Romantics and Civilizers: American Attitudes Toward War, 1898-1902." Dissertation, Yale University, 30/8-A, p. 3386.

This is a study of how Americans reacted to the wars of the period. The author uses the popular press as his basis to suggest that there were two different attitudes: the Romantics, who saw war and warfare as a gallant struggle, while the Civilizers wanted the experts to take over warfare. These ideas also became entangled in the post-war debates over the future of the Army.

437. Bolt, Ernest C., Jr. (1977). *Ballots Before Bullets: The War Referendum Approach to Peace in America, 1914-1941.* Charlottesville, Virginia: University of Virginia Press, 207 pp.

As the war in Europe heated up, Americans opposed to war advocated this concept. Despite the efforts of William J. Bryan and the submission of the concept as a legislative proposal, it did not gain acceptance before America entered the war. Primary sources.

438. Brooks, Edward H. (1950). "The National Defense Policy of the Wilson Administration, 1913-1917." Dissertation, Stanford University. Doctoral Dissertations Accepted by American Universities, 1950, p. 177.

Wilson was opposed to military expansion and his military advisers thought only of creating a force to protect the nation from invasion. Nothing significant was done to improve the military posture of the US. As a result of Wilson's attitudes, America entered World War I woefully unprepared.

439. Chatfield, Charles. (1971). *For Peace and Justice: Pacifism in America, 1914-1941*. Knoxville, Tennessee: University of Tennessee Press, 447 pp.

A study of the anti-war movement, with a brief section on the period between 1914 and 1917, including efforts at keeping the United States out of World War I. Primary and secondary sources.

440. Crouch, Thomas W. (1971). "The Funston-Gambrell Dispute: An Episode in Military-Civilian Relations". *Military History of Texas and the Southwest, 9*, 79-105.

Reverend Gambrell asked General Funston for permission to hold revival meetings among the troops stationed in Texas during the Punitive Expedition. When Funston refused, Gambrell charged the officer with discriminating against Baptists. A heated controversy erupted for the next several months. The author suggests that the episode indicated the still rudimentary nature of the staff system and the need for officers conversant with the problems of civil affairs. Primary sources.

441. Dalton, Kathleen. (1981). "Theodore Roosevelt and the Idea of War." *Theodore Roosevelt Association Journal, 7, No. 4*, 6-12.

Roosevelt felt war would help cleanse American society in general and on the personal level. He saw himself at war with his physical disabilities and found the constant struggle built him up. Primary sources.

442. DeBenedetti, Charles. (1978). *Origins of the Modern American Peace Movement, 1915-1929*. Millwood, New York: KTO Press, 281 pp.

A brief section of this study deals with the pre-1917 era. The author points out the relationship between the peace movement and reform in general, and the growth of a right-wing reaction to efforts to achieve peace. Primary sources.

443. Ekirch, Arthur A., Jr. (1956). *The Civilian and the Military*. New York: Oxford University Press, 340 pp.

A study of the antimilitarism strain in American history. There are two chapters on this period: one on the reactions to the reforms of the Roosevelt era and the other on the preparedness movement. Primary and secondary sources.

444. Gilmore, Russell S. (1975). "Crack Shots and Patriots: The National Rifle Association and America's Military-Sporting Tradition, 1871-1929." Dissertation, University of Wisconsin-Madison, 36/1-A, pp. 480-81.

This organization was a potent pressure group in this period, stressing individual marksmanship and strongly supporting the preparedness movement. It was a powerful organization with a significant impact on the professional military.

445. Hammond, Grant T. (1975). "Plowshares into Swords: Arms Races in International Politics, 1840-1941." Dissertation, Johns Hopkins University, 39/5-A, p. 3115.

In this political science dissertation the author has examined a number of arms races in an effort to define the term and establish some general criteria. One such race involved the United States, Japan, and Great Britain between 1916 and 1922.

446. Huntington, Samuel P. (1957). *The Soldier and the State: The Theory and Politics of Civil-Military Relations*. Cambridge, Massachusetts: Belknap Press of Harvard University Press, 534 pp.

One chapter of this key work describes the military mind set in the period before World War I. Huntington depicts the general isolation which engulfed most military officers, but also examines the contributions of Wood to publicizing the military view for the general public. Primary sources.

447. Huntington, Samuel P. (1961). "Equilibrium and Disequilibrium in American Military Policy." *Political Science Quarterly, 76*, 481-502.

A broad ranging article review of American policy and how it is made. One short section specifically deals with the 1880 to 1916 period. Secondary sources.

448. Kambol, Stephen A. (1980). "Southern Congressmen and the 1912 Army Appropriations Bill." *Southern Studies, 19*, 50-64.

Through an analysis of the speeches and voting of Southerners around the key 1912 appropriations bill, the author tries to test the idea that the South was pro-military. His conclusion is that though they were interested in promoting the efficiency and decreasing the cost of the Army, they were not more so than any other section. Primary sources.

449. Kraft, Barbara S. (1970). "Peacemaking in the Progressive Era: A Prestigious and Proper Calling." *Maryland Historian, 1*, 121-44.

An overview of the various components of the peace movement and its members, including many social leaders. They sought peace or international arbitration treaties. Printed primary and secondary sources.

450. Leonard, Thomas C. (1978). *Above the Battle: War-Making in America from Appomattox to Versailles*. New York: Oxford University Press, 260 pp.

The central focus is how American military and civilian leaders felt about war and war making. War was seen as both good and bad, the enemy as noble and savage, and the new technology as both liberating and confining. Primary sources.

451. Marchand, C. Roland. (1972). *The American Peace Movement and Social Reform, 1898-1918*. Princeton, New Jersey: Princeton University Press, 441 pp.

An account of the rise and fall of the movement, placing it in the general reform context, both in terms of program and leadership. Before World War I it had become one of the acceptable reforms, but the war changed viewpoints. Primary sources.

452. May, Ernest R. (1955). "The Development of Political-Military Consultation in the United States." *Political Science Quarterly, 70*, 161-80.

An account of early consultation, through written communications and the Joint Board, between the services and with the State Department. Primary sources.

453. Nurnberger, Ralph D. (1987). "'Bridling the Passions'." *Wilson Quarterly, 11*, 96-107.

This article is an overview of the peace movement in the United States in the late nineteenth and early twentieth centuries. Nurnberger also discusses the relationship with the Progressive Movement of the same era. No sources cited.

454. Patterson, David S. (1972). "An Interpretation of the American Peace Movement, 1898-1914." *American Studies, 13*, 31-49.

A discussion of the leaders of the movement and why they failed, when war began in Europe, to keep the peace effort alive. Among the ideas the author proposes was that the elitism of the leaders meant no mass following. Primary sources.

455. Patterson, David S. (1976). *Toward a Warless World; The Travail of the American Peace Movement, 1887-1914*. Bloomington, Indiana: Indiana University Press, 339 pp.

A view of the broad diversity of the movement toward world peace, with different approaches ranging from pacifism to international arbitration. Many of the converts to these ideas after 1900 were politically conservative on other issues. The war in Europe exposed many of the internal problems of this broad-based movement. Primary sources.

456. Pohl, James W. (1971). "The Congress and the Secretary of War, 1915: An Instance of Political Pressure." *New Jersey History, 89*, 163-70.

A brief account of a clash between Garrison and Congress over riders which attacked things the General Staff wanted. It was a forerunner of the 1916 debate over Army expansion. Primary sources.

457. Pohl, James W. (1972). "Slayden's Defeat: A Texas Congressman Loses Bid as Wilson's Secretary of War." *Military History of Texas and the Southwest, 10*, 43-50.

In 1912 Democrats in Congress put forward Slayden's name, while Wilson was in the process of making up his cabinet. However he was a friend of Ainsworth, which made him anathema to the General Staff. As a result Wilson chose Garrison. Primary sources.

458. Sellen, Robert W. (1959). "'The Just Man Armed'--Theodore Roosevelt on War." *Military Review, 39, No. 2*, 33-44.

Roosevelt gave much thought to the use of force in affairs between nations. He felt that care should be taken before the military was used, but that it should be ready if needed. No sources cited.

459. Smith, Louis. (1951). *American Democracy and Military Power; A Study of Civil Control of the Military Power in the United States*. Chicago: University of Chicago Press, 370 pp.

General survey of the way the President, Congress, and the Judiciary have tried to control the military. One chapter describes the role of the committees of Congress prior to World War I. Primary sources.

460. Ward, Robert D. (1971). "Stanley Hubert Dent and American Military Policy, 1916-1920." *Alabama Historical Quarterly, 33,* 177-89.

An important member, and chairman, of the House Military Affairs Committee, this southerner had a variety of reasons for his attitudes and votes on the issues of preparedness and Army expansion. Primary sources.

461. Welch, Richard E., Jr. (1973). "Organized Religion and the Philippine-American War, 1899-1902." *Mid-America, 55,* 184-206.

Despite the general view that the churches supported the war and annexation, the author asserts that they were quite divided on the issues. The Catholic Church and many Protestant sects split, being disturbed by the way in which the military conducted the war. Primary sources.

SOCIAL ISSUES

462. Appling, Gregory B. (1979). "Managing American Warrior-Heroism: Awards of the Congressional Medal of Honor, 1863-1973." Dissertation, Cornell University, 40/9-A, pp. 5190-91.

This sociological study examines the reasons given for the awarding of the Congressional Medal of Honor, what these citations can tell us about the goals of the armed forces in giving them out, and whether these goals have changed over time. The author notes that more recent citations seem to be posthumous than in earlier years.

463. Bacevich, Andrew J., Jr. (1982). "Family Matters: American Civilian and Military Elites in the Progressive Era." *Armed Forces and Society, 8,* 405-18.

Though in general military officers were isolated from the rest of American society, the author suggests that this was not true for all of them. Citing several examples, he notes that there was close contact between civilian sectors and the military and that this helped the career of particular officers. Primary and secondary sources.

464. Bond, Horace M. (1943). "The Negro in the Armed Forces of the United States Prior to World War I." *Journal of Negro Education, 12,* 268-87.

Only a small section of this article describes the post-Spanish American War era. It is notable for its listing of commonly accepted stereotypes regarding black participation in the armed services. No sources cited.

465. Brown, Richard C. (1951). "Social Attitudes of American Generals, 1898-1940". Dissertation, University of Wisconsin. Doctoral Dissertations Accepted by American Universities, 1952, p. 206.

An analysis of the ideas of the over 400 individuals who became generals in this time period. The author describes their background, education, ideas which society imparted to the leaders, and the attempts by military men to assume positions of leadership in society. Primary and secondary sources.

466. Christian, Garna L. (1977). "Sword and Plowshare: The Symbiotic Development of Fort Bliss and El Paso, Texas, 1849-1918." Dissertation, Texas Tech University, 38/8-A, p. 5002.

The analysis of the close relationship between town and military post is a key contribution of this study. Among the topics explored are the elements of cooperation and of conflict, including race relations, and the level of social and cultural interchange.

467. Christian, Garna L. (1981). "Rio Grande City: Prelude to the Brownsville Raid." *West Texas Historical Association Year Book, 57*, 118-32.

A group of black soldiers stationed in an isolated community encountered racial hostility from the law enforcement officers and the local population, white and Hispanic. One evening the fort was attacked and the soldiers fired back. Subsequent inquiries did not determine the guilt or innocence of the soldiers. The article illustrates the racial tensions of the area and sets the stage for the Brownsville incident several years after. Primary sources.

468. Fletcher, Marvin E. (1972). "The Black Soldier Athlete in the United States Army, 1890-1916." *Canadian Journal of the History of Sport and Physical Education, 3, No. 2*, 16-26.

Athletic competition in the military was one of the few aspects of interracial contact where blacks and whites could compete against each other. The soldiers often did quite well against their white counterparts. Primary sources.

469. Fletcher, Marvin E. (1974). *The Black Soldier and Officer in the United States Army, 1891-1917*. Columbia, Missouri: University of Missouri Press, 205 pp.

An account of the life of black soldiers and officers both on and off duty as well as a discussion of the impact of racism on them. Includes information on blacks in the Philippine-American War, relations with civilians, athletic competitions, and educational programs. One focus is on the Brownsville Affray and how it reflected the growing racism within the military in the twentieth century. Based on primary and secondary sources.

470. Fletcher, Marvin E. (1978). "War in the Streets of Athens." *Ohio History, 87*, 405-18.

One of the first joint maneuvers between the Ohio National Guard and the Army resulted in a fight and the death of one National Guardsman. Unlike the Brownsville affray of two years later, the Army did little to help the local authorities track down those soldiers who were accused of the shooting. Primary sources.

471. Foner, Jack D. (1974). *Blacks and the Military in American History: A New Perspective*. New York: Praeger, 278 pp.

A brief section of this excellent survey deals with the racism of the Army, the Brownsville Affray, and the black reactions to it.

472. Gatewood, Willard B., Jr. (1972). "Black Americans and the Quest for Empire, 1898-1903." *Journal of Southern History, 38*, 545-66.
The major focus of this article is on the attitudes of the black community on the issue of American overseas expansion. One of the factors that influenced this was the experiences of the black soldiers in Cuba and the Philippines. This convinced most blacks to oppose expansionism and not to move to the Philippines. Primary sources.

473. Gatewood, Willard B., Jr. (1975). *Black Americans and the White Man's Burden, 1898-1903*. Urbana, Illinois: University of Illinois Press, 352 pp.
One chapter of this work describes black soldiers in the Philippine-American War. Gatewood has described the blacks' attitudes toward Filipinos and their reaction to the racism they faced in the Army. There are also appraisals of their performance. Primary sources.

474. Janowitz, Morris. (1960). *The Professional Soldier: A Social and Political Portrait*. New York: The Free Press, 464 pp.
An analysis of the backgrounds, ideas, and goals of professional officers who served between 1900 and 1950. Among the topics covered are: career patterns, motivations, life style, beliefs, and civilian control. A key book in understanding military professionals. Primary sources.

475. Karsten, Peter. (1983). "Ritual and Rank: Religious Affiliation, Father's 'Calling', and Successful Advancement in the U. S. Officer Corps of the Twentieth Century." *Armed Forces and Society, 9*, 427-40.
As an explanation for the small number of Catholics and the large number of Episcopalians in the officer corps, Karsten suggests that this derives from the career patterns of their fathers as much as their religion. He also notes that there was a somewhat high degree of conversion among the Catholics. Secondary sources.

476. Lane, Ann J. (1971). *The Brownsville Affair: National Crisis and Black Reaction*. Port Washington, New York: Kennikat Press, 184 pp.
An account of the Brownsville incident and its effect on the black community. Lane has described the incident itself, as well as the subsequent investigations, the impact on Booker T. Washington and black voters, and the influence it had on the career of Joseph Foraker. Primary and secondary sources.

477. Nalty, Bernard C. (1986). *Strength for the Fight; A History of Black Americans in the Military*. New York: The Free Press, 424 pp.
This excellent general history contains a chapter on two racial incidents involving black soldiers and civilians, the 1906 Brownsville Affray and the 1917 Houston conflict. Primary sources.

478. Reddick, L. D. (1949). "The Negro Policy of the United States Army, 1775-1945." *The Journal of Negro History, 34*, 9-29.
The article describes several ideas which the author feels shaped the Army's policy toward blacks. Only one page covers the period before World War I. Secondary sources.

479. Rich, Bennett M. (1941). *Presidents and Civil Disorder*. Washington, D.C.: Brookings Institution, 235 pp.

A study of the problems that several presidents have encountered with civil disturbances and the use of military force. In this time period this included coal strikes in Colorado and labor disputes at Goldfield, Nevada. Primary and secondary sources.

480. Riordan, Timothy B., III. (1985). "The Relative Economic Status of Black and White Regiments in the Pre-World War I Army: An Example from Fort Walla Walla, Washington." Dissertation, Washington State University, 46/11-A, p. 3392.

Using archaeology to provide the evidence to apply to six indicators of economic status, the author describes the differences "in social position" between blacks and white soldiers. The basis is an analysis of artifacts from the post dump, in use between 1900 and 1910.

481. Robinson, Michael C. and Schubert, Frank N. (1975). "David Fagen: An Afro-American Rebel in the Philippines, 1899-1901." *Pacific Historical Review, 44*, 68-83.

In an era of rising racism and growing black resistance, Fagen deserted the Army and fought on the side of the insurgents. He attained great prowess, at least according to the many reports in the press. He was one of the very few blacks who reacted to the combination of imperialism and racism by fighting against it. Primary sources.

482. Sandos, James A. (1980). "Prostitution and Drugs: The United States Army on the Mexican-American Border, 1916-1917." *Pacific Historical Review, 49*, 621-645.

The expeditionary force in Mexico had to deal with three major problems: prostitution, alcohol, and drugs. Working with major reform groups they tried to regulate prostitution, ban alcohol and generally ignore drugs. Pershing's attempt to regulate rather than abolish worked, but was out of step with much of American society. Primary and secondary sources.

483. Schubert, Frank N. (1974). "The Fort Robinson Y.M.C.A., 1902-1907: A Social Organization in a Black Regiment." *Nebraska History, 55*, 165-79.

Though an isolated post, the black soldiers used the YMCA as a forum for education, social activities, and athletics. The topics of the lectures indicate a close connection with the mainstream concerns of black America. Primary sources.

484. Schubert, Frank N. (1977). "Fort Robinson, Nebraska: The History of a Military Community, 1874-1916." Dissertation, University of Toledo, 38/5-A, pp. 3001-02.

An examination of the community that developed within the post and with the nearby town of Crawford. The addition of black soldiers also added the racial aspect to the community structure. The major peace-time task of these soldiers and officers was coping with industrial disputes.

485. Schubert, Frank N. (1987). "Troopers, Taverns and Taxes: Fort Robinson, NE, and Its Municipal Parasite, 1886-1911." In Garry D. Ryan and Timothy Nenninger, (ed.), *Soldiers and Civilians; The U. S. Army and the American People*. Washington, D.C.: National Archives and Records Administration, 91-103.

This is a description of the interrelationship between a small town and a nearby Army base. Schubert has described how the soldiers were taxed, including taxes on liquor and prostitution, and the impact this had on the finances of the town. Primary sources.

486. Seraile, William. (1985). "Theophilus G. Steward, Intellectual Chaplain, 25th US Colored Infantry." *Nebraska History, 66,* 272-93.

An account of the life and activities of a black chaplain, including his efforts for his troops, his involvement in the mainstream of black life, and his leisure activities. Primary sources.

487. Tate, Michael L. (1974). "Apache Scouts, Police and Judges as Agents of Acculturation, 1865-1920." Dissertation, University of Toledo, 35/6-A, p. 3659.

The majority of this study centers on the Indian War period, but the last section relates the impact of these groups on the Apaches involved. In addition the author describes the growing movement to include the Scouts in the Army.

488. Tate, Michael L. (1986). "From Scout to Doughboy: The National Debate Over Integrating American Indians into the Military, 1891-1918." *Western Historical Quarterly, 17,* 417-37.

Tate describes the efforts to include Native Americans in the pre-war Army and their use in the war itself. Those in favor of the proposal had to battle against the prejudice of most of Congress and American society. Primary sources.

489. Tinsley, James A. (1956). "Roosevelt, Foraker, and the Brownsville Affray." *Journal of Negro History, 41,* 43-65.

An account of the Brownsville Affray, the Senate investigation and the role of Senator Foraker and President Roosevelt in the creation of the Commission of Inquiry. Primary sources.

490. Turcheneske, John A. (1978). "The Apache Prisoners of War at Fort Sill, 1894-1914." Dissertation, University of New Mexico, 39/4-A, p. 3492.

After 1890 one vestige of the Indian Wars was the prisoners that the Army retained in captivity. One group of Apaches, including some Indian scouts, was brought to Fort Sill by the War Department in the 1890s, promised land there, and eventually denied it. This dissertation recounts this "most unprecedented case of injustice."

491. Weaver, John D. (1970). *The Brownsville Raid*. New York: W. W. Norton, 320 pp.

A detailed anecdotal account of the 1906 incident involving the Twenty-fifth Infantry and the subsequent discharge of three companies of the regiment. The author describes the ensuing political storm and its impact on the black community. Weaver believes that the soldiers were not guilty of the crime. Bibliographic essay; primary sources; no specific citations.

492. White, William B. (1968). "The Military and the Melting Pot: The American Army and Minority Groups, 1865-1924." Dissertation, University of Wisconsin, 29/12-A, p. 4443.

The focus of this dissertation is the way in which the military, especially in the nineteenth century, dealt with a variety of ethnic and racial minority groups. Generally the Army's goal has been to integrate them, with the exception of blacks. There have been positive and negative repercussions from these efforts.

493. White, William B. (1976). "The American Indian as Soldier, 1890-1919." *Canadian Review of American Studies, 7,* 15-25.

After 1894 the Army continued to enlist Native Americans but integrated them into other units. The issue of separation or integration continued to be discussed through World War I. Primary sources.

494. Wooster, Robert A. (1985). "The Military and United States Indian Policy, 1865-1903." Dissertation, University of Texas-Austin, 46/10-A, pp. 3140-41.

Though most of the problems were over by the time of the Spanish-American War, the Army continued to monitor Native Americans until 1903. Making things difficult was that this was a minor concern and there was no consensus in the government as to how its policy was to be put into effect.

495. Young, Richard. (1986). "The Brownsville Affray." *American History Illustrated, 21, No. 6,* 10-17.

An account of the 1906 shooting and the subsequent controversy involving the Twenty-fifth Infantry. Young recounts the reaction of the black and white communities, as well as Roosevelt and Foraker, to the incident and the subsequent discharge of the men. No sources cited.

STRATEGY

496. Browning, Robert S., III. (1983). *Two If By Sea: The Development of American Coastal Defense Policy.* Westport, Connecticut: Greenwood Press, 210 pp.

Most of this study deals with the nineteenth century, and only a small section describes 1905 review of the coast defense program by the Taft Board. Primary sources.

497. Hamburger, Kenneth E. (1986). "The Technology, Doctrine, and Politics of U. S. Coast Defenses, 1880-1945: A Case Study in U. S. Defense Planning." Dissertation, Duke University, 47/8-A, p. 3167.

The author examines the technology of the period, how policy was made, and the role of the professionals and politicians in making policy. Each group was parochial in their outlook and never was there a "rational and coherent" analysis of threats and technology.

498. Moore, Jamie W. (1982). "National Security in the American Army's Definition of Mission, 1865-1914." *Military Affairs, 46*, 127-31.
   Being unsure of neither the exact enemy nor the possible threats to the United States, a fortification policy was initiated in the nineteenth century. It reached its fruition in the early twentieth century. The author feels that this process helped define a national security policy. Mainly primary sources.

499. Morton, Louis. (1949). "Military and Naval Preparations for the Defense of the Philippines During the War Scare of 1907." *Military Affairs, 13*, 95-104.
   War with Japan seemed possible in 1907 and Roosevelt pushed the Army and Navy to update their preparations. This article contains long quotes from several documents which illustrate that effort.

500. Morton, Louis. (1959). "War Plan ORANGE: Evolution of a Strategy." *World Politics, 11*, 221-50.
   The beginnings of American strategy to defend the Philippines are outlined. The failure of the Army and Navy to agree was one of the major reasons why no progress was made before 1917. Primary sources.

501. Morton, Louis. (1962). "Interservice Co-operation and Political-Military Collaboration, 1900-38." In Harry L. Coles, (ed.), *Total War and Cold War: Problems in Civilian Control of the Military*. Columbus, Ohio: Ohio State University Press, 131-60.
   Cooperation and conflict between the Army, the Navy, and the State Department are the central focus of this essay, a brief section of which deals with the period before World War I. Primary and secondary sources.

502. Nesmith, Vardell E., Jr. (1977). "The Quiet Paradigm Change: The Evolution of the Field Artillery Doctrine of the United States Army, 1861-1905." Dissertation, Duke University, 38/4-A, pp. 2305-06.
   Through a study of the evolution of field artillery doctrine from direct to indirect fire, the author presents insights into the relationship between technology and a relatively conservative institution. The general tendency was for the doctrine to move in an evolutionary fashion, even if technology made this relatively inefficient.

503. Osterhoudt, Henry J. (1986). "The Evolution of U. S. Army Assault Tactics, 1778-1919: The Search for Sound Doctrine." Dissertation, Duke University, 48/2-A, pp. 467-68.
   An indicator of the growing military professionalism was the way in which the Army studied tactics, evaluated experience, and decided doctrine. Doctrine produced by a series of boards in this period show an Army more sensitive than before to the realities of warfare and the needs of servicemen.

504. Smith, Dale O. (1955). *U. S. Military Doctrine: A Study and Appraisal*. New York: Duell, Sloan and Pearce, 256 pp.
   Though primarily centering on the development of air power theory, the author includes the ideas of such leaders as Root and Bliss. Secondary sources.

505. Taylor, William L. (1964). "The Debate over Changing Cavalry Tactics and Weapons, 1900-1914." *Military Affairs, 28*, 173-83.

Experience and technological change began to raise doubts about the way in the military proposed to use cavalry. For some individuals, experience called into question whether this branch even had a role. The article compares discussions in Europe and America. Primary and secondary sources.

506. Wilson, John B. (1984). "Army Readiness Planning, 1899-1917." *Military Review, 64, No. 7*, 60-73.

By examining tactical organization, the author seeks to understand what the Army saw as its role. This survey includes the several maneuver divisions as well as the call-up caused by the Mexican border problems in 1916. The analysis indicates that the Army prepared to defend the nation from outside attack, not to engage in overseas operations. Primary and secondary sources.

TECHNOLOGY

507. Armstrong, David A. (1982). *Bullets and Bureaucrats: The Machine Gun and the United States Army, 1861-1916*. Westport, Connecticut: Greenwood Press, 239 pp.

A study of how the Army failed to evaluate or understand this new weapon. In this period the Army tested new weapons, with unclear standards, and tried to find the proper niche for the weapon, but with little success. Primary and secondary sources.

508. Azoy, Anastasio C. M. (1941). "Great Guns: A History of the Coast Artillery Corps." *Coast Artillery Journal, 84*, 573-78.

A general history of the Corps in the pre-war period generally concentrating on the organizational changes. In addition some brief note made of the technological changes. No sources cited.

509. Barnhill, John H. (1978). "The Punitive Expedition Against Pancho Villa: The Forced Motorization of the American Army." *Military History of Texas and the Southwest, 14*, 135-45.

Because of the size of the expedition and the terrain, the Army turned to truck transportation. However a number of problems ensued in this first major use of trucks including lack of standardization among the different models and the poor performance of the trucks themselves. The experience forced the Army to motorize and helped prepare it for France. Primary sources.

510. Batchelor, John, and Hogg, Ian V. (1972). *Artillery*. New York: Charles Scribner's Sons, 158 pp.

A brief section details the development of artillery in the period before World War I, though little is included on American innovations. No sources cited.

511. Brinckerhoff, Sidney B., and Chamberlin, Pierce. (1968). "The Army's Search for a Repeating Rifle: 1873-1903." *Military Affairs, 32*, 20-30.
   A description of the long process whereby the Army sought to add a repeating rifle to the arsenal. The vast majority of the article deals with the period prior to 1900, though the repeating rifle that was adopted was developed after 1900. Primary sources.

512. Campbell, Clark S. (1957). *The '03 Springfield*. Beverly Hills, California: Fadco Publishing Co. 344 pp.
   This detailed work describes the history, construction, and production of this famous Army weapon. The book also includes a description, and illustrations, of the weapon and its numerous accessories.

513. Cary, Norman M., Jr. (1980). "The Use of the Motor Vehicle in the United States Army, 1899-1939." Dissertation, University of Georgia, 41/4-A, p. 1730.
   The Army began to use motor vehicles very early in the century, but the experience gained during the Mexican Punitive Expedition made it clear that much remained to be done. Among the problems was the aversion of soldiers to adapt to the new technology and the reluctance of Congress to fund acquisition of vehicles.

514. Chinn, George M. (1951). *The Machine Gun: History, Evolution, and Development of Manual, Automatic, and Airborne Repeating Weapons*. Washington, D.C.: Bureau of Ordnance, Department of the Navy, 3 volumes.
   One section of this massive work describes the developments pioneered by several Americans in this period including Hiram Maxim and John Browning. Chinn has also described the weapons, their evolution, and the reactions of the military to them. Published sources.

515. Ellis, John. (1975). *The Social History of the Machine Gun*. New York: Pantheon, 186 pp.
   An account of the impact of the machine gun. Includes a section on the pre-war neglect of the weapon by all nations, including the United States. Ellis explains how the rapid killing capabilities of the gun fit into the mass slaughter of the war as it developed in Europe in 1914-18. Secondary sources.

516. Hogg, Ian V. (1974). *A History of Artillery*. London: Hamlyn Publishing Group Ltd., 240 pp.
   One chapter describes the developments in the early part of this century in all countries, including the United States. There is material on coastal defense weapons and naval guns. Well illustrated with detailed drawings. No sources cited.

517. Marshall, Max L. (ed.). (1965). *History of the U. S. Army Signal Corps*. New York: F. Watts, 305 pp.
   One chapter details the building of the communications system in Alaska, accomplished by the Army in the first years of this century. No sources cited.

518. Schreier, Konrad F., Jr. (1968). "U. S. Army Field Artillery Weapons, 1866-1918." *Military Collector & Historian, 20*, 40-45.

A descriptive list of breech loading field artillery weapons in the inventory of the Army. The author concludes that we had a larger number of artillery than is generally believed. Secondary sources.

519. Schreier, Konrad F., Jr. (1973). "The U. S. Army 3 Inch Field Gun Model 1902." *Military Collector & Historian, 25*, 185-92.

An account of the evolution and design of the first modern field piece built by the Army. It remained the standard artillery weapon until World War I. Detailed drawings. Primary sources.

520. Speedy, John C., III. (1977). "From Mules to Motors: Development of Maintenance Doctrine for Motor Vehicles by the U. S. Army, 1896-1918." Dissertation, Duke University, 38/8-A, p. 5012.

This dissertation presents a case study of how a bureaucracy responds to technological change. Budgetary limitations, established practices, and civilian experiences shaped the first doctrines on motor vehicle maintenance. However, small numbers of vehicles prevented establishment of an accurate data base. The Mexican Punitive Expedition and World War I created the basis for revised doctrine.

521. Taylerson, A. W. F. (1971). *The Revolver, 1889-1914*. New York: Crown Publishers, Inc., 324 pp.

Though centered on arms available in Britain, considerable attention is devoted to the United States. Included in the chapter on American revolvers are detailed descriptions by company, including illustrations. The work also includes a "Who's Whose", and annotated bibliography. Secondary sources.

522. White, Brian T. (1970). *Tanks and Other Armoured Fighting Vehicles, 1900 to 1918*. New York: Macmillan Company, 199 pp.

A detailed written and illustrated description of 96 different vehicles, a few of which were developed in the United States prior to its entry in the war. No sources cited.

523. Zabecki, David T. (1981). "Dan T. Moore: Founder of the Field Artillery School." *Field Artillery Journal, 49, No. 6*, 58-60.

A brief article in which Zabecki describes the origins of the school in 1911 and the background of the founder. No sources cited.

1919-1941

GENERAL

524. Bernardo, C. Joseph, and Bacon, Eugene H. (1961). *American Military Policy: Its Development Since 1775.* 2nd ed. Harrisburg, Pennsylvania: Stackpole Company, 548 pp.
   Two brief chapters on the interwar period describe the Army, Navy and air power developments. Nothing on social issues, the impact of the Depression, or how American strategy was influenced by domestic and foreign events. Primary and secondary sources.

525. Dupuy, R. Ernest, and Dupuy, Trevor N. (1956). *Military Heritage of America.* New York: McGraw-Hill Book Company, 794 pp.
   Very brief section on the interwar years, but little of the changes occurring are dealt with. Superficial. Secondary sources.

526. Hassler, Warren W., Jr. (1982). *With Shield and Sword: American Military Affairs, Colonial Times to the Present.* Ames, Iowa: Iowa State University Press, 462 pp.
   One chapter of seventeen pages explains this period, including the Navy. Some brief coverage is given to the National Defense Act of 1920 and its impact, manpower problems, and rearmament. Secondary and primary sources.

527. Matloff, Maurice, (ed.). (1969). *American Military History.* Washington, D.C.: Office of the Chief of Military History, United States Army, 701 pp. SD D114.2:M59.
   A team written general history of the Army, whose primary audience was the ROTC. The interwar period is treated in 20 pages.

528. Millett, Allan R., and Maslowski, Peter. (1984). *For the Common Defense: A Military History of the United States of America.* New York: The Free Press, 621 pp.
   Only a few pages of this excellent survey describe the 1920s and 1930s. There is an superior bibliography. Primary and secondary sources.

529. Millis, Walter. (1956). *Arms and Men: A Study in American Military History*. New York: Putnam, 382 pp.

An important analysis of some of the major themes in American military history. In this time period the themes include: the mechanization of warfare and the application of science to war. Secondary sources.

530. Spaulding, Oliver L. (1937). *The United States Army in War and Peace*. New York: G.P. Putnam's Sons, 541 pp.

A few brief pages at the end of this general history describe the changes that occurred after World War I, including the reorganization of 1920. Bibliography but no sources cited.

531. Weigley, Russell F. (1962). *Towards an American Army: Military Thought from Washington to Marshall*. New York: Columbia University Press, 297 pp.

The last chapter of this key work presents the ideas of John McAuley Palmer. He learned from Wood and the experiences of World War I that the best approach to the manpower issue was to depend upon citizen soldiers and universal military training. Primary sources.

532. Weigley, Russell. (1967). *History of the United States Army*. New York: Macmillan Company, 688 pp.

A basic book for the study of the Army. Two chapters cover this time period. Secondary sources.

533. Weigley, Russell. (1986). "The Interwar Army, 1919-1941." In Kenneth J. Hagan and William R. Roberts, (ed.), *Against All Enemies: Interpretations of American Military History from Colonial Times to the Present*. Westport, Connecticut: Greenwood Press, 257-78.

Drawing conclusions from World War I experiences, the Army modified policy in the 1920s. During the next two decades it was affected by strong leaders, technological changes, anti-war feelings and the Depression. Short bibliographic essay. Secondary sources.

BIOGRAPHY

534. Ambrose, Stephen E. (1969). "A Fateful Friendship". *American Heritage, 20, No. 3*, 40-41, 97-103.

Ambrose describes the friendship between Patton and Eisenhower which began in 1919 and continued to 1946. They kept in touch and discussed possible battlefield uses for tanks. No sources cited.

535. Anders, Leslie. (1985). *Gentle Knight; The Life and Times of Major General Edwin Forrest Harding*. Kent, Ohio: Kent State University Press, 384 pp.

Several chapters of this biography describe Harding's service: duty at West Point, Command and General Staff School and Fort Benning; service in China; and editorship of *Infantry Journal*. Primary and secondary sources.

536. Blumenson, Martin. (1972). *The Patton Papers, Volume I: 1885-1940.* Boston: Houghton Mifflin, 996 pp.

Incorporating the writings of Patton, Blumenson has detailed many important events in his life. There are chapters on his years in the Cavalry, on his service in garrison duty, and on the development of the Cavalry and the tank. Primary sources.

537. Blumenson, Martin. (1976). "George S. Patton's Student Days at the Army War College." *Parameters, 5, No. 2,* 25-32.

Blumenson focused on Patton's student thesis, written in the early 1930s. Patton articulated his views on mechanization and on the need to eschew mass armies and develop smaller forces. Primary sources.

538. Blumenson, Martin. (1984). *Mark Clark.* New York: Congdon & Weed, Inc., 306 pp.

Though this biography concentrates on the war years, there are several chapters on the interwar period. Clark's experiences as a young officer, his work at Leavenworth, and his friendship with George Marshall and Dwight Eisenhower are detailed. No sources cited.

539. Blumenson, Martin. (1985). *Patton: The Man Behind the Legend, 1885-1945.* New York: William Morrow and Co., 320 pp.

A relatively brief biography. Two chapters describe Patton in this time period, with one detailing his role in the 1941 maneuvers and the immediate pre-war period. The author also presents the development of Armor and armor doctrine. Selected bibliography cited but no primary sources listed.

540. Coffman, Edward M. (1966). *The Hilt of the Sword: The Career of Peyton C. March.* Madison, Wisconsin: University of Wisconsin Press, 346 pp.

In five chapters, Coffman describes March's work as Chief of Staff and his role in drafting what became the 1920 National Defense Act. Primary sources.

541. Cooling, Benjamin F. (1975). "Dwight D. Eisenhower at the Army War College, 1927-1928." *Parameters, 5, No. 1,* 26-36.

An article largely based on a paper Eisenhower wrote at the War College on an enlisted reserve for the Army. The author relates Eisenhower's ideas to the conditions of the time and adds the comments of his instructors. Primary sources.

542. Editors of the *Army Times.* (1967). *Warrior: The Story of General George S. Patton.* New York: G. P. Putnam's Sons, 222 pp.

One brief chapter of this popular biography describes Patton during the interwar period, including his love-hate relationship with armor. Secondary sources.

543. Fausold, Martin L. (1975). *James W. Wadsworth, Jr.: The Gentleman from New York.* Syracuse, New York: Syracuse University Press, 457 pp.

A biography of a key legislator in the interwar period. He was influential in the 1920 National Defense Act and a prime mover in the 1940 Selective Service legislation. Primary sources.

544. Frye, William. (1947). *Marshall: Citizen Soldier*. Indianapolis, Indiana: Bobbs-Merrill, 397 pp.

Quite sympathetic biography centering on Marshall the man and his experiences. Several chapters detail events of the interwar period. No sources cited.

545. Gugeler, Russell A. (1983). "George Marshall and Orlando Ward, 1939-1941." *Parameters, 13, No. 1*, 28-42.

Ward, secretary to Marshall when the latter served as Chief of Staff, had a good insight in the period of preparation for total war. Among the issues that are described: conflicts with the civilian secretaries, goals for expansion, and relations to the developing Air Force. Primary sources.

546. Hagedorn, Hermann. (1931). *Leonard Wood: A Biography*. New York: Harper and Brothers, 2 volumes, 960 pp.

Six chapters of the second volume cover Wood's post-war service, including his work in the Philippines as Governor. Generally laudatory of the subject. Primary sources.

547. Hatch, Alden. (1950). *George Patton: General in Spurs*. New York: Julian Messner, 184 pp.

Popular biography focusing on the personality of George Patton, with facts included to display the hero growing up toward a battle leader. Several chapters describe Patton in the interwar period, though there is nothing substantive on armor theory or technological changes. No sources cited.

548. Hogg, Ian V. (1982). *The Biography of General George S. Patton*. New York: Hamlyn, 160 pp.

A brief biography, quite well illustrated. In ten pages there is a description of his role in the development of Armor in the 1930s and his participation in the 1940 maneuvers. No sources cited.

549. Holley, I. B., Jr. (1982). *General John M. Palmer, Citizen Soldiers, and the Army of a Democracy*. Westport, Connecticut: Greenwood Press, 814 pp.

A biography of a key individual in the manpower issues of the 1920s and 1930s. Palmer was a crucial figure in shaping the 1920 National Defense Act and the Selective Service Act of 1940. Primary and secondary sources.

550. Hunt, Frazier. (1954). *The Untold Story of Douglas MacArthur*. New York: Devin-Adair Co., 533 pp.

A popular, pro-MacArthur biography. Two chapters contain information on the interwar period including material on his battles for rearmament and dealing with the "Communist" inspired Bonus March. No sources cited.

551. James, D. Clayton. (1970). *The Years of MacArthur, Volume I, 1880-1941*. Boston: Houghton Mifflin Company, 740 pp.

There are several chapters in this excellent work which present the career of MacArthur in the 1920s and 1930s, including his experiences as superintendent of the Military Academy and service in the Philippines. A major section of this book deals with the performance of MacArthur as Chief of Staff during the first part of the Depression, his contacts with the New Deal, and then his return to the Philippines and his role with the Philippine Army. Primary and secondary sources.

552. Lane, Jack C. (1978). *Armed Progressive: General Leonard Wood*. San Rafael, California: Presidio Press, 329 pp.

A section of this biography recounts Wood's attempt to win the Republican presidential nomination in 1920 and his role in shaping and carrying out American policy in the Philippines in the 1920s. Primary sources.

553. Lockmiller, David A. (1955). *Enoch H. Crowder: Soldier, Lawyer, Statesman*. Columbia, Missouri: University of Missouri Studies, 286 pp.

A biography of an important military leader. During the 1920s Crowder was involved in the Cuban government and represented American interests in the country. Primary and secondary sources.

554. Lohbeck, Don. (1956). *Patrick J. Hurley*. Chicago: Henry Regnery Co., 513 pp.

Semi-scholarly biography with one segment in which the author describes Hurley during his tenure as Hoover's Secretary of War. Among the issues discussed are: the movement for Philippine independence, a commission to promote peace, and the Bonus March. Mainly secondary sources.

555. McFarland, Keith D. (1975). *Harry H. Woodring; A Political Biography of FDR's Controversial Secretary of War*. Lawrence, Kansas: University Press of Kansas, 346 pp.

The focus of this biography is Woodring's term of office in the War Department and the controversies that erupted. FDR and Woodring often were at odds, caused partially by policy differences and partially by FDR's desire to control affairs. Primary sources.

556. McFarland, Keith D. (1976). "Woodring vs. Johnson: F.D.R. and the Great War Department Feud." *Army, 26, No. 3*, 36-42.

The conflict between Woodring and Assistant Secretary Louis Johnson over policy was encouraged by FDR as part of his effort to enhance his own power. Depending on which position the president wanted to encourage on rearmament or air force expansion, FDR chose his adviser. Though the War Department was split by this divide and rule strategy, FDR did it on purpose. No sources cited.

557. Manchester, William. (1978). *American Caesar: Douglas MacArthur, 1880-1964*. Boston: Little, Brown, 793 pp.

A well written, often personality oriented, account of MacArthur, with two chapters on his interwar experiences. Some have questioned Manchester's scholarship. Primary and secondary sources.

558. Morison, Elting E. (1960). *Turmoil and Tradition: A Study of the Life and Times of Henry L. Stimson*. Boston: Houghton Mifflin, 686 pp.

Two chapters of this detailed biography describe the beginning of Stimson's second term of service as Secretary of War, though only as a general overview of the major issues. Primary sources.

559. Mosley, Leonard. (1982). *Marshall, Hero For Our Times*. New York: Hearst Books, 570 pp.

A biography which mixes anecdotes with information about Marshall the soldier. Brief chapters describe the interwar period, the death of his first wife, and his remarriage. Source notes; no footnotes. Primary sources.

560. Murray, Lawrence L. (1972). "General John J. Pershing's Bid for the Presidency in 1920--'The Boys Will Never Call Him "Papa"'." *Nebraska History, 53*, 216-52.

An account of the effort by Pershing and others to secure for the general the 1920 Republican nomination. He failed in several primaries, including one in his home state of Nebraska, largely because he had no real organization, not because there was an anti-military feeling. Primary sources.

561. O'Connor, Richard. (1961). *Black Jack Pershing*. Garden City, New York: Doubleday & Company, Inc., 431 pp.

Two chapters describe his life after the AEF, with attention to the man but little to the Army in which he served. Aimed at the general public. Primary sources; chapter bibliographies; no specific citations.

562. Payne, Robert. (1951). *The Marshall Story; A Biography of General George C. Marshall*. New York: Prentice-Hall, 344 pp.

A popular account, in which the author tries to understand the officer, but merely succeeds in retelling stories about him. There is one chapter on his experiences in the interwar period, including life in China. No sources cited.

563. Peake, Louis A. (1977). "West Virginia's Best Known General Since 'Stonewall Jackson': John L. Hines." *West Virginia History, 38*, 226-35.

A brief biographical sketch of his career, with several pages on his service as Chief of Staff in the 1920s. Primary sources.

564. Perry, Milton F., and Parke, Barbara W. (1957). *Patton and His Pistols: The Favorite Side Arms of General George S. Patton, Jr.* Harrisburg, Pennsylvania: The Stackpole Company, 138 pp.

One chapter describes his interwar career, including his role in the Bonus March incident and his growing interest and display of pistols. Primary and secondary sources.

565. Petillo, Carol M. (1981). *Douglas MacArthur: The Philippine Years*. Bloomington, Indiana: Indiana University Press, 301 pp.

This scholarly study seeks to present the relationship between MacArthur and the Islands during his several tours there, including his service after his retirement from the US Army. In addition the author has also tried to understand the personality of MacArthur and the impact of his Philippine service. Primary and secondary sources.

566. Pogue, Forrest C. (1963). *George C. Marshall: Education of a General, 1880-1939*. New York: Viking Press, 421 pp.

An excellent scholarly account of Marshall the man and soldier. Several chapters detail his career including his work with Pershing after the war, his duty in China, and his tour at the Infantry School at Fort Benning. Primary and secondary sources.

567. Pogue, Forrest C. (1966). *George C. Marshall: Ordeal and Hope, 1939-1942*. New York: Viking Press, 491 pp.

A continuation of an excellent biography of this key leader, now as Chief of Staff in the rearmament period. Half of the book describes the period before Pearl Harbor. There is also a section debunking the idea of a conspiracy to lead the US into a war. Primary and secondary sources.

568. Reese, John R. (1984). "Supply Man: The Army Life of Lieutenant General Henry S. Aurand, 1915-1952." Dissertation, Kansas State University, 45/11-A, p. 3436.

According to Reese, Aurand was a new type of Army officer, a military manager of field supply. He wrote a manual on the topic and taught the subject at the Army War College. In World War II he made a major contribution to the success of the Allies through his understanding of logistics.

569. Semmes, Harry H. (1955). *Portrait of Patton*. New York: Appleton-Century-Crofts, Inc., 308 pp.

A biography by an officer who served under Patton. One chapter recounts the interwar years, with an emphasis on the 1941 Louisiana maneuvers. No sources cited.

570. Smith, Cornelius C., Jr. (1977). *Don't Settle for Second; Life and Times of Cornelius C. Smith*. San Rafael, California: Presidio Press, 229 pp.

A biography of a career officer who commanded the Tenth Cavalry and served on the electoral commission in Nicaragua. The author makes considerable use of quotations from materials written by the subject.

571. Smythe, Donald. (1972). "Battle of the Books: Pershing versus March." *Army, 42, No. 9*, 30-32.

A brief description of the way these two commanders wrote about each other in their accounts of World War I. Pershing virtually ignored March, while March criticized the AEF commander. Primary sources.

572. Smythe, Donald. (1975). "Literary Salvos: James G. Harbord and the Pershing-March Controversy." *Mid-America, 57*, 173-83.

Round three in the battle of the histories of World War I was written by a friend, and former subordinate, of Pershing's, who defended his conduct against the attacks of General March. Primary sources.

573. Smythe, Donald. (1984). "Pershing after the Armistice, 1918-1919." *Missouri Historical Review, 79*, 43-64.

Though the war ended in November 1918, Pershing's tasks did not. As Smythe details in this article, Pershing had problems getting what he felt was the proper respect from General Foch; he was concerned about the health of his soldiers; and he was troubled by the end of promotions as a result of General March's orders. Primary sources.

574. Smythe, Donald. (1986). *Pershing: General of the Armies*. Bloomington, Indiana: Indiana University Press, 399 pp.

While most of this biography by the leading scholar on Pershing concentrates on World War I, there are brief chapters dealing with Pershing's return home, his effort to win a presidential nomination, his work as Chief of Staff and the battle of the memoirs. Primary and secondary sources.

575. Stewart, Roy P. (1981). "Raymond S. McLain: America's Greatest Citizen Soldier." *Chronicles of Oklahoma, 59,* 4-30.

A description of the career of a businessman who participated in the National Guard in the interwar years and distinguished himself at the 1941 maneuvers. Subsequently he was promoted to general officer rank and performed well in World War II. No sources cited.

576. Toner, James H. (1977). "Douglas MacArthur: Colorful Leader, Colorless Times." *Social Science, 52,* 212-20.

An account of MacArthur as military manager during the 1920s and 1930s, including public relations problems stemming from the Bonus March. Printed primary and secondary sources.

577. Tuchman, Barbara. (1970). *Stilwell and the American Experience in China, 1911-45.* New York: Macmillan Company, 621 pp.

Much of this detailed biography describes Joseph Stilwell and the Chinese revolution and Civil War. In addition his role as Military Attaché during the Sino-Japanese War is also recounted. The book is a biography and a history of Americans' relation to China and Asia itself. Primary and secondary sources.

578. Twichell, Heath, Jr. (1974). *Allen: The Biography of an Army Officer, 1859-1930.* New Brunswick, New Jersey: Rutgers University Press, 358 pp.

A detailed biography of a general who was involved in a variety of activities, including commander of the American occupation forces in Germany. Primary sources.

579. Vandiver, Frank E. (1977). *Black Jack: The Life and Times of John J. Pershing.* College Station, Texas: Texas A&M Press, 2 volumes, 1178 pp.

The last chapter describes Pershing's post-World War I activities including his service as Chief of Staff. Personal anecdotes predominate. Primary sources.

CONFLICTS

580. Bolger, Daniel P. (1987). "Cruel Russian Winter." *Military Review, 67,* No. 6, 63-77.

This is a brief presentation of the history of the North Russian front [1918-1920], and the American role. Though the American troops had little impact on the war in Russia, they performed their arduous duty quite well. Printed primary and secondary sources.

581. Calhoun, Frederick S. (1983). "The Wilsonian Way of War: American Armed Power from Veracruz to Vladivostok." Dissertation, University of Chicago, 44/7-A, p. 2223.

The author compares the different military interventions and finds a variety of different themes. The two interventions in Russia and Siberia, claims the author, "witnessed Wilson's efforts to establish the principle of international cooperation."

582. Dobson, Christopher, and Miller, John. (1986). *The Day They Almost Bombed Moscow: The Allied War in Russia 1918-1920.* New York: Atheneum, 288 pp.

A popular history of the various campaigns in Russia and Siberia during and after the end of World War I. Though concentrating mainly on the British role, some material about the American Army is included. No footnotes; selected bibliography of secondary sources included.

583. Gardner, Lloyd C. (1976). *Wilson and Revolutions: 1913-1921.* Philadelphia: Lippincott, 149 pp.

Part of a series of short paperbacks for classroom use on policy alternatives, this one focuses mainly on American intervention into the Russian revolution. In addition there are a series of documents illustrating the process. No sources cited.

584. Goldhurst, Richard. (1978). *The Midnight War: The American Intervention in Russia, 1918-1920.* New York: McGraw-Hill, 288 pp.

A popular account of the planning and execution of Wilson's intervention in Russia and Siberia. Brief chapters cover the many aspects of this complex event. Mainly secondary sources.

585. Goldhurst, Richard. (1979). "Steadying Efforts: The War at Archangel, 1918-1919." *Wisconsin Magazine of History, 62,* 200-16.

A short amount of text supplemented with many photographs of the 339th Infantry in North Russia in the period after the end of World War I. No sources cited.

586. Gordon, Dennis. (1983). *Quartered in Hell: The Story of the American North Russia Expeditionary Force 1918-1919.* Missoula, Montana: Doughboy Historical Society and G.O.S., Inc., 320 pp.

A history of the North Russia force based upon the recollections of individual soldiers and officers. This is supplemented with additional text, maps, and photographs.

587. Halliday, Ernest M. (1960). *The Ignorant Armies; The Anglo-American Archangel Expedition: 1918-1919.* London: Weidenfeld and Nicolson, 232 pp.

A detailed account, centering on individuals, of the North Russia expedition, including a discussion of why it began, the conditions the soldiers operated under, and the reasons why they left. The author feels that the expedition had as one of its goals the destruction of the Bolshevik Revolution. No sources cited though there are brief general source notes.

588. Hanna, William. (1984). "American Intervention into Siberia." *American History Illustrated, 19, No. 2,* 8-11, 44-47.

An account of the reasons for the intervention into Siberia and of the history of the Siberian Expeditionary Force itself. No sources cited.

589. Hayes, Harold B., III. (1982). "The Iron(ic) Horse From Nikolsk." *Military Review, 62, No. 5,* 18-28.

A narrative of one part of the American expedition to Siberia and its attempts to remain neutral among the contending factions, including the Japanese. Making the task more difficult was one officer's assistance to the Soviet's in the guise of being neutral. Primary and secondary sources.

590. Hunt, George A. (1931). *The History of the Twenty-Seventy Infantry*. Honolulu, Hawaii: Honolulu Star-Bulletin, 204 pp.
The book includes a variety of materials on the Siberian intervention, in which this regiment played a role.

591. Jackson, Robert. (1972). *At War with the Bolsheviks: The Allied Intervention into Russia, 1917-1920*. London: Tom Stacey, Ltd. 251 pp.
A general history of the war in Russia and Siberia with the major focus on Britain and brief attention paid to the American role. Primary and secondary sources.

592. Kennan, George F. (1958). *Soviet-American Relations, 1917-1920; II, The Decision to Intervene*. Princeton, New Jersey: Princeton University Press, 513 pp.
Mainly an account of the reasons for the American intervention and later the withdrawal of American troops from Russia and Siberia. Includes a brief narrative of the expeditions that arose from those decisions. Primary sources.

593. Kennan, George F. (1959). "American Troops in Russia; the True Record." *Atlantic, 203, No. 1*, 36-42.
A description, according to Kennan, of why the US went into Russia and Siberia in 1918-1919 and what was accomplished. No sources cited.

594. Lasch, Christopher. (1962). "American Intervention in Siberia: A Reinterpretation." *Political Science Quarterly, 77*, 205-23.
After presenting evidence against a variety of commonly held theories, Lasch suggests his own: that the US intervened because we believed that we were combating a German induced conspiracy aimed at having the Central Powers take over Siberia. Primary sources.

595. Long, John W. (1982). "American Intervention in Russia: The North Russian Expedition, 1918-1919." *Diplomatic History, 6*, 45-68.
Wilson wanted to secure a resolution of the conflict in Russia and when this proved to be impossible, he ordered American troops withdrawn. The author does not accept the idea that there was an ideological motivation to the intervention. Primary sources.

596. Luckett, Judith A. (1984). "The Siberian Intervention: Military Support of Foreign Policy." *Military Review, 64, No. 4*, 54-63.
General William Graves was one of the first officers commanding a military force with a limited diplomatic goal. The author uses an account of the experiences of the expedition to draw lessons for similar situations in the future. Primary and secondary sources.

597. Maddox, Robert J. (1967). "President Wilson and the Russians." *American History Illustrated, 2, No. 1*, 40-48.
A general account of the events leading up to Wilson's decision to send troops to Russia and what happened subsequently. No sources cited.

598. Maddox, Robert J. (1977). "Doughboys in Siberia." *American History Illustrated, 12, No. 5*, 10-21.
An account of the SEF, including material on its origins, problems in trying to remain neutral or stay out of conflict with the various factions battling in Siberia, and final withdrawal. No sources cited.

599. Maddox, Robert J. (1977). *The Unknown War with Russia: Wilson's Siberian Intervention*. San Rafael, California: Presidio Press, 156 pp.
In an effort to stop Bolshevism, Wilson ordered the American intervention in Siberia. This account describes the decision and the problems which the expeditionary force faced. Primary and secondary sources.

600. Manning, Clarence A. (1952). *The Siberian Fiasco*. New York: Library Publishers, 210 pp.
This narrative of the Siberian intervention begins with the premise that it was primarily motivated to change the outcome of the Russian civil war. Manning believes the attempt failed. Few sources cited, mainly secondary.

601. Nolan, William F. (1978). "America's Participation in the Military Defense of Shanghai, 1931-1941." Dissertation, Saint Louis University, 39/3-A, pp. 1762-63.
An account of the efforts of a number of nations to defend their sectors of the city during the conflict between China and Japan. One section describes the actions of the Thirty-first Infantry during the fighting in 1932.

602. O'Connor, Richard. (1974). "Yanks in Siberia." *American Heritage, 25, No. 5*, 10-17, 80-83.
This is a general account of the Siberian expedition and the problems they encountered in trying to be neutral. No sources cited.

603. Pelzel, Sophia R. (1946). *American Intervention in Siberia, 1918-1920*. Philadelphia: n.p., 98 pp.
Published version of a dissertation. The author views American intervention from the perspective of its role in American policy in the Far East as well as the traditional view of the expedition arising from anti-Soviet intentions. Only a small section actually describes the SEF. Primary sources.

604. Richard, Carl J. (1986). "'The Shadow of a Plan': The Rationale Behind Wilson's 1918 Siberian Intervention." *The Historian, 49*, 64-84.
A review of six theories advanced to account for American involvement. Richard argues that defeating Germany was the prime motivation, though overthrow of the Bolsheviks was secondary. Primary and secondary sources.

605. Shapiro, Sumner. (1973). "Intervention in Russia (1918-1919)." *United States Naval Institute Proceedings, 99, No. 4*, 52-61.
An account of the decision to intervene and its consequences at the time and in subsequent US-USSR relations. No sources cited.

606. Silverlight, John. (1971). *The Victor's Dilemma: Allied Intervention in the Russia Civil War*. New York: Weybright and Talley, 392. pp.
A good general history of the wars in Russia and Siberia. Though focusing mainly on the British role, the American expedition is discussed. Primary and secondary sources.

607. Trani, Eugene P. (1976). "Woodrow Wilson and the Decision to Intervene in Russia: A Reconsideration." *Journal of Modern History, 48*, 440-61.
The decisive factor, according to Trani, was his desire to placate the Allies, especially the British, who were urging him to join them against the Bolsheviks. Primary and secondary sources.

608. Trask, David F. (1961). *The United States in the Supreme War Council: American War Aims and Inter-Allied Strategy, 1917-1918*. Middleton, Connecticut: Wesleyan University Press, 244 pp.
One chapter focuses on the decision to intervene in Russia in 1918 and the factors that led the United States to accept the idea. The author suggests that Wilson participated in the expedition in an effort to limit what the Allies did in Russia as well as from opposition to the new Bolshevik regime. Primary and secondary sources.

609. Unterberger, Betty M. (1955). "President Wilson and the Decision to Send American Troops to Siberia." *Pacific Historical Review, 24,* 63-74.
A discussion of the reasons why Wilson, reluctantly, decided to allow American troops to intervene in the Civil War in Siberia. Among the factors was a desire to curb Japanese expansionism and maintain the open door policy in the Far East. Primary sources.

610. Unterberger, Betty M. (1956). *America's Siberian Expedition, 1918-1920: A Study of National Policy*. Durham, North Carolina: Duke University Press, 271 pp.
The Siberian experience is described from the American perspective. The author explains why we intervened in the first place, what were some of the problems that the SEF encountered, why the expedition returned, and what the consequences of the expedition were. Primary and secondary sources.

611. Westfall, Virginia C. (1968). "AEF Siberia -- The Forgotten Army." *Military Review, 48, No. 3,* 11-18.
A brief description of the AEF in Siberia centering around the recollections of General Robert Eichelberger, who was a captain in the expeditionary force.

612. White, John A. (1950). *The Siberian Intervention*. Princeton, New Jersey: Princeton University Press, 471 pp.
A general history of Siberia and the whole Allied intervention in Siberia in 1919-1920. White places the American role in a general context. Primary and secondary sources.

613. Williams, William A. (1963). "American Intervention in Russia, 1917-1920." *Studies on the Left, 3, No. 4,* 24-48 and *4, No. 1,* 39-57.
An attempt to understand the background of the policy makers involved in the decisions to invade Russia in 1917. The author feels the decision was based on the American opposition to the radical nature of the Revolution. Primary sources.

ECONOMIC ISSUES

614. Bernstein, Barton J. (1966). "The Automobile Industry and the Coming of the Second World War." *Southwestern Social Science Quarterly, 47,* 22-33.
In 1940 the automobile industry was called upon to help the defense buildup, but they were reluctant to participate. Fearful of being charged as merchants of death, they did not really cooperate until 1942. Primary sources.

615. Blackman, John L., Jr. (1967). *Presidential Seizure in Labor Disputes.* Cambridge, Massachusetts: Harvard University Press, 351 pp.

Blackman has produced a general study on this issue, though some cases from 1941 are included as examples. Primary sources.

616. Blum, Albert A. (1963). "Birth and Death of the M-Day Plan." In Harold Stein, (ed.), *American Civil-Military Decisions; A Book of Case Studies.* Birmingham, Alabama; University of Alabama Press, 61-96.

A description of the creation of the Industrial Mobilization Plan during the interwar period, the sources of the proposal, and the reasons for its demise. The author argues that it was FDR's need to keep control of the bureaucracy that caused the plan to be significantly modified in 1940. Primary sources.

617. Fairchild, Byron, and Grossman, Jonathan. (1959). *The Army and Industrial Manpower (United States Army in World War II: The War Department).* Washington, D.C.: Office of the Chief of Military History, Department of the Army, 291 pp. SD D114.7:W19/v.7.

The first chapter of this official history explains the industrial mobilization planning done by the War Department in the 1920s and 1930s. The focus is on the preparations the Army made for the utilization of labor. Primary sources.

618. Funigiello, Philip J. (1969). "Kilowatts for Defense: The New Deal and the Coming of the Second World War." *Journal of American History, 56,* 604-620.

In the late 1930s the War Department and the Federal Power Commission began to plan for possible power needs in a future war. The supporters of public and private power debated their roles and there was bureaucratic infighting in the government. As a result, nothing was really done until the US entered World War II. Primary sources.

619. Koistinen, Paul A. C. (1970). "The 'Industrial-Military Complex' in Historical Perspective: The InterWar Years." *Journal of American History, 55,* 819-839.

Interwar industrial planning was based on the model of World War I and was created with great assistance from industry. The Industrial Mobilization Plan developed, but later rejected by FDR, assumed war industries would be regulated by the military and the industries themselves. Despite this failure, the planning was not in vain because the War Department was attuned to the problems of industrial mobilization. Primary sources.

620. Koistinen, Paul A. C. (1980). *The Military-Industrial Complex: A Historical Perspective.* New York: Praeger, 168 pp.

A series of essays, most published previously, on this topic. The first contains an overview of the relations between the military and the industrial sector. There is also an essay on the interwar period. Primary sources.

621. Lotchin, Roger W. (1979). "The City and the Sword: San Francisco and the Rise of the Metropolitan-Military Complex, 1919-1941." *Journal of American History, 65,* 996-1020.

Spurred by its declining position vis-a-vis Los Angeles, San Francisco actively sought naval projects to be built there and Army units to be stationed in the city. The military cooperated and encouraged this effort. The result was a close relationship that was significant for both groups. Primary sources.

622. McGlade, Jacqueline. (1983). "The Zoning of Fort Crook: Urban Expansionism vs County Home Rule." *Nebraska History, 64*, 21-34.

The decision in 1940 to locate a bomber plant in the Omaha area led to competition among municipalities over which had authority to zone the area. It was a struggle between a rural county and Omaha, with the rural area winning. Primary sources.

623. Molander, Earl A. (1976). "Historical Antecedents of Military-Industrial Criticism." *Military Affairs, 40*, 59-63.

While beginning before World War I, criticism of the military accelerated after 1919. The "Merchants of Death" theory was not the beginning, but the continuation of attacks on the military. Mainly primary sources.

624. Renshaw, Patrick. (1986). "Organized Labour and the United States War Economy, 1939-1945." *Journal of Contemporary History, 21*, 3-22.

The expansion for the war helped boost the economy and in turn helped shape the ideas of the labor leaders toward the role that government should play in the economy. Rearmament helped establish the CIO and converted many individuals to Keynesianism. Primary sources.

625. Smith, Gibson B. (1972). "Rubber for Americans: The Search for an Adequate Supply of Rubber and the Politics of Strategic Materials, 1934-1942." Dissertation, Bryn Mawr College, 33/10-A, pp. 5662-63.

Several planners, including Herbert Feis, felt in the 1930s that we needed to stockpile certain raw materials, including rubber, against the threat of Japan. Despite general indifference, they were able to accomplish part of their aim, and this became vital in the first years of the war.

626. Smith, R. Elberton. (1959). *The Army and Economic Mobilization (United States Army in World War II: The War Department)*. Washington, D.C.: Office of the Chief of Military History, Department of the Army, 749 pp. SD D114.7:W19/v. 5.

Five chapters in this work deal with the interwar period and industrial mobilization planning. Among the topics covered are: procurement planning, the Industrial Mobilization Plan, and the interwar munitions programs. Primary sources.

627. Watson, Mark S. (1948). "First Vigorous Steps in Re-Arming, 1938-39." *Military Affairs, 12*, 65-78.

This article is taken from Watson's book on the Chief of Staff in World War II [#924]. Primary sources.

628. Yoshpe, Harry B. (1951). "Economic Mobilization Planning Between the Two World Wars." *Military Affairs, 15*, 199-204 and *Military Affairs, 16*, 71-83.

The Army planed for the mobilization of industry in a future war, but the resulting program proved to be flawed by a number of false assumptions. The plans provided only limited help in the succeeding war. No sources cited.

629. Yoshpe, Harry B. (1965). "Bernard M. Baruch: Civilian Godfather of the Military M-Day Plan." *Military Affairs, 29,* 1-15.

Based on his experiences in World War I, Baruch helped the Army to prepare industrial mobilization plans for a future conflict. He did this through lectures to the Army War College and assistance to the creators of the Industrial Mobilization Plan. Because of political reasons, the plan was eventually rejected. Primary sources.

EDUCATION

630. Ambrose, Stephen E. (1966). *Duty, Honor, Country: A History of West Point.* Baltimore, Maryland: Johns Hopkins Press, 357 pp.

This is a detailed history of the academy, centering around the role of key individuals. Two chapters describe MacArthur as superintendent and the implementation of the MacArthur reforms. Primary sources.

631. Ball, Harry P. (1983). *Of Responsible Command: A History of the U. S. Army War College.* Carlisle Barracks, Pennsylvania: Alumni Association of the U. S. Army War College, 534 pp.

Five chapters describe the interwar period in this detailed history. Among the topics covered: the impact of World War I on the course of study, the role of the college vis-a-vis the General Staff, the impact of General William Connor in shaping the curriculum, and the impact of the approaching war on the college. Primary sources.

632. Bauer, Theodore. (1983). *History of the Industrial College of the Armed Forces, 1924-1983.* Washington, D.C.: Alumni Association of the Industrial College of the Armed Forces, 137 pp.

Bauer explains the creation and role of the Army Industrial College. He also describes the course of study at the school and the Industrial Mobilization Plans they helped draw up. Secondary sources.

633. Davies, Richard G. (1984). "Of Arms and the Boy: A History of Culver Military Academy, 1894-1945." Dissertation, Indiana University, 45/5-A, p. 1313.

In the years after World War I this military school evolved, effected by the methods and techniques of the educational establishment. Emphasis was now placed on preparing adolescents for college with military training downplayed.

634. Dupuy, Richard E. (1951). *Men of West Point; The First 150 Years of the United States Military Academy.* New York: Sloane, 486 pp.

This narrative history of some of the Academy graduates has three brief chapters on this time period including information on educational reforms and on some key graduates, such as Malin Craig. Brief chapter notes.

635. Fleming, Thomas J. (1969). *West Point: The Men and Times of the United States Military Academy.* New York: William Morrow & Company, Inc., 402 pp.
An anecdotal account of the Academy, its graduates, and officers. In describing this period the author discusses MacArthur and his attempt to make changes in the curriculum and recounts some of the activities at the Academy. Secondary and primary sources.

636. Forman, Sidney. (1950). *West Point: A History of the United States Military Academy.* New York: Columbia University Press, 255 pp.
A short section of this general history delineates the reforms initiated by Douglas MacArthur in the 1920s and how the Military Academy evolved in the 1930s. Some primary, but mainly secondary sources.

637. Hirshauer, Victor B. (1975). "The History of the Army Reserve Officers' Training Corps 1916-1973." Dissertation, Johns Hopkins University, 39/6-A, p. 3774.
During the 1920s and 1930s the goal of the program, generally successful, was to produce Reserve officers for duty in emergencies. It is a quite unique partnership between colleges and the Army.

638. Kraus, John D. (1978). "The Civilian Military Colleges in the Twentieth Century: Factors Influencing Their Survival." Dissertation, University of Iowa, 39/8-A, pp. 4760-61.
An analysis of schools with a military environment but no direct connection with the federal government. They incorporated a military system into their educational structure for a variety of reasons. Three survive and remain healthy from the eleven the Army classified in 1903.

639. Lyons, Gene M., and Masland, John W. (1959). *Education and Military Leadership: A Study of the ROTC.* Princeton, New Jersey: Princeton University Press, 283 pp.
Twelve pages describe the development of ROTC from the National Defense Act of 1920 to World War II. Primary and secondary sources.

640. Nunn, Jack H. (1979). "MIT: A University's Contributions to National Defense." *Military Affairs, 43,* 120-25.
Several paragraphs in this article outline the different roles that MIT played in the interwar period. The contributions include the ROTC program and the research undertaken by its students and faculty.

641. Pappas, George S. (1967). *Prudens Futuri: The U. S. Army War College, 1901-1967.* Carlisle, Pennsylvania: The Alumni Association of the US Army War College, 338 pp.
During the interwar period, the curriculum was modified to better train high level commanders. Pappas has included information about the officers and areas of instruction for most classes in the 1920s, but has presented little information on the 1930s. Primary sources.

642. Phillips, Helen C. (1967). *United States Army Signal School, 1919-1967*. Fort Monmouth, New Jersey: U. S. Army Signal Center and School, 325 pp.

A detailed history, written from the perspective of the school's commander, with several chapters describing the interwar period. The purpose of the school was to standardize communication training within the Army and National Guard. The author has also presented the course of training. Primary sources; documents included in text.

643. Roop, David D. (1985). "Collegiate Cavalry: R.O.T.C. at the University of Arizona, 1921-1941." *Arizona and the West, 27*, 55-72.

The cavalry unit, part of the compulsory ROTC program, was an attractive educational program. One of the enticements for students was a chance to participate in a championship polo team. Primary sources.

644. Rulon, Philip R. (1979). "The Campus Cadets: A History of Collegiate Military Training, 1891-1951." *Chronicles of Oklahoma, 57*, 67-90.

An article on the development and impact of military training at Oklahoma State University. A brief section describes the period after World War I and the expansion of the ROTC program. Primary and secondary sources.

645. Vollmar, William J. (1976). "The Issue of Compulsory Military Training at The Ohio State University, 1913-1973." Dissertation, Ohio State University, 37/2-A, pp. 1182-83.

Though firmly established by 1920, ROTC soon came under attack. Students and pacifist groups tried to end the compulsory aspect of the program, but they had little chance of success. Little attention was paid to the concept of educating military officers at a civil school.

ENGINEERS

646. _____. (1985). *The Federal Engineer, Damsites to Missile Sites; A History of the Omaha District, U. S. Army Corps of Engineers*. Washington, D.C.: U. S. Corps of Engineers, Omaha District, 279 pp. SD D103.2:F31.

A detailed description of a number of the dams and reservoirs built to control flooding and improve navigation on the upper Missouri River. Primary and secondary sources.

647. _____. (1986). *The History of the US Army Corps of Engineers*. Washington, D.C.: Government Printing Office, 132 pp. SD D103.43:360-1-21.

This official volume is a brief history of the military and civil operations of the Corps of Engineers. No sources cited but a bibliography included.

648. Alperin, Lynn M. (1977). *Custodians of the Coast; History of the United States Army Engineers at Galveston*. Galveston, Texas: U. S. Army Corps of Engineers, 318 pp. SD D103.2:C96.

Alperin has written an account of the role of the Engineers in developing the Texas coastal region through harbor development projects at Galveston, Houston, and other sites, and the building of a section of the Intercoastal Waterway. Primary and secondary sources.

649. Branyan, Robert L. (1974). *Taming the Mighty Missouri; A History of the Kansas City District, Corps of Engineers, 1907-1971*. Kansas City, Missouri: U. S. Army Corps of Engineers, Kansas City District, 128 pp. SD D103.2:M69o/2.

A variety of activities of the Engineers including flood control and navigation improvements are recounted in this offical history. Mainly secondary sources with some interviews included.

650. Brown, D. Clayton. (1987). *The Southwestern Division: 50 Years of Service*. Washington, D.C.: U. S. Army Corps of Engineers, Southwestern Division, 196 pp. SD D103.2:So5/2.

A brief chapter describes the creation of the division in 1937 and its early flood control and navigation projects. Primary and secondary sources.

651. Buker, George E. (1981). *Sun, Sand and Water; A History of the Jacksonville District, U. S. Army Corps of Engineers, 1821-1975*. Jacksonville, Florida: U. S. Army Corps of Engineers, Jacksonville District, 288 pp. SD D103.2:Su7.

The projects covered in this work include: flood control, Intercoastal Waterway construction and maintenance, and harbor dredging and expansion. Primary and secondary sources.

652. Cass, Edward C. (1982). "Flood Control and the Corps of Engineers in the Missouri Valley, 1902-1973." *Nebraska History, 63*, 108-22.

After Congress gave them the authority to participate in civilian oriented flood control projects, the Engineers moved ahead. Fairly rapidly they surveyed the river system and then began to construct flood control projects. They proceeded with the activities despite the competition of the Bureau of Reclamation. Primary sources.

653. Chambers, John W., II. (1980). *The North Atlantic Engineers: A History of the North Atlantic Division and Its Predecessors in the U. S. Army Corps of Engineers, 1775-1975*. New York: U. S. Army Corps of Engineers, North Atlantic Division, 167 pp.

A brief history of the Corps of Engineers in the eastern part of the country. Chambers has described a variety of civil projects, such as dredging ship channels and harbor improvements, which occupied the attention of the Corps in this time period. Mainly printed secondary sources.

654. Clay, Floyd M., and Williams, Bobby Joe. (1986). *A Century on the Mississippi; A History of the Memphis District, U. S. Army Corps of Engineers, 1876-1981*. Washington, D.C.: U. S. Army Corps of Engineers, Memphis District, 357 pp. SD D103.2:M69/10.

A description of the efforts of the Engineers to control the flooding of the Mississippi and keep it navigable. Three chapters present the impact of the major flood in 1927, the subsequent plan to fix the river banks to prevent a deluge from occurring again, and its first major test during the flood of 1937. Primary sources.

655. Cotton, Gordon A. (1979). *A History of The Waterways Experiment Station, 1929-1979*. Vicksburg, Mississippi: U. S. Army Corps of Engineers, Waterways Experiment Station, 196 pp + appendices.

Established in the late 1920s, this organization was created to use modeling techniques in working out possibilities for controlling and channeling a variety of waterways, especially the Mississippi. During its first decade it labored on a variety of cut-off plans and helped prepare for the construction phase. Primary sources.

656. Cowdrey, Albert E. (1971). *The Delta Engineers; A History of the United States Army Corps of Engineers In the New Orleans District*. New Orleans, Louisiana: U.S. Army Corps of Engineers, New Orleans District, 91 pp.

Cowdrey has written a brief account of the Engineers and their attempts to control flooding and provide a navigable waterway. A section of the book describes the 1927 flood and the resulting improvements. Primary and secondary sources.

657. Cowdrey, Albert E. (1977). *Land's End; A History of the New Orleans District, U. S. Army Corps of Engineers, and Its Lifelong Battle with the Lower Mississippi and Other Rivers Wending Their Way to the Sea*. New Orleans, Louisiana: U. S. Army Corps of Engineers, New Orleans District, 118 pp. SD D103.2:L23.

An official history of this district. For this period the author has detailed the major efforts to control the flooding of the Mississippi by building levees and river diversion projects. Primary and secondary sources.

658. Cowdrey, Albert E. (1980). *A City For The Nation; The Army Engineers and the Building of Washington, D.C., 1790-1967*. Washington, D.C.: Historical Division, Office of Administrative Services, Office of the Chief of Engineers, 77 pp.

This pamphlet recounts the role of the Engineers in the construction of many of the important public buildings of this time period including the Pentagon. Primary and secondary sources.

659. Davis, Virgil. (1977). *A History of the Mobile District, United States Army Corps of Engineers, 1815 to 1971*. Mobile, Alabama: U. S. Corps of Engineers, South Atlantic Division, Mobile District, 109 pp. SD 103.2:M71/815-971.

Davis has written a description of the projects engaged in by the Corps of Engineers in this district. One chapter deals with the projects of the interwar period, especially the completion of the Intercoastal Waterway. Primary and secondary sources.

660. Dobney, Fredrick J. (1978). *River Engineers on the Middle Mississippi; A History of the St. Louis District, U. S. Army Corps of Engineers*. Washington, D.C.: U. S. Army Corps of Engineers, St. Louis District, 177 pp. SD D103.2:M69i.

A brief description of the efforts of the Engineers in the St. Louis area to control the Mississippi and make it usable for shipping. Secondary sources.

661. Drescher, Nuala M. (1982). *Engineers for the Public Good: A History of the Buffalo District, U. S. Army Corps of Engineers*. Buffalo, New York: U. S. Army Corps of Engineers, Buffalo District, 328 pp. SD D103.2:En3/4.

Different kinds of projects were engaged in by these Engineers including harbor facilities in Buffalo and Cleveland, lighthouses on the Great Lakes, and power houses on the Niagara River. Primary and secondary sources.

662. Fine, Lenore, and Remington, Jesse A. (1972). *The Corps of Engineers: Construction in the United States*. Washington, D.C.: Office of the Chief of Military History, United States Army, 747 pp.

Though primarily about World War II, this work includes a number of chapters on the interwar period, especially the defense buildup. There are descriptions of construction programs for airfields and new training camps. There is also an explanation of the problems of dealing with civilian contractors and controlling costs. Primary sources.

663. Granger, Mary L. (1968). *History of the Savannah District, 1829-1968*. Savannah, Georgia: U. S. Army Corps of Engineers, Savannah District, 114 pp.

A brief account of the programs supervised by the Engineers, including harbor improvements, the Intercoastal Waterway and river navigation in the Savannah area. No sources listed.

664. Green, Sherman. (1969). *History of the Seattle District, 1896-1968*. Seattle, Washington: U. S. Army Corps of Engineers, Seattle District, chapters individually numbered.

A poorly written history of the Engineers in Seattle, containing only a brief mention of their work during this period, such as river and harbor improvements. No sources cited.

665. Hagwood, Joseph J., Jr. (1976). *Commitment to Excellence; A History of the Sacramento District, U. S. Army Corps of Engineers, 1929-1973*. Washington, D.C.: U. S. Army Corps of Engineers, Sacramento District, 289 pp. SD D103.2:Sa1/2/929-73.

Four chapters of this offical history describe the early years of this district. Among the projects the Engineers undertook were river dredging, hydraulic mining debris removal, and flood control. Primary and secondary sources.

666. Hagwood, Joseph J., Jr. (1981). *Engineers at the Golden Gate; A History of the San Francisco District, U. S. Army Corps of Engineers, 1866-1980*. San Francisco, California: U. S. Army Corps of Engineers, San Francisco District, 452 pp. SD D103.2:G56/866-980.

An account of the activities of the Corps of Engineers in Northern California including building fortifications at the entrance to San Francisco Bay and construction of Treasure Island for the 1939 World's Fair. Primary and secondary sources.

667. Hartzer, Ronald B. (1984). *To Great and Useful Purpose; A History of the Wilmington District, U. S. Army Corps of Engineers*. Washington, D.C.: n.p., 172 pp. SD D103.2:W68.

The Engineers in this district in North Carolina constructed part of the Intercoastal Waterway, dredged harbors, tried to stop beach erosion, and dealt with flood damage. Primary and secondary sources.

668. Hoften, Ellen van. (1970). *History of the Honolulu Engineer District, 1905-1965*. Honolulu, Hawaii: U. S. Army Corps of Engineers, 133 pp.

Hoften has written brief chapters on the construction of harbors and harbor defenses in Hawaii and Midway and on the defense buildup in 1940-1941. Printed primary and secondary sources.

669. Johnson, Leland R. (1975). *The Falls City Engineers; A History of the Louisville District, Corps of Engineers, United States Army*. Washington, D.C.: U. S. Army Corps of Engineers, Louisville District, 347 pp. SD D103.2:F19.

The major project in this time period, as presented in Johnson's official history, involved trying to control the flooding of the Ohio River and its tributaries. The damage caused by the 1937 flood showed that much needed to be done and the Corps accelerated its activities. Primary and secondary sources.

670. Johnson, Leland R. (1977). *Men, Mountains, and Rivers; An Illustrated History of the Huntington District, U. S. Army Corps of Engineers, 1754-1974*. Washington, D.C.: U. S. Army Corps of Engineers, Huntington District, 322 pp. SD D103.2:H 92/754-974.

A description of the activities of the Corps of Engineers in part of the Ohio Valley, with projects in Ohio and West Virginia; their attempts to control flooding; and the continuation of the canalization of the Ohio River. Mainly secondary sources.

671. Johnson, Leland R. (1978). *Engineers on the Twin Rivers; A History of the Nashville District, Corps of Engineers, United States Army*. Washington, D.C.: U. S. Army Corps of Engineers, Nashville District, 329 pp. SD D103.2:T92.

A history of the Engineers and their work on the Tennessee and Cumberland Rivers, including flood control and navigation projects. Primary and secondary sources.

672. Kanarek, Harold. (1978). *The Mid-Atlantic Engineers: A History of the Baltimore District, U. S. Army Corps of Engineers, 1774-1974*. Baltimore, Maryland: U. S. Army Corps of Engineers, Baltimore District, 196 pp. SD D103.2:B21/774-974.

The major work of this group of Engineers in the first part of this century was river and harbor navigation. Secondary projects included harbor fortifications and, after 1936, flood control. Primary and secondary sources.

673. Klawonn, Marion J. (1977). *Cradle of the Corps; A History of the New York District, U. S. Army Corps of Engineers, 1775-1975*. New York: U. S. Army Corps of Engineers, New York District, 310 pp. SD D103.2:N42y/775-975.

The major projects undertaken by the Corps in this district during the interwar period involved the maintenance of New York harbor and the control of floods on the Hudson River. Primary sources used but not cited.

674. Larson, John W. (1980). *Those Army Engineers; A History of the Chicago District, U. S. Army Corps of Engineers*. Washington, D.C.: U. S. Army Corps of Engineers, Chicago District, 307 pp. SD D103.2:C43/4.

Among the activities undertaken by the Engineers in this area were the construction of the Illinois Waterway, development of harbors in Illinois and Wisconsin for recreational and commercial use, and flood control. Some primary and secondary sources cited.

675. Larson, John W. (1981). *Essayons; A History of the Detroit District, U. S. Army Corps of Engineers*. Detroit, Michigan: U. S. Army Corps of Engineers, Detroit District, 215 pp. SD D103.2:Es7.

As described by Larson, two of the major concerns of the Engineers in this district were the channels connecting the Great Lakes, such as Sault Saint Marie, and the harbors from Mackinac Island to Toledo. Primary sources.

676. Maass, Arthur. (1951). *Muddy Waters; The Army Engineers and the Nation's Rivers*. Cambridge, Massachusetts: Harvard University Press, 306 pp.

An attack upon the Corps of Engineers as an institution out of control of the President and Congress. Included as supporting evidence are examples from the flood and reclamation projects of the 1930s. Primary sources.

677. Merritt, Raymond H. (1980). *Creativity, Conflict and Controversy: A History of the St. Paul District, U. S. Army Corps of Engineers*. Washington, D.C.: U. S. Army Corps of Engineers, St. Paul District, 461 pp. SD D103.2:Sa2p.

Major projects undertaken by this group of Engineers included deepening part of the Upper Mississippi and controlling flooding in parts of Wisconsin, Minnesota and North Dakota. Primary sources.

678. Moore, Jamie W. (1981). *The Lowcountry Engineers; Military Missions and Economic Development in the Charleston District, U. S. Army Corps of Engineers*. Charleston, South Carolina: U. S. Army Corps of Engineers, Charleston District, 140 pp. SD D103.2:L95.

A brief history of the Engineers and their activities in this region including harbor improvements, coastal fortifications, and construction of part of the Intercoastal Waterway. Primary and secondary sources.

679. Morgan, Arthur E. (1971). *Dams and Other Disasters; A Century of the Army Corps of Engineers in Civil Works*. Boston: Porter Sargent, 422 pp.

An attack upon the Corps and its negative impact on the environment. Morgan cites the Corps' opposition to a hydraulic laboratory in the 1920s, conflicts over changing the course of the Mississippi, and resistance to reservoirs in flood control plans. Printed primary sources.

680. Parkman, Aubrey. (1978). *Army Engineers in New England; The Military and Civil Work of The Corps of Engineers in New England, 1775-1975*. Waltham, Massachusetts: U. S. Army Corps of Engineers, New England Division, 319 pp. SD D103.2:N42e/2/775-975.

A description of the variety of activities performed by the Engineers in New England including building flood control projects and constructing harbor defenses. Primary sources.

681. Quinn, Mary-Louise. (1977). *The History of the Beach Erosion Board, U. S. Army, Corps of Engineers, 1930-63*. Fort Belvoir, Virginia: Department of Defense, Department of the Army, Corps of Engineers, Coastal Engineering Research Center, 181 pp. SD D103.42/8:77-9.

One aspect of coastal engineering begun in the 1930s, was this engineering agency. This official history of the Board describes how the Corps began to deal with the problems of beach erosion, a task assigned to the Engineers by Congress in 1935. Mainly secondary sources.

682. Reuss, Martin. (1982). "The Army Corps of Engineers and Flood-Control Politics on the Lower Mississippi." *Louisiana History, 23*, 131-48.

Reuss describes how politics and nature shaped the decisions of the Corps of Engineers and Congress on a 1930s Louisiana flood control project. Primary sources.

683. Reynolds, Carroll F. (1950). "The Development of Military Floating Bridging by the United States Army." Dissertation, University of Pittsburgh. Doctoral Dissertations Accepted by American Universities, 1949-1950, p. 47.

One chapter examines the World War I experiences of the Engineers in military bridging and the impact that this had on interwar developments. As heavier equipment developed the Engineers strove to increase the weight carrying capacity while still keeping the equipment mobile. Much significant work was done before our entry into the war.

684. Richmond, Henry R., III. (1970). *The History of the Portland District, Corps of Engineers, 1871-1969*. Portland, Oregon: U.S. Army Corps of Engineers, Portland District, 273 pp.

A brief account of the various activities of this group of Engineers. Richmond has included material on the development of coastal harbors, expansion of river navigation on the Columbia, and the building of Bonneville Dam. No sources cited.

685. Scheufle, Roy W. (1969). *The History of the North Pacific Division, U. S. Army Corps of Engineers, 1888-1965*. Portland, Oregon: U. S. Army Corps of Engineers, North Pacific Division, 53 pp.

This official history contains a brief chapter on the 1930s, including material on projects on the Columbia River. Biographical sketches of Division Commanders are also included. Published primary and secondary sources.

686. Snyder, Frank E., and Guss, Brian H. (1974). *The District: A History of the Philadelphia District, U. S. Army Corps of Engineers, 1866-1971*. Philadelphia, Pennsylvania: U. S. Army Corps of Engineers, Philadelphia District, 263 pp. SD D104.2:P53.

A variety of projects undertaken by the Corps of Engineers in this area are described including the Intercoastal Waterway, harbor dredging, canal building, and river improvements. Numerous illustrations. Secondary sources.

687. Thompson, Erwin N. (1985). *Pacific Ocean Engineers; History of the U. S. Army Corps of Engineers in the Pacific, 1905-1980*. Washington, D.C.: U. S. Army Corps of Engineers, Pacific Ocean Division, 460 pp. SD D103.2:En3/7/905-80.

Included in this officially sponsored work are accounts of fortification construction in Hawaii, construction of airbases, and harbor improvement in Honolulu. Primary and secondary sources cited.

688. Turhollow, Anthony F. (1975). *A History of the Los Angeles District, U. S. Army Corps of Engineers, 1898-1965*. Los Angeles: U. S. Army Corps of Engineers, Los Angeles District, 440 pp. SD D103.2:L89A/898-965.

An account of the Los Angeles district, with the greatest attention paid to projects affecting water resources. The programs undertaken during the interwar period included harbor projects in San Diego and Los Angeles, and flood control throughout the region. Primary and secondary sources.

689. Tweet, Roald. (1984). *A History of The Rock Island District, U. S. Army Corps of Engineers, 1866-1983*. Washington, D.C.: U. S. Army Corps of Engineers, Rock Island District, 441 pp. SD D103.2:R59/4.
    One chapter of this work describes the post-World War I efforts to widen the upstream navigational channel on the Mississippi. Primary sources.

690. Ware, James. (1979). "Soldiers, Disasters, and Dams: The Army Corps of Engineers and Flood Control in the Red River Valley, 1939-1946." *Chronicles of Oklahoma, 57*, 26-33.
    A brief account of how the Engineers studied the conditions in the area, reported on this to Congress and then shaped the ensuing legislation. Ware also recounts the efforts of local groups to get a project and how they helped convince Congress. Primary sources.

691. Welsh, Michael. (1985). "The United States Army Corps of Engineers in the Middle Rio Grande Valley, 1935-1955." *New Mexico Historical Review, 60*, 295-316.
    One of the keys to growth in the Albuquerque area has been a supply of fresh water and freedom from floods. This has been provided by projects built by the Corps of Engineers. Their active role in the area began in the late 1930s. Primary sources.

692. Welsh, Michael E. (1985). *A Mission in the Desert; Albuquerque District, 1935-1985*. Washington, D.C.: U. S. Army Corps of Engineers, Albuquerque District, 262 pp. SD D103.2:M69/9/935-85.
    Two of the early flood control dams constructed by the Engineers in New Mexico are described, including the various problems encountered in their construction. Primary sources.

LOGISTICS

693. Aronsen, Lawrence R. (1982). "From World War to Limited War: Canadian-American Industrial Mobilization for Defence." *International Review of Military History, 52*, 208-245.
    This article examines events from the late 1930s to the early 1950s. In the early period the author shows how Canada and the US meshed their war production capabilities through planning and coordination. Primary sources.

694. Green, Constance M., Thomson, Harry C., and Roots, Peter C. (1955). *The Ordnance Department: Planning Munitions for War (United States Army in World War II: The Technical Services)*. Washington, D.C.: Office of the Chief of Military History, Department of the Army, 542 pp. SD D114.7:Or 2.
    Though concentrating heavily on the war period, there are several chapters of this official history on the pre-1941 era at the Ordnance Department. The organization of the department, the impact of Lend-Lease, and the training of personnel are among the topics covered. Primary sources.

695. Huston, James A. (1966). *The Sinews of War: Army Logistics, 1775-1953*. Washington, D.C.: Office of the Chief of Military History, United States Army, 789 pp. SD D114.2:W19.
    A brief section describes the impact of World War I on organization and planning for supply operations. Mainly secondary but some primary sources.

696. Leighton, Richard M., and Coakley, Robert W. (1955). *Global Logistics and Strategy, 1940-1943 (United States Army in World War II: The War Department)*. Washington, D.C.: Office of the Chief of Military History, Department of the Army, 780 pp. SD D114.7:W19/v. 4.

About 1/7th of this work describes the pre-war period and the issue of rearmament, preparedness and logistical support of the Allies. Primary documents.

697. Risch, Erna. (1962). *Quartermaster Support of the Army: A History of the Corps 1775-1939*. Washington, D.C.: Quartermaster Historian's Office, Office of the Quartermaster General, 796 pp. SD D106.8/3:Q2/775-939.

One chapter details the interwar period of the Corps. Among the topics covered are: transportation, industrial mobilization planning, and the impact of the Depression. Primary sources.

MANAGEMENT

698. Boylan, Bernard L. (1967). "Army Reorganization 1920: The Legislative Story." *Mid-America, 49*, 115-28.

Debate on the legislation dealt with such issues as the status of the National Guard, the size of the Army and the continuation of the draft. The result was legislation which shaped the post-war Army: a small professional force with little role in international affairs. Primary sources.

699. Franklin, Ben G. (1943). "The Military Policy of the United States, 1918-1933: A Study of the Influence of World War I on Army Organization and Control." Dissertation, University of California, Berkeley. Doctoral Dissertations Accepted by American Universities, 1942-1943, p. 78.

Three aspects of interwar policy are examined: the National Guard and its upgrade to the second line of defense; the general staff and its power, especially over supply and industrial mobilization; and the problem of manpower mobilization planning. The author explains how the lessons of World War I were applied.

700. Hammond, Paul Y. (1961). *Organizing for Defense: The American Military Establishment in the Twentieth Century*. Princeton, New Jersey: Princeton University Press, 403 pp.

An account of the development of the organizational structure of the armed forces. One chapter briefly examines the origins of the Staff system and the role of the Secretary of War and notes the impact that war had on the structure. Primary sources.

701. Haydon, Frederick S. (1952). "War Department Reorganization, August 1941-March 1942." *Military Affairs, 16*, 12-29, 97-114.

As war approached, there was a debate within the War Department as to how that organization should be structured. One plan envisioned a GHQ heading the combat arm, much as in World War I. Though the issues were discussed, no solution was arrived at until after the US entered the war. Primary sources.

702. Hewes, James E., Jr. (1975). *From Root to McNamara: Army Organization and Administration, 1900-1963*. Washington, D.C.: Center of Military History, United States Army, 452 pp. SD D114.17:Or3/900-63.

A brief part of this official history presents the reorganization that George Marshall put into effect after he became Chief of Staff in 1939. Secondary sources.

703. Nelson, Otto L. (1946). *National Security and the General Staff*. Washington, D.C.: Infantry Journal Press, 608 pp.

A detailed, and somewhat pedestrian, history of the General Staff. One chapter describes the interwar development of the Staff. Among the topics covered: the 1920 National Defense Act's provisions, and interwar planning. Numerous charts and documents are included in the text. Published primary sources.

MANPOWER

704. Blum, Albert A. (1967). *Drafted or Deferred: Practices Past and Present*. Ann Arbor, Michigan: University of Michigan, Graduate School of Business Administration, 275 pp.

The first chapter presents a history of the passage of the 1940 Selective Service Act, while the second describes the process whereby it was decided who should make the decisions on which individuals and groups should be drafted. Primary and secondary sources.

705. Blum, Albert A., and Smyth, J. Douglas. (1970). "Who Should Serve: Pre-World War II Planning for Selective Service." *Journal of Economic History, 30*, 379-404.

Planning by the Army involved discussions with the AFL and CIO, which often held views which clashed with those of the Army. Because of this the manpower plans were often unrealistic. Primary sources.

706. Clifford, John G. (1973). "Grenville Clark and the Origins of Selective Service." *Review of Politics, 35*, 17-40.

Clifford describes the links, in terms of philosophy and personnel, between the Plattsburg movement and the effort to enact Selective Service in 1940. He also presents the key role that Clark took in the effort. Primary sources.

707. Clifford, J. Garry, and Spencer, Samuel R., Jr. (1986). *The First Peacetime Draft*. Lawrence, Kansas: University Press of Kansas, 320 pp.

An account of the 1940 public debate over the adoption of the first peacetime conscription. Grenville Clark was the leader, pushing the concept in spite of little enthusiasm from President Roosevelt or the War Department. The discussion also reflected the divisions in America about how to react to the war in Europe and whether to aid Britain. Primary sources.

708. Conway, Theodore J. (1986). "The Great Demobilization: Personnel Demobilization of the American Expeditionary Force and the Emergency Army, 1918-1919: A Study in Civil-Military Relations." Dissertation, Duke University, 47/8-A, p. 3166.

With almost no preparation, the Army put into operation a generally successful demobilization program. Though repeating many of the mistakes from the past, the Army did study these old errors and this had an impact on future efforts.

709. Cooling, Benjamin F., III. (1968). "Enlisted Grade Structure and the Army Reorganization Act of 1920." *Military Affairs, 31*, 187-94.

The pay and structure of the enlisted ranks was greatly confused as a result of the great expansion of World War I. Attempts were made in 1919-1920 to bring order to the chaos. Complicating the decision was the rise of new technical specialists. The final solution recognized most of the changes. Primary sources.

710. Crossland, Richard B., and Currie, James T. (1984). *Twice the Citizen: A History of the United States Army Reserve, 1903-1983*. Washington, D.C.: Office of the Chief, Army Reserve, 325 pp. SD D101.22:140-14.

One chapter describes the creation of the Officers' Reserve Corps, the Citizens' Military Training Camps and other interwar measures to build up a reserve force. There is also information on the call-up of the reservists in 1940-1941. Primary and secondary sources.

711. Gillam, Richard. (1968). "The Peacetime Draft: Voluntarism to Coercion." *Yale Review, 57*, 495-517.

A discussion of the topic, especially in this century, with a small section on the debates in 1940-1941 concerning the draft. No sources cited.

712. Grant, Philip A., Jr. (1979). "The Kansas Congressional Delegation and the Selective Service Act of 1940." *Kansas History, 2*, 196-205.

An account of how Kansas Congressmen voted on this issue. The author suggests that party affiliation and the attitudes of the citizens of Kansas influenced the Congressmen's negative view on the proposal. Primary sources.

713. Griffith, Robert K., Jr. (1979). "Quality Not Quantity: The Volunteer Army During the Depression." *Military Affairs, 43*, 171-77.

This article is an examination of the impact of harsh economic conditions on the ability of the Army to recruit volunteers. The author also discusses the influence of the New Deal on the Army and its recruiting efforts. Primary sources.

714. Griffith, Robert K., Jr. (1980). "Conscription and the All-volunteer Army in Historical Perspective." *Parameters, 10, No. 3*, 61-69.

An account of this issue, with a major section devoted to volunteering in the 1920s and 1930s. Griffith describes the recruiting process and the type of men who enlisted. Primary and secondary sources.

715. Griffith, Robert K., Jr. (1982). *Men Wanted for the U. S. Army: America's Experience with an All-Volunteer Army Between the World Wars*. Westport, Connecticut: Greenwood Press, 259 pp.

A study of how the Army recruited in prosperity and depression, who they got, and what kind of a enlisted force they became. The process was shaped by general attitudes about the Army and Congressional parsimony. Parallels are drawn with the 1970s. Primary sources.

716. Hamilton, Maxwell. (1985). "Some Called Us 'Cannon Fodder'." *Retired Officer, 41, No. 7*, July 1985, 24-28.

A description of the Citizens' Military Training Camps operating in the 1920s, why people went, and what they learned there. The article includes information on the author's personal experiences. No sources cited.

717. House, Jonathan M. (1982). "John McAuley Palmer and the Reserve Components." *Parameters, 12, No. 3*, 11-18.

The debate over the role of the citizen soldier versus the professional soldier has been strongly influenced by Palmer. He helped to shape the 1920 National Defense Act with his views and influenced Marshall as well. Primary and secondary sources.

718. Kreidberg, Marvin A., and Henry, Merton G. (1955). *History of Military Mobilization in the United States Army, 1775-1945*. Washington, D.C.: Office of the Chief of Military History, Department of the Army, 721 pp.

Several chapters discuss important developments in the interwar period including the mobilization plans, the roles envisioned for the National Guard, and industrial mobilization. There is also a chapter on how these plans were put into effect in 1940-1941. Published primary and secondary sources.

719. Mitchell, John B. (1967). "Army Recruiters and Recruits Between the World Wars." *Military Collector & Historian, 19*, 76-81.

A description of recruiting methods and the recruits in this time period. Mitchell suggests those aspects of the Army which seemed to attract individuals to join the service. Primary sources.

720. Mooney, Chase C., and Layman, Martha E. (1952). "Some Phases of the Compulsory Military Training Movement, 1914-1920." *Mississippi Valley Historical Review, 38*, 633-56.

The debate over the shape of the post-war military involved this issue. The final result, in the National Defense Act, was not what the proponents had hoped for. Primary sources.

721. Napoli, Donald S. (1978). "The Mobilization of American Psychologists, 1938-1941." *Military Affairs, 42*, 32-36.

In the late 1930s a number of psychologists, for a variety of reasons, offered their services to the Army. The service put them to use developing procedures for classifying recruits and handling other personnel problems. When the war began, the psychologists continued in a role they had already established. Primary and secondary sources.

722. O'Sullivan, John. (1982). *From Voluntarism to Conscription; Congress and Selective Service, 1940-1945.* New York: Garland Publishing, Inc., 284 pp.

About half of this published version of the dissertation deals with the debate in the country and in Congress over the question of selective service. It also describes how the country came to accept the concept that individuals had to serve in the military. Primary sources.

723. Porter, David L. (1979). *The Seventh-sixth Congress and World War II, 1939-1940.* Columbia, Missouri: University of Missouri Press, 236 pp.

Porter presents the changing ideas of the Congress regarding affairs in Europe and preparedness and provides the background for the passage of the Selective Service Act of 1940. The author tries to explain which groups supported the different positions and why. Primary sources.

724. Sibley, Mulford Q., and Jacob, Philip E. (1952). *Conscription and Conscience; The American State and the Conscientious Objector, 1940-1947.* Ithaca, New York: Cornell University Press, 580 pp.

The authors describe the development of the Selective Service legislation in 1940 and its application to COs in 1940 and 1941. They also discuss which groups fell into this category. Primary and secondary sources.

725. Sperry, James R. (1969). "Organized Labor and Its Fight Against Military and Industrial Conscription, 1917-1945." Dissertation, University of Arizona, 30/2-A, p. 668.

Labor saw conscription as a tool that would be used against the unions, based on their experience in World War I, and opposed the concept. Their fear was heightened by the industrial mobilization plans of the 1930s, which they also saw as anti-union. The 1940 debates found the labor movement divided, but support for conscription grew as war approached.

726. Ward, Robert D. (1974). "Against the Tide: The Preparedness Movement of 1923-1924." *Military Affairs, 38,* 59-61.

In the mid-1920s the War Department tried to win public support for its view on Army expansion, but the effort was a failure. The peace organizations of the period and the executive and legislative branches reacted negatively to the effort. The military could not convince anyone that an enemy was in sight.

MISCELLANEOUS

727. _____ . (1976). *The Army Lawyer: A History of the Judge Advocate General's Corps, 1775-1975.* Washington, D.C.: U. S. Army, Judge Advocate General's Corps, 278 pp.

One chapter describes the Ansell-Crowder dispute, 1920 revision of the Articles of War, and the work of the Corps in the interwar period. Printed primary and secondary sources.

728. Alexander, Thomas G. (1965). "Ogden's 'Arsenal of Democracy,' 1920-1955." *Utah Historical Quarterly, 33,* 237-47.

A brief history of the Ogden Arsenal, including its development in 1920 and expansion in the late 1930s. Primary sources.

729. Arrington, Leonard J., and Alexander, Thomas G. (1965). "The U. S. Army Overlooks Salt Lake Valley: Fort Douglas, 1862-1965." *Utah Historical Quarterly, 33*, 326-50.

A general history of the post with brief references to the period after World War I, especially the use of the post as a Citizens' Military Training Camp and as site for a CCC camp. Primary sources.

730. Anders, Leslie. (1976). "The Watershed: Forrest Harding's *Infantry Journal*, 1934-1938." *Military Affairs, 40*, 12-16.

Under the editorship of Forrest Harding this publication pointed the direction that the Army was to take--mechanization and modernized warfare. Though it stirred up great controversy, it was a forum for new ideas. Primary sources.

731. Bacon, Edwin L., and Todd, Frederick P. "Memories of the Dress of the Seventh New York: 1925-1940." *Military Collector & Historian, 26*, 200-10.

A description of the fatigue and dress uniforms of this National Guard unit. Illustrations.

732. Bayne-Jones, Stanhope. (1968). *The Evolution of Preventive Medicine in the United States Army, 1607-1939.* Washington, D.C.: Office of the Surgeon General, Department of the Army, 255 pp. SD D104.2:P92.

One chapter describes the interwar period, including developments in education and drug research. In addition organizational changes and the significance of preventive medicine is examined. Secondary sources.

733. Bidwell, Bruce W. (1986). *History of the Military Intelligence Division, Department of the Army General Staff: 1775-1941.* Frederick, Maryland: University Publications of America, 625 pp.

A detailed history of one section of the General Staff. A large part of this work deals with the interwar period. The Division was hurt by budgetary cutbacks and did not begin to grow until 1940. The section engaged in domestic intelligence gathering, developed aerial surveillance techniques, and expanded its code breaking abilities. Primary sources.

734. Bower, Stephen E. (1984). *A History of Fort Benjamin Harrison, 1903-1982.* Washington, D.C.: Command History Office, US Army Soldier Support Center, Fort Benjamin Harrison, Indiana, 179 pp. SD D101.2:f77 b/2.

A brief chapter on the interwar years including the Citizens' Military Training Camps and the CCC at the post. Primary sources.

735. Brown, Terry W. (1967). "The Crowder-Ansell Dispute: The Emergence of General Samuel T. Ansell." *Military Law Review, 35*, 1-45.

Affected by some proceedings he felt were unfair, General Ansell advocated a series of changes in the rules governing military justice. After a heated controversy with General Crowder, his superior, Ansell saw some of his recommendations accepted in the 1920 revision of the Articles of War. Even more of his ideas came to be implemented in the Uniform Code of Military Justice, adopted in the 1950s. Primary sources.

736. Bruun, Michael C. (1979). "U. S. Army Service Dress Rank Chevrons -- 1905 to 1926." *Military Collector & Historian, 31*, 65-73.

A description and detailed list of the insignia worn on dress coats to indicate branch and rank. Primary sources.

737. Cavanaugh, Philip M., and Kloster, Donald E. (1985). "The Forgotten U. S. Army 1936 Officer's Dress Blue Uniform." *Military Collector & Historian, 37*, 165-67.

Though the Army abolished a dress uniform requirement after World War I, there was a demand that it be reinstated. In 1936 they prescribed one, but two months later replaced it with a new dress uniform. Primary sources.

738. Collins, John M. (1972). "Depression Army." *Army, 22, No. 1*, 8-14.

A description of the Army at the end of the Depression era from the position of the enlisted man. The article includes information on pay, training, and equipment. No sources cited.

739. Cooling, B. Franklin. (1971). "U. S. Army Support of Civil Defense: The Formative Years." *Military Affairs, 35*, 7-11.

Because of improvements in airplanes, by the 1930s the Army began to advocate preparations for defense. Even further planning efforts were made in 1940 and 1941. However the Army tried to avoid direct responsibility for implementing those plans. A general overview of the issue. Printed primary and secondary sources.

740. Eastwood, Harland, Sr. (1983). *Fort Whitman on Puget Sound 1911-1945*. Lopez, Washington: Twin Anchors Co., 85 pp.

Brief typewritten manuscript on this coastal defense post in the Puget Sound area. During much of this period it was garrisoned by two individuals. Primary sources.

741. Foster, Gaines M. (1983). *The Demands of Humanity: Army Medical Disaster Relief*. Washington, D.C.: Center of Military History, United States Army, 188 pp. SD D114.17:H88.

A brief history of the relief activities of the Army Medical Department. The book includes some pages on the efforts to deal with several disease epidemics overseas and floods in the United States. Primary and secondary sources.

742. Generous, William T., Jr. (1973). *Swords and Scales: The Development of the Uniform Code of Military Justice*. Port Washington, New York: Kennikat Press, 250 pp.

While most of this work explains the evolution of the military law code after 1940, the first chapter presents information on Samuel Ansell and his role in the development of the 1920 Articles of War. Though the reform was not as great as Ansell had hoped for, it remained the policy until World War II. Primary sources.

743. Gushwa, Robert L. (1977). *The Best and Worst of Times: The United States Army Chaplaincy, 1920-1945*. Washington, D.C.: Office of the Chief of Chaplains, Department of the Army, 227 pp. SD D101.2:C36/5/v.4.

About one third of this volume deals with chaplains in the 1920s and 1930s. In the first decade there was an effort made to upgrade the professional background of the chaplains. In the second the chaplains had to deal with the problems of the Depression and also minister to the CCC adjuncts of the Army. Secondary and primary sources.

744. Honeywell, Roy J. (1958). *Chaplains of the United States Army.* Washington, D.C.: Office of the Chief of Chaplains, Department of the Army, 376 pp. SD 101.2:C36/3.

General history of the Chaplains. One chapter is devoted to the interwar period. Legislative changes are noted, especially the impact of the National Defense Act of 1920. Also discussed are organizational changes, the impact of the pacifist movement, and the duties performed by the chaplains. Primary and secondary sources.

745. Kegel, James. (1981). "Lest We Forget: A Tribute to the Unknown Soldier." *American History Illustrated, 16, No. 7,* 16-22.

An account of the ceremonies surrounding the choosing and burying of the Unknown Soldier in 1921. No sources cited.

746. Kumamoto, Bob. (1979). "The Search for Spies: American Counterintelligence and the Japanese American Community, 1931-1942." *Amerasia Journal, 6, No. 2,* 45-76.

In the 1920s American military and civilian intelligence agencies began to fear Japanese expansionism and possible Nisei cooperation and began surveillance of the group. In the late 1930s they compiled lists of those whom they felt were security risks. These 2000 were arrested even before the round-up of the whole Japanese-American community. Primary sources.

747. Lax, John, and Pencak, William. (1982). "Creating the American Legion." *South Atlantic Quarterly, 81,* 43-55.

The authors describe the origins of the Legion, citing the Red Scare and the desire of the soldiers to keep alive the spirit of the AEF in the face of the country's seeming inattention to their needs. Primary sources.

748. Lewis, George G., and Mewha, John. (1955). *History of Prisoner of War Utilization by the United States Army, 1776-1945.* Washington, D.C.: Department of the Army, 278 pp. SD D101.22:20-213.

One chapter covers the development of laws involving prisoners, such as the 1929 Geneva Convention and discussion of plans in the immediate pre-war period. Primary sources.

749. Lindley, John M. (1974). "'A Soldier is Also a Citizen': The Controversy over Military Justice in the U. S. Army, 1917-1920." Dissertation, Duke University, 35/8-A, p. 5308.

A study of the conflict over military justice within the Army and with Congress. In 1917 Brigadier General Samuel Ansell questioned the legality of several court-martial proceedings. He argued that soldiers should receive the same protection as civilians. While the Army rejected his suggestions, Congress considered them when revising the Articles of War in 1919 and 1920.

750. Mahon, John K., and Danysh, Romana. (1972). *Army Lineage Series: Infantry, Part I: Regular Army.* Washington, D.C.: Office of the Chief of Military History, United States Army, 938 pp. SD D114.11:In3/pt.1.

Though mainly an account of the lineage of Army infantry units, there is an introductory section which traces the history of the organization of this branch. Ten pages of that section describe the interwar period.

751. Margulies, Herbert F. (1979). "The Articles of War, 1920: The History of a Forgotten Reform." *Military Affairs, 43*, 85-89.

The Articles of War were revised after World War I and in the process the code of military justice and court-martial procedure was liberalized. Involved in this process were conflicts within the War Department and between conservative and progressive elements in Congress. Primary and secondary sources.

752. McCormick, David C. (1970). "A History of the United States Army Band to 1946." Dissertation, Northwestern University, 31/7-A, p. 3585.

The organization was established in 1922 by General Pershing to be the principal musical contingent of the Army. This work describes the personnel, their activities, and relations with civilian musical activities, especially during the Depression.

753. McKenney, Janice E. (1985). *Army Lineage Series: Air Defense Artillery.* Washington, D.C.: Center of Military History, United States Army, 429 pp. SD D114.11:Ar7.

An account of the lineage of these units, many of which began as artillery or coast artillery in the Nineteenth Century. A bibliography is included with some unit lineages.

754. Minott, Rodney G. (1962). *Peerless Patriots; Organized Veterans and the Spirit of Americanism.* Washington, D.C.: Public Affairs Press, 152 pp.

A study of the creation of veterans' organizations and their ideas about society, especially what America should and should not be. Primary sources.

755. Morris, Cheryl H. (1973). "Alice M. Robertson: Friend or Foe of the American Soldier?" *Journal of the West, 12*, 307-16.

This Oklahoma Congresswoman was elected on a platform of helping soldiers, but she opposed the bonus bill in 1922. As a result she lost her bid for re-election. Primary sources.

756. Rader, Frank J. (1973). "Harry L. Hopkins: The Works Progress Administration and National Defense, 1935-1940." Dissertation, University of Delaware, 34/10-A, pp. 6573-74.

Hopkins used his position to help the defense establishment build a variety of projects, such as buildings on military posts and highways. In the territories the military took direct control of the projects. Later Hopkins would bring his pro-military outlook to the office of Secretary of Commerce.

757. Rader, Frank J. (1976). "Work Relief and National Defense: Some Notes on WPA in Alaska." *Alaska Journal, 6*, 54-59.

In the territories, the WPA was more than likely to combine national defense and work relief. This included highway and road construction and airport building. Primary sources.

758. Rader, Frank J. (1979). "The Works Progress Administration and Hawaiian Preparedness, 1935-1940." *Military Affairs, 43*, 12-17.

In secret Roosevelt placed the Hawaiian WPA under the control of the War Department, who used it to help build military fortifications in the Hawaiian Islands. The author explains why the process was done secretly and how it related to the increasing role of the military in Hawaiian governance. Mainly primary sources.

759. Reid, Bill G. (1967). "Agrarian Opposition to Franklin K. Lane's Proposal for Soldier Settlement, 1918-1921." *Agricultural History, 41,* 167-79.
     A proposal to settle World War I veterans on unused federal agricultural lands aroused tremendous opposition from farm groups, who feared the new competition. As a result the plan failed. Primary sources.

760. Roberts, Bobby L. (1978). "The Relationship Between War and Society as Reflected in the Writings of Five Military Historians, 1919-1945." Dissertation, University of Arkansas, 39/6-A, p. 3740.
     The experiences of World War I affected the writing of several significant military historians in the next decades. Among the Americans discussed in this dissertation are Hoffman Nickerson, Alfred Vagts and Quincy Wright. They expanded the meaning of military history and examined the impact of war on different institutions in society.

761. Sawicki, James A. (1981). *Infantry Regiments of the US Army.* Dumfries, Virginia: Wyvern Publications, Inc., 682 pp.
     A general history of the branch along with coats of arms, regimental lineages and divisional structure in World War I and II. No sources cited.

762. Sawicki, James A. (1985). *Cavalry Regiments of the US Army.* Dumfries, Virginia: Wyvern Publications, Inc., 415 pp.
     General history of the branch, both mounted and mechanized, along with coats of arms and regimental lineages. No sources cited.

763. Scipio, L. Albert. (1986). *The 24th Infantry at Fort Benning.* Silver Springs, Maryland: Roman Publications, 373 pp.
     A history of Fort Benning and the regiment which served there during most of the interwar period. Profusely illustrated. Covers activities, athletics, family life, and social activities in this black unit. Primary sources.

764. Sherman, Edward F. (1970). "The Civilianization of Military Law." *Maine Law Review, 22,* 3-103.
     A major study of this facet of military life. The author explains the nature of the revisions proposed by Ansell, why they were opposed and the gutted reforms embodied in the National Defense Act of 1920. Reform continued after World War II. Primary and secondary sources.

765. Silverman, Albert J. (1980). "Kidnapping the Kaiser." *American History Illustrated, 14, No. 9,* 36-43.
     Eight Americans decided in late 1918 to try to kidnap Kaiser Wilhelm II and take him to the Paris Peace Conference. Though the plan failed, it got the attention of many people. No sources cited.

766. Slackman, Michael. (1984). "The Orange Race: George S. Patton, Jr.'s Japanese-American Hostage Plan." *Biography, 7,* 1-49.
     While in Hawaii in the 1930s, Patton devised a plan to stop any possible problems with the local Japanese by arresting their leaders on the occasion of an outbreak of war. The proposal reflects the accepted attitudes of whites in Hawaii at the time. Primary sources, including a copy of the original document.

767. Smith, Cornelius C., Jr. (1981). *Fort Huachuca: The Story of a Frontier Post*. Washington, D.C.: n.p., 417 pp. SD D101.2:F77hu.

This book contains several chapters on the interwar period including the information on the stationing of black soldiers and the Indian scouts. Primary sources.

768. Smythe, Donald. (1981). "Honoring the Nation's Dead: General Pershing's American Battle Monuments Commission." *American History Illustrated, 16, No. 2*, 26-33.

Pershing took the leadership of a program to commemorate the World War I dead by the building of suitable monuments in France. The project was completed in the 1930s. No sources cited.

769. Soderbergh, Peter A. (1966). "*Aux Armes*!: The Rise of the Hollywood War Film, 1916-1930." *South Atlantic Quarterly, 65*, 509-22.

In this early period the different attitudes of Hollywood toward war, both pro and con, were developed. Especially in the 1920s, one could see the stereotypical soldiers and battle scenes already evolving. No sources cited.

770. Stubbs, Mary L., and Connor, Stanley R. (1969). *Army Lineage Series: Armor-Cavalry, Part I: Regular Army and Army Reserve*. Washington, D.C.: Office of the Chief of Military History, United States Army, 477 pp. SD D114.11:Ar5/pt.1.

The lineage book begins with a history of the organization of Armor and Cavalry, with nine pages devoted to both during the interwar period. The unit lineages also include bibliographies.

771. Stubbs, Mary L., and Connor, Stanley R. (1972). *Army Lineage Series: Armor-Cavalry, Part II: Army National Guard*. Washington, D.C.: Office of the Chief of Military History, United States Army, 297 pp. SD D114.11:Ar5/pt. 2.

There is a brief history of the Cavalry including about ten pages that cover this period, with material on both tanks and cavalry. In addition the unit lineages contain individual bibliographies.

772. Wade, Gary H. (1986). "World War II Division Commanders." *Military Review, 63, No. 3*, 61-67.

An examination of the pre-war careers of a number of generals who had combat commands in World War II. Among the factors examined are age, duty assignments, military education, and efficiency reports. No sources cited.

773. Weiner, Frederick W. (1970). "How Many Stars for Pershing?" *Army, 20, No. 12*, 28-34 and *Army, 21, No. 1*, 42-48

An analysis of evidence, including statues, that indicates that John Pershing never had a higher rank than general and never wore more than four stars. Printed primary and secondary sources.

774. Wesbrook, Stephen D. (1980). "The Railey Report and Army Morale, 1941: Anatomy of a Crisis." *Military Review, 60, No. 6*, 11-24.

In late 1941 the Army experienced a morale crisis, as many soldiers wanted to return home. A reporter investigated the situation and found bad conditions. The problem was that the soldiers had no clear understanding of the world situation or why they should remain in the service. Nothing was done. Primary sources.

NATIONAL GUARD

775. Alexander, Thomas G., and Arrington, Leonard J. (1965). "Utah's First Line of Defense: The Utah National Guard and Camp W. G. Williams, 1926-1965." *Utah Historical Quarterly, 33*, 141-56.
   The development of the Utah National Guard and their summer training camp, with a brief section on the interwar years. Primary sources.

776. Barry, Herbert. (1939). *Squadron A: A History of Its First Fifty Years, 1889-1939*. New York: Association of Ex-members of Squadron A, Inc., 390 pp.
   A brief section of this book deals with the activities of this part of the New York National Guard in the 1920s and 1930s. No sources cited.

777. Black, Lowell D. (1976). "The Negro Volunteer Militia Units of the Ohio National Guard, 1870-1954: The Struggle for Military Recognition and Equality in the State of Ohio." Dissertation, Ohio State University, 37/5-A, p. 3122.
   This dissertation describes the service performed by blacks in the Ohio Guard and by their efforts to establish a firm footing in the organizational structure. The author also examines the position in society of the black officers and how this influenced their role in the Guard.

778. Colby, Elbridge. (1977). *National Guard of the United States: A Half Century of Progress*. Manhattan, Kansas: Military Affairs/Aerospace Historian, chapters individually paged.
   A typescript publication with two chapters on the period after World War I, including material on the 1920 National Defense Act. Primary and secondary sources including National Guard reports.

779. Cooper, Jerry, and Smith, Glen. (1986). *Citizens as Soldiers: A History of the North Dakota National Guard*. Fargo, North Dakota: North Dakota Institute for Regional Studies, 447 pp.
   An excellent history of a state guard. The authors describe the various activities and the development during the depression. Primary and secondary sources.

780. Cropp, Richard. (1962). *"The Coyotes": A History of the South Dakota National Guard*. Mitchell, South Dakota: South Dakota Board of Military Affairs and the National Guard Officers Association, 220 pp.
   General history of the Guard with one chapter on this period, which includes descriptions of the training camps and organizational structure. No footnotes; chapter bibliography with some primary sources noted.

781. Daugherty, Robert L. (1974). "Citizen Soldiers in Peace: The Ohio National Guard, 1919-1940." Dissertation, Ohio State University, 35/2-A, p. 1000.
   According to the author, in this time period, the Ohio National Guard was successful in maintaining itself, despite public opposition to "all things military." In Ohio the Guard received a constant level of support and was viewed as a useful emergency force.

782. Daugherty, Robert L. (1976). "Problems in Peacekeeping: The 1924 Niles Riot." *Ohio History, 85*, 280-92.

As a result of a planned meeting of the KKK and the public reaction against it, the Ohio National Guard had to be sent in to restore order. Primary and secondary sources.

783. Derthick, Martha. (1965). *The National Guard in Politics*. Cambridge, Massachusetts: Harvard University Press, 202 pp.

Part of one chapter describes the Guard's defense of its power in the interwar era, including its use of the National Guard Bureau within the War Department itself. Primary sources.

784. Fowles, Brian D. (1982). "A History of the Kansas National Guard, 1854-1975." Dissertation, Kansas State University, 43/12-A, p. 4011.

The deficiencies of the Kansas Guard began to be remedied in the 1920s. More federal money and the agricultural depression of the 1920s encouraged increased attendance at drill and summer camp. This proces of rejuvenation was accelerated during the Depression.

785. Hill, Jim D. (1964). *The Minute Man in Peace and War: A History of the National Guard*. Harrisburg, Pennsylvania: Stackpole Co., 585 pp.

A history of the Guard and its defense against attacks from the Army. Several chapters describe the National Defense Act of 1920 [seen as a major victory], the impact of the Depression, and the interwar era joint maneuvers. Bibliographic notes at the end of chapters; mainly secondary sources.

786. Hudson, James J. (1952). "The California National Guard, 1903-1940." Dissertation, University of California, Berkeley. Doctoral Dissertations Accepted by American Universities, 1953, pp. 228.

Among the topics covered in this dissertation are: the reorganization of the Guard following the 1920 National Defense Act; the role of the Guard in helping civilians after natural calamities, such as the 1933 Long Beach earthquake; and the service of the Guard in civil disorders, such as the 1934 strike in San Francisco.

787. Hudson, James J. (1982). "The Role of the California National Guard During the San Francisco General Strike of 1934." *Military Affairs, 46*, 76-83.

A strike by longshoremen in 1934 soon led to violence and the Governor sent in the National Guard to restore order. They did this very effectively, and despite a general strike, conditions remained quiet. The author cites this episode as an effective use of the National Guard in dealing with civil disorder. Primary sources.

788. Johnson, Charles, Jr. (1976). "Black Soldiers in the National Guard, 1877-1949." Dissertation, Howard University, 37/7-A, p. 4531.

Focusing on the organizations which made up the 93rd Division, the author examines the attitudes towards blacks in the National Guard and the problems this created for those trying to serve their state. Black officers also faced hurdles, especially when the units were nationalized.

789. Krenek, Harry L. (1979). "A History of the Texas National Guard Between World War I and World War II." Dissertation, Texas Tech University, 40/8-A, p. 4717.
   The author contends that in this time period the Texas National Guard played "an active and important" role. While training went on, the Guard most frequently assisted communities in dealing with national disasters. The Texas Guard also was involved in large scale police duty, such as in labor disturbances and race riots.

790. Lens, Sidney. (1973). *The Labor Wars: From the Molly Maguires to the Sitdowns*. Garden City, New York: Doubleday, 366 pp.
   Included in the narrative are some incidents involving National Guardsmen, such as the San Francisco strike of 1934. Secondary sources.

791. Mahon, John K. (1983). *History of the Militia and the National Guard*. New York: Macmillan, 374 pp.
   A scholarly account of the growth of the National Guard. One chapter describes the interwar period, including the impact of the 1920 National Defense Act, the role of the Guard in labor disputes, and the changes brought by the 1940 mobilization. Primary and secondary sources.

792. Milner, Elmer R. (1979). "An Agonizing Evolution: A History of the Texas National Guard, 1900-1945." Dissertation, North Texas State University, 40/3-A, pp. 1651-52.
   A relatively brief history of the Texas National Guard. After World War I the organization grew in "quality and quantity." The Depression accentuated the growth, as pay attracted many recruits to training camp. When war approached, the author believes the Guard was "reasonably" prepared.

793. Newland, Samuel J. (1986). "Twenty Years at Haskell: Indian Units in the Kansas National Guard." *Military Collector & Historian, 38*, 114-117.
   Students at Haskell Institute, an Native American educational institution, were a component of the Kansas Guard. There was both a machine gun and a cavalry unit and they received much public attention. Primary sources.

794. O'Brien, Larry D. (1975). "The Ohio National Guard in the Coal Strike of 1932." *Ohio History, 84*, 127-44.
   The Ohio Guard acted as a neutral force in the labor dispute, trying, fairly successfully, to prevent violence between the owners and the strikers. Primary sources.

795. Roberts, Richard C. (1973). "History of the Utah National Guard, 1894-1954." Dissertation, University of Utah, 34/4-A, p. 1838.
   Roberts presents his dissertation as a case study of National Guard development. The Utah Guard played a variety of roles: source of soldiers for combat, preserver of order, and strike breaker. As more federal funds were provided, it came under greater federal control.

796. Weiner, Frederick B. (1940). "The Militia Clause of the Constitution." *Harvard Law Review, 54*, 181-220.
   A review of the legislation and court decisions involving the relations between the national government and the National Guard. The article includes material on the impact of the National Defense Act of 1920. Primary sources.

OVERSEAS

797. Bacevich, Andrew J. (1983). "American Military Diplomacy, 1898-1949: The Role of Frank Ross McCoy." Dissertation, Princeton University, 43/7-A, p. 2423.

The author contends that American officers have had a role in the formulation and conduct of diplomacy and uses McCoy as a case study. He received assignments overseas from all of the presidents in this time period.

798. Bletz, Donald F. (1972). *The Role of the Military Professional in U. S. Foreign Policy.* New York: Praeger, 320 pp.

Only a brief section of this work provides an historical background, with only a few pages on the interwar period. Secondary sources.

799. Cornebise, Alfred E. (1981). *The AMAROC News, The Daily Newspaper of the American Forces in Germany, 1919-1923.* Carbondale, Illinois: Southern Illinois University Press, 248 pp.

Based partially on the newspaper, this is an account of the experiences of the American troops in Germany. Among the topics explored are the impact of the war upon the Americans and Germans, what the American occupiers did in their leisure time, and how they managed life overseas. Many quotations from the paper.

800. Cornebise, Alfred E. (1982). *Typhus and Doughboys: The American Polish Typhus Relief Expedition, 1919-1921.* Newark, Delaware: University of Delaware Press, 188 pp.

In the aftermath of World War I, a major epidemic of typhus broke out in Poland. The brunt of the Allied relief effort was born by a unit of American military officers and enlisted men headed by Harry Gilchrist. They helped deal with the epidemic as well as other problems. Primary sources.

801. Cornebise, Alfred E. (1982). "Der Rhein Entlang: The American Occupation Forces in Germany, 1918-1923, A Photo Essay." *Military Affairs, 46,* 183-89.

A brief survey of the American occupation forces in Germany after World War I, their mission, how it was accomplished, and the impact of the occupation on the soldiers. Good selection of pictures.

802. Cruz, Romeo V. (1974). *America's Colonial Desk and the Philippines, 1898-1934.* Quezon City, Philippines: University of the Philippines Press, 247 pp.

This is an account of the Bureau of Insular Affairs and its relationship with the Philippines. It was the chief agency of the US government to deal with the Islands. The author argues that the Bureau protected the interests of the US while claiming that it was trying to help the Philippines. Primary sources.

803. Dziuban, Stanley W. (1959). *Military Relations Between the United States and Canada: 1939-1945 (United States Army in World War II: Special Studies).* Washington, D.C.: Office of the Chief of Military History, Department of the Army, 432 pp. SD D114.7:C16.

Though the total work concentrates on events after the United States entered the war, the first section provides a good background on the pre-war cooperation between these two nations. Primary sources.

804. Finney, Charles G. (1961). *The Old China Hands*. Garden City, New York: Doubleday and Company, 258 pp.

An account of the Fifteenth Infantry in Tientsin in the 1920s and 1930s, based on the personal experiences of the author. The regiment became involved in the Chinese Civil War and the beginnings of the war between China and Japan. No sources cited.

805. Flint, Roy K. (1980). "The United States Army on the Pacific Frontier, 1899-1939." In Joe C. Dixon, (ed.), *The American Military and the Far East: Proceedings of the Ninth Military History Symposium, United States Air Force Academy, 1-3 October 1980*. Washington, D.C.: United States Air Force Academy, 1980, 139-59. SD D301.78:980.

The paper examines the garrisoning of US positions in Hawaii, the Philippines and China and the impact that this had upon the Army. Among the changes: development of new strategies. No sources cited.

806. Foster, Gaines M. (1981). "Typhus Disaster in the Wake of War: The American-Polish Relief Expedition, 1919-1920." *Bulletin of the History of Medicine, 55,* 221-32.

An example of employing the Army in a quasi-political mission of nation building and health reform. The Relief Expedition provided supplies and technical knowledge to help the new nation meet this health emergency. Primary sources.

807. Fraenkel, Ernst. (1944). *Military Occupation and the Rule of Law: Occupation Government in the Rhineland, 1918-1923*. New York: Oxford University Press, 267 pp.

A detailed account of the occupation of Germany, the prosecution of war criminals, and the relations with the Weimar Government. The author meant the book to provide object lessons for the forthcoming occupation. No sources cited but bibliography included.

808. Herndon, James S., and Baylen, Joseph O. (1975). "Col. Philip R. Faymonville and the Red Army, 1934-43." *Slavic Review, 34,* 483-505.

The first American Military Attaché to the USSR, Faymonville was quite sympathetic to the country. This influenced his reports and made him blind to problems, including the impact of the 1937 purges. Primary sources.

809. Hinkle, Stacy C. (1967). *Wings and Saddles: The Air and Cavalry Punitive Expedition of 1919*. El Paso, Texas: Texas Western Press, 45 pp.

A force of American cavalry moved into Mexico in 1919 in an effort to pursue some bandits and locate some prisoners. They accomplished most of their goals. Primary sources.

810. Hinkle, Stacy C. (1968-1969). "Wings and Saddles: The Air and Cavalry Punitive Expedition of 1919." *Aerospace Historian, 15, No. 4,* 30-36, 44-45 and *16, No. 1,* 28-33.

Hinkle describes a successful chase after some bandits who had captured American flyers in Mexico. The operation involved joint cavalry-air corps work. No sources cited.

811. Lacy, James F. (1977). "Origins of the United States Army Advisory System: Its Latin American Experience, 1922-1941." Dissertation, Auburn University, 38/8-A, p. 5000.

By 1941 there were nine active mission in Latin America. The author suggests that these set precedents for later systems and made a significant contribution to the Good Neighbor Policy as well as helping the nations take an active role in hemispheric defense.

812. Langer, John D. (1976). "The 'Red General': Philip R. Faymonville and the Soviet Union, 1917-52." *Prologue, 8*, 209-221.

This officer believed that the Russians were our natural allies and developed an interest in the nation before World War I. Then in 1919-1920 he was involved in the Siberian expedition. In the 1930s he was our Military Attaché, but was often blinded by his interest in the country. This later led to accusations of disloyalty. Primary sources.

813. Morton, Louis A. (1960). "Army and Marines on the China Station: A Study in Military and Political Rivalry." *Pacific Historical Review, 29*, 51-74.

Command in China was divided between the Army and the Marines with the State Department exercising final authority. This led to a constant tug of war among the three groups and eventually to measures designed to coordinate issues among them. Primary sources.

814. Nelson, Keith L. (1975). *Victors Divided: America and the Allies in Germany, 1918-1923*. Berkeley, California: University of California Press, 441 pp.

An account of why American forces occupied the Rhine region in Germany, what they did, and how this occupation fit into the developing foreign policy of Wilson and Harding. Primary and secondary sources.

815. Onorate, Michael P. (1967). "Leonard Wood and the Philippine Cabinet Crisis of 1923." *Journal of East Asiatic Studies, 11, Part II*, 1-74.

The article describes an incident in the term of office of Wood as Governor-General. There is extensive background on Philippine politics and the role of Wood in those issues. Onorate suggests that Wood was a military leader who had problems when he had to act as a politician. Primary and secondary sources.

816. Onorate, Michael P. (1971). "Governor General Leonard Wood and His Administration: A Reappraisal." *Asian Forum, 3*, 237-44.

A review of different perspectives scholars have taken on the role of Leonard Wood in the Philippines in the 1920s and an analysis of what Wood did based on a close study of a variety of primary sources. The author concludes that Wood really did not run the government, the Filipinos did. Primary sources.

817. Rasmussen, John C., Jr. (1972). "The American Forces in Germany and Civil Affairs, July 1919-January 1923." Dissertation, University of Georgia, 33/19-A, pp. 6849-50.

Creating an administration from scratch, American forces administered a portion of the Rhineland for four years. They won the support of the local population through their supervision of affairs rather than direct control. The lessons learned here were applied when the Americans next occupied Germany after World War II.

818. Stoesen, Alexander R. (1966). "The End of the American Watch on the Rhine." *The Proceedings of the South Carolina Historical Association, 1966,* 18-26.

A brief overview of the occupation, in which both the domestic political reaction and the policies of the American troops in Germany are discussed. One central theme is the continuing conflict with the French occupation leaders. Primary sources.

819. Winkler, Fred H. (1966). "The War Department and Disarmament, 1926-1935." *The Historian, 28,* 426-46.

The disarmament negotiations the US participated in during this period presented the General Staff with a problem: how to adhere to American policy while still maintaining what they felt was an adequate defense force. At times they found themselves in opposition to the State Department and even the President. Primary sources.

POLITICAL ISSUES

820. Alonso, Harriet H. (1986). "'To Make War Legally Impossible': A Study of the Women's Peace Union, 1921-1942." Dissertation, State University of New York at Stony Brook, 47/8-A, pp. 3165-66.

A study of one element of the anti-war movement of the period. They were only able to convince one Congressman to introduce a constitutional amendment against war. Their limited success provide an awareness of the problems facing the anti-war movement.

821. Aubrey, James R., and Comer, Richard L. (1985). "The Maverick as Hero: Military Schools in American Popular Culture." *Air University Review, 26, No. 1,* 98-107.

The authors suggest that one can gain an insight into the popular attitudes toward the military by examining how mavericks at military school are pictured in books and films. Generally the sources had a favorable view of the independent cadet who resisted the pressures of the school. The article includes a list of books and films about military schools.

822. Barthell, Daniel W. (1972). "The Committee on Militarism in Education, 1925-1940." Dissertation, University of Illinois-Urbana, Champaign, 33/10-A, p. 5647.

One aspect of the anti-war movement in this period was the effort to eliminate military training at educational institutions. This organization, founded by pacifists, had a great deal of influence, and succeeded in convincing Congress to reduce appropriations for ROTC. The CME was opposed by such groups as the American Legion and the War Department.

823. Bolt, Ernest C., Jr. (1977). *Ballots Before Bullets: The War Referendum Approach to Peace in America, 1914-1941.* Charlottesville, Virginia: University of Virginia Press, 207 pp.

Proposed prior to World War I, the concept of a war referendum gained popularity again after the conclusion of the war. It was proposed in Congress a number of times, especially in the 1930s in the form of the Ludlow amendment. It reflects a strain of anti-war sentiment deep in American society. Primary and secondary sources.

824. Braeman, John. (1982). "Power and Diplomacy: The 1920's Reappraised." *The Review of Politics, 44*, 342-69.

The author describes the different interpretations of American military and foreign policy in the period and then presents his own view. He feels that the policies adopted were realistic given the world order and power relationships in existence. Secondary sources.

825. Brax, Ralph S. (1979). "When Students First Organized Against War: Student Protest During the 1930's." *New York Historical Society Quarterly, 63*, 228-55.

Student anti-militarism joined together with two left-wing organizations in the 1930s to form the first organized anti-war movements. Though it died out in World War II, it formed the seeds for the protests of the 1960s. Primary sources.

826. Caine, Philip D. (1966). "The American Periodical Press and Military Preparedness During the Hoover Administration." Dissertation, Stanford University, 27/12-A, p. 4189.

The author studied the periodical press to see whether there was any real interest in preparedness and also to examine the relationship between the Hoover administration and the public on the issue. Caine found that the media covered the issue, especially in regards to the disarmament negotiations, but generally ignored the Army. Hoover did little to use the media to influence opinion.

827. Chatfield, Charles. (1971). *For Peace and Justice: Pacifism in America, 1914-1941*. Knoxville, Tennessee: University of Tennessee Press, 447 pp.

A study of the anti-war movement in this time period, including attempts at disarmament, neutrality legislation, and to keep America out of the growing conflict in Europe. The author concludes with an analysis of why the pacifists failed to gain a consensus for their views. Primary sources.

828. Chatfield, Charles. (1972). "Alternative Antiwar Strategies of the Thirties." *American Studies, 13*, 81-93.

The problems of the 1930s split the peace movement over issues of arms limitation, neutrality legislation, and neutral mediation. They failed to unite and neutrality became identified with isolationism. Primary sources.

829. Cottrell, Bob. (1983). "The Social Gospel of Nicholas Comfort." *Chronicles of Oklahoma, 61*, 386-413.

This religious leader at the University of Oklahoma campaigned against the military and war. He attacked the ties between the military and economic problems. Though himself criticized for these attitudes, he publicly persisted. Primary sources.

830. Davis, Roger G. (1970). "Conscientious Cooperators: The Seventh-day Adventists and Military Service, 1860-1945." Dissertation, George Washington University, 31/7-A, p. 3464.

A section of this dissertation describes the pacifism of this movement during the 1930s. They also prepared for non-combatant service by developing a Medical Cadet Corps. By 1941 over 5,000 Adventists had received this form of training.

831. DeBenedetti, Charles. (1972). "Alternative Strategies in the American Peace Movement in the 1920's." *American Studies, 13*, 69-79.
    Peace groups were determined to prevent the recurrence of violence among nations and strove to achieve this through introducing discipline in European politics. They accepted American nationalism and hoped to channel it away from militarism and toward peace. Primary sources.

832. DeBenedetti, Charles. (1978). *Origins of the Modern American Peace Movement, 1915-1929*. Millwood, New York: KTO Press, 281 pp.
    The majority of this major study describes events of the 1920s. The author relates efforts to get the US to join the World Court, to participate in international arbitration, and to ratify the Kellogg-Briand Treaty. The ties between the reform movement and the peace movement are also delineated, as well as the impact of the 1920s on the group. Primary sources.

833. Eagan, Eileen M. (1981). *Class, Culture, and the Classroom: The Student Peace Movement of the 1930s*. Philadelphia: Temple University Press, 319 pp.
    The student movement focused on a number of peace and war issues in this period, including opposition to compulsory ROTC and antagonism to involvement in any future war. The Spanish Civil War caused divisions in the organization and later conflicts did more damage. However the legacy of the movement could be seen in the 1960s. Primary sources.

834. Ehrhart, Robert C. (1975). "The Politics of Military Rearmament, 1935-1940: The President, the Congress, and the United States Army." Dissertation, University of Texas-Austin, 36/10-A, p. 6893.
    The debate was shaped by both the perceptions of the overseas threat and how best to meet it, and the relationship between the Congress, the president, and the military establishment. Though Congress framed the legislation, it was within parameters that the president set. However, by the summer of 1940 there was a broad consensus that rearmament must proceed.

835. Ekirch, Arthur A., Jr. (1956). *The Civilian and the Military*. New York: Oxford University Press, 340 pp.
    A history of antimilitarism in America. There is a description of the efforts to reduce the size of the armed forces, opposition to military education, and the rearmament program. Primary and secondary sources.

836. Eyck, F. Gunther. (1972). "Secretary Stimson and the European War, 1940-1941." *Parameters, 2, No. 1*, 40-51.
    Stimson felt his goal was to prepare the Army for a possible war. He supported aid to Britain, which he felt was buying us time to rearm, the continuation of the draft in 1941, and the expansion of the armaments industry. Primary sources.

837. Girard, Jolyon P. (1974). "Congress and Presidential Military Policy: The Occupation of Germany, 1919-1923." *Mid-America, 56*, 211-20.
    For four years after World War I Presidents Wilson and Harding kept an occupation force in Germany without any Congressional approval. Though Congress protested, it was not until 1923 that the troops were removed, encouraged by a strong resolution of the US Senate. Primary sources.

838. Glen, John M. (1983). "Secular Conscientious Objection in the United States: The Selective Service Act of 1940." *Peace and Change, 9,* 55-71.

The groups opposed to compulsory military service argued successfully for expansion of the conscientious objector provisions from those originally envisioned when the legislation was proposed. Non-religious groups were included and a variety of ways of meeting the obligation were recognized. Primary sources.

839. Griffin, Walter R. (1968). "Louis Ludlow and the War Referendum Crusade, 1935-1941." *Indiana Magazine of History, 64,* 267-88.

This Indiana Representative was the leader in the unsuccessful effort to make declarations of war contingent upon a popular vote. His crusade represents one approach to the issue of war stemming from his analysis of the events leading to World War I and his view of the growing tension overseas. Primary sources.

840. Haglund, David G. (1980). "George C. Marshall and the Question of Military Aid to England, May-June 1940." *Journal of Contemporary History, 15,* 745-60.

In the discussions over military aid, Marshall strongly opposed sending assistance. He wanted to keep resources in order to first build up the American Army. Primary and secondary sources.

841. Hammond, Grant T. (1975). "Plowshares into Swords: Arms Races in International Politics, 1840-1941." Dissertation, Johns Hopkins University, 39/5-A, p. 3115.

Hammond has examined a number of arms races in an effort to define the term and establish some general criteria for them. One such race involved the United States, Japan, Germany, the USSR, and Great Britain between 1938 and 1939.

842. Harrelson, Elmer H. (1971). "Roosevelt and the United States Army, 1937-1940: A Study in Challenge-Response." Dissertation, University of New Mexico, 32/7-A, pp. 3920-21.

A study of how FDR dealt, budgetarily, with the Army, and what forces led him to decide how much to ask for the service. The author suggests that Roosevelt responded to international events by increasing his requests, but that even in 1940, he felt that military assistance would keep the US out of war and thus avoid the need for a major expansion.

843. Harrison, Richard A. (1985). "Testing the Water: A Secret Probe Towards Anglo-American Military Co-operation in 1936." *International History Review, 7,* 214-34.

Secretary of War Woodring suggested to the British War Office that the US and Britain should discuss the common problems of industrial mobilization and tank design. After meetings in both London and Washington the request was withdrawn. The author thinks that FDR used this as a trial balloon to see how cooperation between the two nations would work. Primary sources.

844. Hawkes, James H. (1965). "Antimilitarism at State Universities: The Campaign Against Compulsory ROTC, 1920-1940." *Wisconsin Magazine of History, 49*, 41-54.

The antimilitary groups concentrated on a variety of targets, including getting rid of the poison on the college campuses. The Committee on Militarism in Education was a leader in this effort. Though it succeeded on a few campuses, it was generally unsuccessfully, especially at the land grant institutions. Primary sources.

845. Huntington, Samuel P. (1957). *The Soldier and the State: The Theory and Politics of Civil-Military Relations*. Cambridge, Massachusetts: Belknap Press of Harvard University Press, 534 pp.

In this significant book, Huntington explains the isolation of the military in the interwar period and the way in which the military profession developed in this vacuum. Primary sources.

846. Huntington, Samuel P. (1961). "Equilibrium and Disequilibrium in American Military Policy." *Political Science Quarterly, 76*, 481-502.

A broad ranging article review of American policy and how it is made. One short section describes interwar period. Secondary sources.

847. Huzar, Elias. (1943). "Military Appropriations, 1933-1942." *Military Affairs, 7*, 141-50.

A discussion of what the Army asked for, who determined the figures, and how the final amounts were set. One goal of the article is to try to fix the blame for the Army's lack of preparation in 1941.

848. Huzar, Elias. (1950). *The Purse and the Sword: Control of the Army By Congress Through Military Appropriations 1933-1950*. Ithaca, New York: Cornell University Press, 417 pp.

An analysis of the process whereby Congress determines spending levels for the military, including the proposed budgets and the final appropriations. Huzar compares pre- and post-war situations, and includes suggestions for tighter Congressional control. Primary sources.

849. Jensen, Joan M. (1987). "The Army and Domestic Surveillance on Campus." In Garry D. Ryan and Timothy Nenninger, (ed.), *Soldiers and Civilians; The U. S. Army and the American People*. Washington, D.C.: National Archives and Records Administration, 153-78.

This article concentrates on anti-military, especially anti-ROTC, protests during the 1920s and 1930s and how the War Department reacted to them. Primary sources.

850. Johnson, Charles W. (1968). "The Civilian Conservation Corps: The Role of the Army." Dissertation, University of Michigan, 30/1-A, p. 248.

Despite its opposition to the idea, the Army was given a key role in the CCC. They trained the men, organized the camps, and kept the records for the agency. The program was valuable for the service, however, for it helped train reserve officers and improve the condition of some Army posts.

851. Johnson, Charles W. (1972). "The Army and the Civilian Conservation Corps, 1933-42." *Prologue, 4*, 139-56.

With the creation of the CCC, the Army was unwillingly thrust into a new role--trainer of civilians in peacetime. Forced into abandoning their regular duties, the Army put its resources into developing the CCC. Because of a fear that the Army would use this for military training purposes, the discipline level was minimal. Mainly primary sources.

852. Killigrew, John W. (1960). "The Impact of the Great Depression on the Army, 1929-1936." Dissertation, Indiana University, 21/12, pp. 3759-60.

A study of how the Army reacted to the Depression. Among the topics covered in this dissertation are: manpower targets; training goals; the Army and the CCC; research and development; equipment procurement; and relations with FDR.

853. Lisio, Donald J. (1967). "A Blunder Becomes Catastrophe: Hoover, the Legion, and the Bonus Army." *Wisconsin Magazine of History, 51*, 37-50.

A description of Hoover and his relations with the American Legion after the Bonus marchers were dispersed by the use of force. Though he showed political ineptitude in both instances, they did not become major issues in the election itself. Primary sources.

854. MacCarthy, Esther J. (1977). "The Catholic Periodical Press and Issues of War and Peace: 1914-1946." Dissertation, Stanford University, 38/3-A, p. 1602.

A content analysis of the press to determine attitudes, especially whether the just war theory was accepted. The author found that there differences between lay and official publications, and that there was little opposition to war in the press. Another finding was the similarities with the Jewish press which emphasized service with citizenship.

855. Maddox, Robert J. (1967). "William E. Borah and the Crusade to Outlaw War." *The Historian, 29*, 2200-20.

An account of the motivations and accomplishments of the Idaho senator in his efforts in the 1920s to outlaw war. Maddox also explains why Borah dropped the topic after the Kellogg-Briand Treaty was signed. Primary sources.

856. McNeal, Patricia F. (1974). "The American Catholic Peace Movement 1928-1972." Dissertation, Temple University, 35/6-A, pp. 3645-46.

During the 1920s and 1930s the movement was quite small, but took several organizational forms. One group concentrated on Catholic workers, another organized conscientious objectors. The greatest growth came after World War II.

857. Miller, Robert A. (1973). "The United States Army during the 1930s." Dissertation, Princeton University, 34/8-A, pp. 5069-70.

The 1930s saw a variety of trends in the Army: there were divergences because of differences over national strategic policy; problems caused by budgetary cuts; and difficulties in weapons development because of the budget cuts and policy differences. Most of the bureaucracy was unable to handle these problems.

858. Miller, Robert M. (1956). "The Attitudes of the Major Protestant Churches in America Toward War and Peace, 1919-1929." *The Historian, 19,* 13-38.

These churches supported a reduction in armaments and opposed anything they considered militaristic. They were in agreement with much of American society in these positions. Primary sources.

859. Moellering, Ralph L. (1968). "Some Lutheran Reactions to War and Pacifism, 1917 to 1941." *Concordia Historical Institute Quarterly, 41,* 121-31.

Within some church synods there were some individuals who argued for pacifism and against the concept of a just war, especially after the experiences of World War I. They were also spurred on by the efforts at world peace in the 1920s. However this was just a minority and scarcely present in other synods. Primary sources.

860. Nelson, John K. (1967). *The Peace Prophets: American Pacifist Thought, 1919-1941.* Chapel Hill, North Carolina: University of North Carolina Press, 153 pp.

A series of essays on how the pacifists used their analysis of the causes of war and on their efforts to arrive at universal peace. Mainly based on contemporary periodicals.

861. Peterson, Patti M. (1972). "Student Organizations and the Antiwar Movement in America, 1900-1960." *American Studies, 13,* 131-148.

A survey article with seven pages on the student antiwar movement in the 1920s and 1930s, with emphasis on the latter decade. Primary sources.

862. Powers, Thomas L. (1978) "The United States Army and the Washington Conference, 1921-1922." Dissertation, University of Georgia, 39/6-A, pp. 3781-82.

This is a study of the failure of the Army to influence the formulation of American foreign policy. The Washington Conference dealt with issues central to the Army such as weapons and size of armies. Instead of a unified voice, the Army spoke with many, competing ones. The result was no influence and a treaty which led to budgetary cut-backs and Army isolation.

863. Putnam, Carl M. (1973). "The CCC Experience." *Military Review, 53, No. 9,* 49-62.

A description of the role that the Army took in the operation of the CCC, and the lessons that could be learned from that for future programs. The Army was responsible for training and organizing the group, its first mass mobilization since World War I, but it tried to avoid the idea that it was using the organization as an avenue for militarism. Secondary sources.

864. Salmond, John A. (1967). *The Civilian Conservation Corps, 1932-1942: A New Deal Case Study.* Durham, North Carolina: Duke University Press, 240 pp.

A study of the administration of the CCC, including the role of the Army in the process. The author also discusses the issue of the inclusion of military training as part of the program. Primary sources.

865. Schaffer, Ronald. (1969). "The War Department's Defense of ROTC, 1920-1940." *Wisconsin Magazine of History, 53*, 108-20.

An account of the defense of the program against antimilitary groups and against criticism from college and university officials. The War Department worked through civilian allies and avoided direct confrontations with antimilitarists. Primary sources.

866. Sherraden, Michael W. (1981). "Military Participation in a Youth Employment Program: The Civilian Conservation Corps." *Armed Forces and Society, 7*, 227-45.

The article is an attempt to evaluate the effectiveness of the military in administering the CCC. The author concludes that the Army did an efficient job. At the same time they also used the program to improve the managerial skills of its reserve officers. Primary and secondary sources.

867. Tarr, Curtis W. (1962). "Unification of America's Armed Forces: A Century and a Half of Conflict, 1798-1947." Dissertation, Stanford University, 22/12-A, pp. 4339-40.

After a brief historical introduction, Tarr describes the unification issue during World War II and the post-war period.

868. Trask, David F. (1966). "General Tasker Howard Bliss and the 'Sessions of the World,' 1919." *Transactions of the American Philosophical Society, New Series, 56, Part 8*, 80 pp.

An account of the activities of General Bliss during the negotiations in Versailles leading to the final treaty. He was but one of five plenipotentiaries that Wilson appointed and the only officer. Bliss argued for a democratic Germany and self-determination for the peoples of Europe, but at times found himself in conflict with Wilson and House. Primary and secondary sources.

869. Trotter, Agnes A. (1966). "The Development of Merchants of Death Theory of American Intervention in the First World War, 1914-1937." Dissertation, Duke University, 27/2-A, p. 448.

This study explores the origin and development of the idea that the American munitions industry maneuvered the United States into World War I. The concept was accepted in the 1930s because of the era's anti-business and anti-war attitudes. The groups served as scapegoats for current problems.

870. Walker, Henry P. (1974). "American Isolationism and the National Defense Act of 1920." *Military Review, 44, No. 10*, 14-23.

Though Congress created a sizable Army in the 1920 legislation, post-war isolationism encouraged them to do little to put life into it. They did not appropriate money for the authorized manpower. A number of citizen groups opposed the military itself and most of the general public ignored it. Mainly primary sources.

871. Weinrich, William A. (1971). "Business and Foreign Affairs: The Roosevelt Defense Program, 1937-1941." Dissertation, University of Oklahoma, 32/7-A, p. 3940.

Responding to criticism, some business groups in the late 1930s opposed military expansion and favored isolationism. However, others supported a contrary program and were proponents of Lend-Lease in 1940. Since this sector of society was divided, they really did not influence Roosevelt's policy.

872. Wilson, E. Raymond. (1975). "Evolution of the C.O. Provisions in the 1940 Conscription Bill." *Quaker History, 64*, 3-15.

A discussion of the way in which the provisions of the 1940 Act dealt with the issue of conscientious objectors. The author, who participated in the discussions, also indicates the issues ignored, such as pay for special detached service. Primary sources.

873. Wilson, John R. (1971). "Herbert Hoover and the Armed Forces: A Study of Presidential Attitudes and Policy." Dissertation, Northwestern University, 32/6-A, p. 3234.

Hoover had good relations with the Army and it expanded. He believed in preparedness and desired to preserve the peace. The author calls the resulting policy "economical preparedness through independent internationalism."

874. Wilson, John R. (1974). "The Quaker and the Sword: Herbert Hoover's Relations with the Military." *Military Affairs, 38*, 41-47.

Despite his pacifism, Herbert Hoover had warm relations with his military advisers. Hoover hated war, wanted economy in government, and believed that preparedness would act as a deterrent. When the Depression hit, and international efforts at collective security failed, Hoover was more concerned about economy than military preparedness. Primary sources.

875. Wiltz, John E. (1963). *In Search of Peace: The Senate Munitions Inquiry, 1934-36*. Baton Rogue, Louisiana: Louisiana State University Press, 277 pp.

A description of the forces that led to the Nye Committee investigation, their findings, and the consequences of the hearings. The author argues that the investigation and the concurrent neutrality legislation sprang from similar forces and that the positive results outweighed the negative. Primary sources.

876. Woito, Robert. (1987). "Between the Wars." *Wilson Quarterly, 11*, 108-21.

Focuses on the impact of the peace movement in shaping the policy of the United States, especially in the 1930s. No sources cited.

SOCIAL ISSUES

877. Appling, Gregory B. (1979). "Managing American Warrior-Heroism: Awards of the Congressional Medal of Honor, 1863-1973." Dissertation, Cornell University, 40/9-A, pp. 5190-91.

This sociological study examines the reasons given for the awarding of Congressional Medals of Honor, what they can tell us about the goals of the armed forces in giving them out, and whether these have changed over time. Among other items, the author notes that "rank influences the kinds of behavior for which awardees are decorated."

878. Bodenger, Robert C. (1971). "Soldiers' Bonuses: A History of Veterans' Benefits in the United States, 1776-1967." Dissertation, Pennsylvania State University, 32/11-A, p. 6328.

Assistance to former soldiers has a long history, including continued controversy, and has cost the government a great deal of money. This general survey of the topic incorporates material on this time period, including the issue of "adjusted compensation."

879. Brown, Richard C. (1951). "Social Attitudes of American Generals, 1898-1940". Dissertation, University of Wisconsin. Doctoral Dissertations Accepted by American Universities, 1952, p. 206.

An analysis of the ideas of over 400 individuals who became generals in this time period. The author describes their background and education, the ideas which society imparted to the leaders, and the attempts by military men to assume positions of leadership in society. Primary and secondary sources.

880. Coffman, Edward M., and Herrly, Peter F. (1977). "The American Regular Army Officer Corps Between the World Wars: A Collective Biography." *Armed Forces and Society, 4*, 55-74.

An examination of the officer corps in this period on the following criteria: age, sectional origin, higher education, and enlisted experience. The authors describe the typical officer and his career pattern. Primary sources.

881. Dalfiume, Richard M. (1969). *Desegregation of the U. S. Armed Forces: Fighting on Two Fronts, 1939-1953*. Columbia, Missouri: University of Missouri Press, 252 pp.

Two brief chapters describe the racial situation in the 1920s and 1930s and the battles in 1940-1941 to end segregation within the armed forces. Primary and secondary sources.

882. Dalfiume, Richard M. (1969). "Military Segregation and the 1940 Presidential Election." *Phylon, 30*, 42-55.

An account of the efforts by the black community to have blacks included on an equal basis in the armed services. It became a major issue in the 1940 election and blacks tried to use this to pressure Roosevelt for changes. The results were more surface than real. Primary sources.

883. Daniels, Roger. (1971). *The Bonus March; An Episode of the Great Depression*. Westport, Connecticut: Greenwood Publishing Corporation, 370 pp.

Included in this detailed account are several chapters on the Army and its efforts to move the marchers out of Washington. The author argues strongly that MacArthur caused the Army to evict the marchers with the use of force. Primary sources.

884. Jensen, Joan M. (1983). "All Pink Sisters: The War Department and the Feminist Movement in the 1920s." In Lois Scharf and Joan M. Jensen, (ed.), *Decades of Discontent, The Women's Movement, 1920-1940*. Westport, Connecticut: Greenwood Press, 199-222.

An account of the Women's International League for Freedom and Peace, its efforts against militarism, and the reaction of the War Department to the effort. The process illustrates splits in the women's movement as well as the War Department's reaction to the 1920s peace movement. Primary sources.

885. Johnson, Charles. (1972). "The Army, the Negro and the Civilian Conservation Corps: 1933-1942." *Military Affairs, 36,* 82-88.

Though the black community wanted fairness in the way in which the CCC operated, the military was not really interested in achieving this goal. Some local commanders enforced segregation, others did not. Similarly arguments over adding black officers found the War Department little interested in giving them an opportunity to command. Primary sources.

886. Killigrew, John W. (1962). "The Army and the Bonus Incident." *Military Affairs, 26,* 59-65.

A brief overview of the use of troops and tear gas against supposedly communist led demonstrators in Depression-era Washington. The end result was the dispersal of the people and a lot of unfavorable publicity for the Army. Primary sources.

887. Lisio, Donald J. (1974). *The President and Protest: Hoover, Conspiracy, and the Bonus Riot.* Columbia, Missouri: University of Missouri Press, 346 pp.

A detailed account of the BEF and the military, including the roles of Hurley and MacArthur in the decision to use force. Lisio feels that Hoover took the blame for the poor decisions of the military. Primary sources.

888. McGoff, Kevin. (1978). "The Bonus Army." *American History Illustrated, 12, No. 10,* 28-35.

An account of the BEF, with one page describing how the Army dispersed the marchers. No sources cited.

889. McGuire, Phillip. (1978). "Judge William H. Hastie and Army Recruitment, 1940-1942." *Military Affairs, 42,* 75-79.

A brief article on one aspect of Hastie's effort to get more blacks included in the Army on an integrated basis: his attempt to have the Army use the black press as an advertising medium. Though this particular program failed, he did succeed in bringing in more blacks. Primary sources.

890. Nalty, Bernard C. (1986). *Strength for the Fight; A History of Black Americans in the Military.* New York: The Free Press, 424 pp.

This excellent general history contains a brief chapter on the 1920s and 1930s and the impact of the policy of segregation on blacks. There is also material on the growing black protests about this policy. Primary sources.

891. Parks, Robert J. (1973). "The Development of Segregation in U. S. Army Hospitals, 1940-1942." *Military Affairs, 37,* 145-50.

A description of the largely futile effort before Pearl Harbor to get black physicians into the military hospital system. In the end segregated hospitals were developed as the Army's solution to this particular problem. Primary sources.

892. Patton, Gerald W. (1981). *War and Race: The Black Officer in the American Military, 1915-1941.* Westport, Connecticut: Greenwood Press, 214 pp.

Despite the title, the vast majority of the work deals with World War I. There are three chapters on the efforts of non-Regular Army black officers who served in the war to find a spot in the plans for a future conflict. Primary and secondary sources.

893. Price, John W. (1971). "The Army Evicts the Bonus Marchers." *Military Review, 51, No. 5,* 56-65.

This is an account of the Bonus March and the use of the Army to remove the marchers from Washington. It was an exercise in restoring law and order which led to an excessive use of force. The author places a large part of the blame on General MacArthur. Primary sources.

894. Reddick, L. D. (1949). "The Negro Policy of the United States Army, 1775-1945." *The Journal of Negro History, 34,* 9-29.

The article examines several ideas which the author feels shaped the policy the Army practiced toward blacks. One page deals with the period before World War II, especially 1940-41. Secondary sources.

895. Rich, Bennett M. (1941). *Presidents and Civil Disorder.* Washington, D.C.: Brookings Institution, 235 pp.

A study of the problems that several presidents have encountered with civil disturbances and the use of military force. In this time period this included coal strikes in West Virginia, the Bonus Army and a 1941 strike at North American Aviation. Primary sources.

896. Vivian, James F., and Vivian, Jean H. (1967). "The Bonus March of 1932: The Role of General George Van Horn Moseley." *Wisconsin Magazine of History, 51,* 26-36.

An account of the affair from the perspective of the Deputy Chief of Staff. The authors indicate that the military had a significant role in the decisions, maybe even more than Hoover himself. Primary sources.

897. Weaver, John D. (1963). "Bonus March." *American Heritage, 14, No. 4,* 18-23, 92-97.

A general narrative of the Bonus March itself and the events which led to the Army being used to drive the veterans out of Washington. Weaver makes no real attempt to describe the attitudes within the Army on the use of force. No sources cited.

STRATEGY

898. Atwater, William F. (1986). "United States Army and Navy Development of Joint Landing Operations, 1898-1942." Dissertation, Duke University, 48/5-A, p. 1287.

Building upon the disaster of Gallipoli, the Army and Navy developed a doctrine for landing operations. Though most scholars credit the Marine Corps with this innovation, the author believes that this is overstated and that the Army and Navy contributed as much. He also believes that most of the doctrine that was developed was inadequate.

899. Cerami, Joseph R. (1987). "Training: The 1941 Louisiana Maneuvers." *Military Review, 67, No. 10,* 34-43.

Analysis of the maneuvers and the view of combat they gave potential generals forms the focus of this article. Cerami views the training from the perspective of the lessons it can teach current leaders. Primary sources.

900. Child, John. (1979). "From 'Color' to 'Rainbow': U. S. Strategic Planning for Latin America, 1919-1945." *Journal of Interamerican Studies and World Affairs, 21,* 233-60.

American war plans evolved from considering the area an American lake to the beginnings of bilateral strategy. Multilateral planning was envisioned by the State Department, but not by War and Navy. Primary and secondary sources.

901. Cooling, Benjamin F. (1965). "The Tennessee Maneuvers, June, 1941." *Tennessee Historical Quarterly, 24,* 265-80.

The first maneuvers of the newly reorganized Second Army were held in Tennessee. Notable was the use of armor by Patton and light planes as spotters for artillery. Flaws were observed which were worked on in later maneuvers that year. Primary sources.

902. Cooling, B. Franklin, III. (1967). "The Arkansas Maneuvers, 1941." *Arkansas Historical Quarterly, 26,* 103-22.

This describes the second phase of the maneuvers of the Second Army, leading up to the late 1941 maneuvers in Louisiana. The Arkansas war games involved a number of relatively untested National Guard units. It helped highlight the weaknesses of the divisions and led to further training. Primary sources.

903. Doherty, Thomas. (1985). "Blitzkrieg for Beginners: The Maneuvers of 1940 in Central Wisconsin." *Wisconsin Magazine of History, 68,* 83-107.

In these series of maneuvers, the Wisconsin National Guard tried to show that it was ready for any future conflicts. Old and new methods of transportation and weaponry were tried out and some were found deficient. Primary sources.

904. Dyster, Paul A. (1984). "In the Wake of the Tank: The 20th-Century Evolution of the Theory of Armored Warfare." Dissertation, Johns Hopkins University, 45/3-A, p. 937.

A cross-national examination of the development of the theory and practice of armored warfare. While technological change has been constant, the military has managed to deal with it through a process of "innovation and adaptation."

905. Gabel, Christopher R. (1981). "The U. S. Army GHQ Maneuvers of 1941." Dissertation, Ohio State University, 42/10-A, p. 4553.

After the expansion and training of the Army in 1940-1941, the autumn maneuvers were key tests of progress. They demonstrated problems in armor doctrine and gave higher commanders needed experience. As a result, the US entered the war with a combat-ready Army.

906. Gole, Henry G. (1985). "War Planning at the War College in the Mid-1930s." *Parameters, 15, No. 1,* 52-64.

In the mid-1930s some Army officers began to envision a war scenario with Germany as the chief enemy and the US allied with other nations. Planners at the Army War College began to work on this idea long before it became accepted policy in the RAINBOW plans. This helped planners on the General Staff deal with these issues in the late 1930s. Secondary sources.

907. Greene, Fred. (1961). "The Military View of American National Policy, 1904-1940." *American Historical Review, 66,* 354-76.

Feeling in a vacuum when planning, military leaders articulated their own version of American policy. Especially in the 1930s the planners saw the possibility of a war with Japan arising from a need to defend American interests in the Philippines. Primary sources.

908. Hamburger, Kenneth E. (1986). "The Technology, Doctrine, and Politics of U. S. Coast Defenses, 1880-1945: A Case Study in U. S. Defense Planning." Dissertation, Duke University, 47/8-A, p. 3167.

The author examines the technology of the period, how policy was made, and the role of the professionals and politicians in making policy. Each group was parochial in the process and never was there a "rational and coherent" analysis of threats and technology.

909. House, Jonathan M. (1984). "Designing the Light Division, 1935-44." *Military Review, 64, No. 5,* 39-47.

Beginning with the experiences of World War I, in the post-war period the Army considered a new divisional structure for a future conflict. The thrust of the implemented changes led to a smaller, more concentrated organization, with integrated firepower. The structure was revised during the ensuing war because combat was different than had been envisioned. Secondary sources.

910. Johnsen, William T. (1986). "Forging the Foundations of the Grand Alliance: Anglo-American Military Collaboration, 1938-1941." Dissertation, Duke University, 47/8-A, p. 3158.

Informal staff negotiations prior to American entry into the war set the stage for successful military, political, and economic collaboration after 1941. It was a process that evolved as a result of personal contacts.

911. Kirchner, D. P., and Lewis, E. R. (1968). "American Harbor Defenses: The Final Era." *United States Naval Institute Proceedings, 94, No. 1,* 84-98.

A pictorial essay about the development of American harbor defenses in the 1920s and 1930s, including weapons and fortifications. No sources cited.

912. Larsen, Lawrence H. (1976). "The United States Army's 1919 Contingency Plan to Defend North Dakota Against an Unspecified Invader From Canada." *North Dakota History, 43, No. 4,* 22-27.

An example of military planning in a vacuum. A small group of Engineers developed a plan to defend the US by a variety of means, including invading Canada. Primary sources.

913. Larsen, Lawrence H. (1986). "The 1919 United States Army's Canadian Invasion Plan Revisited." *Heritage of the Great Plains, 19,* 15-22.

An account of Larsen's 1976 article and the public reaction to it in the United States and Canada. Primary sources.

914. Lewis, Emanuel R. (1970). *Seacoast Fortifications of the United States: An Introductory History.* Washington, D.C.: Smithsonian Institution Press, 145 pp.

A brief history of coastal fortifications. One chapter describes the interwar building program. Numerous photographs greatly supplement the text. Primary and secondary sources.

915. Matloff, Maurice. (1966). "The American Approach to War, 1919-1945." In Michael Howard, (ed.), *The Theory and Practice of War: Essays Presented to Captain B. H. Liddell Hart on His Seventieth Birthday*. New York: Frederick A. Praeger, 213-43.

A discussion of American war planning. Between 1919 and 1939 it centered on defense of the US and the Pacific. In the 1939-1941 period the planners were much more realistic in terms of coalition warfare and the impact of modern technology. Secondary sources.

916. May, Ernest R. (1955). "The Development of Political-Military Consultation in the United States." *Political Science Quarterly, 70*, 161-80.

This is a description of interwar efforts at coordination, especially under FDR and the Standing Liaison Committee. Primary sources.

917. McGlasson, W. D. (1980). "Mobilization 1940: The Big One." *National Guard, 34, No. 8*, 10-23.

An account of the call-up of the National Guard in September 1940, including anecdotes of the experiences of individual Guardsmen. No sources cited.

918. McGlasson, W. D. (1981). "The Great '41 Maneuvers." *National Guard, 35, No. 10*, 10-13, 36, 38.

From the general to the particular, this account of the various levels of maneuvers covers them all in brief fashion. Stories from Guardsmen illustrate the problems, such as lack of weapons, facing those participating in this last pre-war test of the Army. No sources cited.

919. Morton, Louis. (1959). "War Plan ORANGE: Evolution of a Strategy." *World Politics, 11*, 221-50.

The defense of the Philippines against Japan was accepted as a joint Army-Navy problem. However the services had difficulty agreeing on what each should do. The process was also affected by the Washington Naval Treaty, and later the unwillingness of the nation to assume an offensive posture in the Far East. Primary sources.

920. Morton, Louis A. (1960). "National Policy and Military Strategy." *Virginia Quarterly Review, 36*, 1-17.

Discussion of this issue with several examples including the evolution of American policy toward the defense of the Philippines in the 1920s and 1930s and War Plan ORANGE. No sources cited.

921. Morton, Louis. (1962). "Interservice Co-operation and Political-Military Collaboration, 1900-38." In Harry L. Coles, (ed.), *Total War and Cold War: Problems in Civilian Control of the Military*. Columbus, Ohio: Ohio State University Press, 131-60.

Cooperation and conflict between the Army, the Navy, and the State Department are the central focus of this essay. Though much of the time there was little coordination, in the immediate period before World War II this process reversed itself, especially on an informal level. Primary and secondary sources.

922. Murray, G. Patrick. (1972). "The Louisiana Maneuvers: Practice for War." *Louisiana History, 13*, 117-38.
Several months before we entered the war, the Army staged large scale war games involving the Second and Third Armies. With little prearranged they were a real test of command and technology. Lessons of a political and military nature were learned. Primary sources.

923. Preston, Richard A. (1974). "Buster Brown Was Not Alone: American Plans for the Invasion of Canada, 1919-1939." *Canadian Defence Quarterly, 3, No. 4*, 47-58.
A discussion of planning, both on the Canadian and American sides, of a hypothetical war between the two countries. Though the Canadian plans were done by one man in the early 1920s, students at the American Army War College continued to make such plans into the 1930s. Primary sources.

924. Preston, Richard A. (1974). "Buster Brown Was Not Alone--A Postscript." *Canadian Defence Quarterly, 4, No. 1*, 11-12.
The author updates his previous article with material from the General Staff indicating their level of planning. The Americans assumed that Canada would participate in a war with Great Britain against the US. Primary sources, though not cited specifically.

925. Schaffer, Ronald. (1973). "General Stanley D. Embick: Military Dissenter." *Military Affairs, 37*, 89-95.
During the 1920s and 1930s General Embick was a formulator of strategy and an advocate of a limited defense perimeter, a position which often put him at odds with the rest of the military leadership. In his view, Hawaii and the Philippines were not the keys to America's defense. Primary and secondary sources.

926. Vinson, J. Chalmers. (1957). "Military Force and American Policy, 1919-1939." In Alexander DeConde, (ed.), *Isolation and Security: Ideas and Interests in Twentieth-Century American Foreign Policy*. Durham, North Carolina: Duke University Press, 56-81.
A discussion of this period in terms of: the failure of efforts to coordinate military and diplomatic policy; the attitudes of Americans toward the use of force; and the background to the Ludlow war referendum amendment. Bibliographic notes.

927. Watson, Mark S. (1950). *Chief of Staff: Prewar Plans and Preparations (United States Army in World War II: The War Department)*. Washington, D.C.: Historical Division, Department of the Army, 551 pp. SD D114.7:W19/v. 1.
This significant volume presents a number of key issues in the interwar period, centered on the Chief of Staff level of the Army. These include: the role of the General Staff; rearmament and its objectives; arming of the Allies in 1940; and the coordination between foreign policy and military preparedness. Primary sources.

928. Weigley, Russell F. (1973). "The Role of the War Department and Army." In Dorothy Borg and Shumpei Okamoto with Dale K. A. Finlayson, *Pearl Harbor as History; Japanese-American Relations, 1931-1941*. New York: Columbia University Press, 165-88.

This essay examines the military's lack of interest in foreign affairs and the impact that this had on civilian policy planning. Weigley also discusses the strategy of holding the Philippines despite the knowledge of many that they were indefensible. Primary and secondary sources.

929. Weigley, Russell F. (1981). "Shaping the American Army of World War II: Mobility Versus Power." *Parameters, 11, No. 3*, 13-21.

During the 1920s and 1930s the Army still remained oriented toward a border constabulary with horses playing a significant role. On the other hand, the Civil War had provided a tradition of power in the use of force. These two concepts underlay the debates of the interwar period on the future of the Army. Mainly secondary sources.

930. Wheeler, Gerald E. (1969). "National Policy Planning between the World Wars: Conflict between Ends and Means." *Naval War College Review, 21, No. 6*, 54-69.

Beginning with a discussion of the background of the period, the author explains the ideas that shaped the military planning of the 1920s and 1930s. He contrasts the Army and the Navy efforts in this area. One major conclusion is that the planners and the nation should have some agreement on what the national goals are. No sources cited.

931. Wilson, John B. (1983). "Mobility versus Firepower: The Post-World War I Infantry Division." *Parameters, 13, No. 3*, 47-52.

Based on different interpretations of World War I experiences, the Army debated whether they should emphasize mobility or firepower. The result was a decision to create a division oriented toward firepower. Primary sources.

932. Woolley, William J. (1985). "Patton and the Concept of Mechanized Warfare." *Parameters, 15, No. 3*, 71-80.

In the interwar period there was a debate over the use of the internal combustion engine and its role in warfare. Studying the changes in Patton's attitudes in this period gives an insight into how officers dealt with these issues. The author concludes that Patton's service with tanks helped influenced his thinking, but that he viewed mechanization within a traditional framework. Primary sources.

TECHNOLOGY

933. Addington, Larry H. (1976). "The U. S. Coast Artillery and the Problem of Artillery Organization, 1907-1954." *Military Affairs, 40*, 1-6.

The realities of World War I posed a threat to the Coast Artillery, which was only partially resolved in the National Defense Act of 1920. The mission of the Corps and its relation to the other branches would continue to be debated for the next several decades. Primary and secondary sources.

934. Batchelor, John, and Hogg, Ian V. (1972). *Artillery*. New York: Charles Scribner's Sons, 158 pp.

A brief section details the progression of artillery in the period between the wars, especially the impact of World War I on American developments. No sources cited.

935. Batchelor, John, and Hogg, Ian V. (1973). *Rail Gun*. New York: Charles Scribner's Sons, 61 pp.

Several pages of this lavishly illustrated work describes American railway weapons, most of which came out of the World War I experience. Many were used in coastal defense installations. No sources cited.

936. Beaver, Daniel R. (1983). "Politics and Policy: The War Department Motorization and Standardization Program for Wheeled Transport Vehicles, 1920-1940." *Military Affairs, 47*, 101-108.

The author uses the procurement of trucks to indicate how policy, often ineffective, shaped the development of technology. Arguments within and without the Army arose over who should design the trucks, the level of standardization, and the types for each branch. Primary and secondary sources.

937. Brophy, Leo P., and Fisher, George J. B. (1959). *The Chemical Warfare Service: Organizing for War (United States Army in World War II, The Technical Services)*. Washington, D.C.: Office of the Chief of Military History, Department of the Army, 498 pp. SD D114.7:C42/v.1

Two chapters describe the World War I experiences and the gas warfare developments in the interwar period. There is a discussion of the issue of chemical warfare and the attitudes toward it inside the military and in the government. Primary sources.

938. Campbell, Clark S. (1957). *The '03 Springfield*. Beverly Hills, California: Fadco Publishing Co. 344 pp.

This detailed work describes the history, construction, and production of this famous Army weapon, which after World War I continued to be produced. Campbell also describes, and illustrates, the weapon and its numerous accessories.

939. Cary, Norman M., Jr. (1980). "The Use of the Motor Vehicle in the United States Army, 1899-1939." Dissertation, University of Georgia, 41/4-A, p. 1730.

Though the Army began to use motor vehicles early in the century, the major expansion came after World War I. By 1939 the horse and mule were almost totally gone. This dissertation details how the Army, despite handicaps, such as bureaucratic infighting, adapted technology to the military needs.

940. Gabel, Christopher R. (1984). "Evolution of US Armor Mobility." *Military Review, 64, No. 3*, 54-63.

During the 1930s two trends emerged in the Army: the mechanized forces added armor, which increased protection but reduced tank mobility; the antitank units reduced the firepower of their weapons to increase their mobility. The experiences of World War II indicate that the mechanization advocates had pursued the proper course. Primary sources.

941. Gillie, Mildred H. (1947). *Forging the Thunderbolt: A History of the Development of the Armored Force*. Harrisburg, Pennsylvania: Military Service Publishing Company, 330 pp.
  About half of this work details the developments in the 1920s and 1930s. Since the book is based on the papers of General Chaffee, it naturally focuses on him. Issues discussed include mechanization, the role of the Cavalry, and the contributions of Walter Christie.

942. Gourley, Scott R. (1985). "The Westervelt Board." *Field Artillery Journal*, 53, No. 5, 27-29.
  An account of a post-war Army board convened to study the future of the artillery. They recommended weapons and a plan for motorization. This influenced developments in the next decades. No sources cited.

943. Grow, Robert W. (1987). "The Ten Lean Years; From the Mechanized Force (1930) To the Armored Force (1940). *Armor, 96, No. 1*, 22-30 and 96, No. 2, 25-33.
  Based on his own personal experiences, the author has written an account of the development of mechanization and mobility in the Army during the Depression. He explores the opposition from some elements in the service and the mechanical problems of the equipment. No sources cited.

944. Hacker, Barton C. (1982). "Imaginations in Thrall: The Social Psychology of Military Mechanization, 1919-1939." *Parameters, 12, No. 1*, 50-61.
  A cross-national examination of the words individuals used to characterize tanks and tank warfare. Primary sources.

945. Harstad, Peter T., and Fox, Diana J. (1975). "Dusty Doughboys on the Lincoln Highway: The 1919 Army Convoy in Iowa." *The Palimpset, 56*, 66-87.
  A description of the convoy, its origins, and its impact on Iowa. The experience pointed out the deficiencies of the road system as it then existed and the possibilities for the future. Through Eisenhower, who was a part of the convoy, it laid the groundwork for the much later interstate highway system. General list of sources used.

946. Heiberg, H. H. D. (1976). "Organize a Mechanized Force." *Armor, 85, No. 5*, 8-11, 48-51.
  An account of the development of a mechanized group in the Army in the 1930s. The article includes descriptions of the group's equipment and the role of General Chaffee. No sources listed.

947. Hofmann, George F. (1973). "The Demise of the U. S. Tank Corps and Medium Tank Development Program." *Military Affairs, 37*, 20-25.
  An illustration of the conflict in the 1920s as to whether tanks should be used independently or as an adjunct to the Infantry. Also an example of how bureaucratic politics shapes weapons programs. Primary sources.

948. Hofmann, George F. (1973). "Tactics vs Technology--The US Cavalry Experience." *Armor, 82, No. 5*, 10-14.
  Debates in the post-war era concerned the future of the Cavalry and how its tactics could be used by motorized vehicles. The addition of light vehicles and tanks to the Cavalry in the end of the decade accentuated the arguments. World War II resolved the issue in favor of mechanization. No sources cited.

949. Hofmann, George F. (1975). "A Yankee Inventor and the Military Establishment: The Christie Tank Controversy." *Military Affairs, 39*, 12-18.

A conflict between an individual inventor and the committee approach to military ordnance development during the 1920s and 1930s. Also involved were different views within the Army as to how to use tanks. While the Cavalry and Infantry were interested, the Ordinance Department did not like the way in which the vehicle was developed. Primary sources.

950. Hofmann, George F. (1986). "The Troubled History of the Christie Tank." *Army, 36, No. 5*, 54-65.

Private entrepreneur and innovator versus the US Army, suggests the author, is one way to look at the military's attempt to develop a convertible tank in the 1920s and 1930s. However, he notes that most of the problems developed from Christie's inability to meet the needs of the Army. No sources cited.

951. Hogg, Ian V. (1974). *A History of Artillery*. London, England: Hamlyn Publishing Group Ltd., 240 pp.

A chapter describes the impact of World War I on artillery development and its manifestations in the next two decades. The work includes coast defense weapons, anti-aircraft guns, and artillery pieces attached to the Army. No sources cited.

952. Hogg, Ian V. (1980). *Armour in Conflict: The Design and Tactics of Armoured Fighting Vehicles*. New York: Jane's, 208 pp.

Though most of the work details tanks in war situations, one chapter describes the interwar period and developments in the US and overseas. Emphasis is on theory of tank use more than actual construction. Secondary sources.

953. Ickes, Harry E. (1951). "The Development of the 60-inch Antiaircraft Searchlight by the United States Army." Dissertation, University of Pittsburgh. Doctoral Dissertations Accepted by American Universities, 1950-1951, p. 50.

Ickes describes the experiences of the war on searchlight construction and use and how attempts were made in the interwar period to make improvements in light sources and reflectors. It was seen as a key weapon in anti-aircraft programs.

954. Jones, Ralph E., Rarey, George H., and Icks, Robert J. (1933). *The Fighting Tanks Since 1916*. Washington, D.C.: National Service Publishing Company, 325 pp.

An early work describing the use and development of tanks during and after World War I. The American aspects are brief, with twenty pages on the tanks of the period. The authors suggest that while the future is unclear as to which direction tank developments will go, they will be an important component of any future conflict. No sources cited.

955. Kelly, Vicki L. (1976). "In the Shadow of Fame: The San Jacinto Ordnance Depot, 1939-1964." *Military History of Texas and the Southwest, 13*, 39-45.

An account of the development and role of the depot, concentrating on World War II and later. No sources listed.

956. Kemeny, Jim. (1983). "Professional Ideologies and Organizational Structure: Tanks and the Military." *European Journal of Sociology, 24*, 223-40.

An analysis of the evolution of tank doctrine in three countries including the United States, the interplay between different levels of command, and the way in which the final results were derived. Secondary sources.

957. Macksey, Kenneth. (1981). *The Tank Pioneers*. New York: Jane's, 228 pp.

A multi-national approach, noting the inter-action between developers in Britain, Germany, and the United States. One chapter details the work of Walter Christie and his relations with the Army, while another describes the 1930s and Chaffee's efforts. Secondary sources.

958. Macksey, Kenneth, and Batchelor, John H. (1970). *Tank: A History of the Armoured Fighting Vehicle*. London: Macdonald & Co., 160 pp.

Included in this detailed study, profusely illustrated with vivid drawings, is information on the tanks that Walter Christie designed and other 1930s American vehicles, many of which were throwbacks to older, discarded designs. No sources cited.

959. McKenney, Janice E. (1978). "More Bang for the Buck in the Interwar Army: The 105-mm Howitzer." *Military Affairs, 42*, 80-86.

During the interwar period the Artillery attempted to balance mobility and firepower. The discussions over the adoption of the 105-mm howitzer are a case study of how these decisions were made or rather not made. Discussions within the Army, with Congress, and the impact of foreign events are considered. Primary sources mainly.

960. Miller, Edward G. (1985). "Armor's First Struggle." *Armor, 94, No. 2*, 13-17.

A brief account of the development of US armor doctrine and the establishment of the Armor branch between the wars. Arguments developed over whether tanks were to be separate or a support for infantry. Doctrine and technology were divergent, which created problems for the forces in World War II. Few sources cited.

961. Mountcastle, John W. (1979). "Trial By Fire: U. S. Incendiary Weapons, 1918-1945." Dissertation, Duke University, 40/4-A, p. 2228.

Though the US Chemical Warfare Service had begun development of flame weapons during World War I, they abandoned them shortly after the end of the war. When World War II renewed a need for such weapons, they had to begin anew. The majority of this dissertation thus deals with World War II.

962. Nenninger, Timothy K. (1969). "The Development of American Armor 1917-1940, Part II: The Tank Corps Reorganized." *Armor, 78, No. 2*, 34-38.

A description of the evolution and stagnation of the Tank Corps in the 1920s. Though officers discussed the proper utilization of tanks, there was little development because of budgetary constraints.

963. Nenninger, Timothy K. (1969). "The Development of American Armor 1917-1940, Part III: The Experimental Mechanized Forces." *Armor, 78, No. 3,* 33-39.

Following the British example, in the late 1920s the Americans began to develop a separate mechanized force. In 1930 this force participated in a series of maneuvers, but later in the year MacArthur ordered it disbanded and told the Infantry and Cavalry to mechanize individually. Primary and secondary sources listed for this and Part II.

964. Nenninger, Timothy K. (1969). "The Development of American Armor 1917-1940, Part IV: A Revised Mechanization Policy." *Armor, 78, No. 5,* 45-49.

During the 1930s the Infantry and Cavalry cautiously began to mechanize. Many officers, especially in the Cavalry, were opposed. Budgetary constraints also limited experimentation. Debate began over the proper use of tanks and their armor weights. Primary and secondary sources.

965. Nofi, Albert A. (1973). "Mechanized Warfare: Experiment and Experience, 1935-40." *Strategy and Tactics, November 1973,* 5-14.

An overview of efforts to integrate tanks and infantry into battle plans and the outcome of this process in the first years of the war. Written to accompany a combat simulation game. One section describes the American efforts. No sources listed.

966. Ogorkiewicz, Richard M. (1968). *Design and Development of Fighting Vehicles.* Garden City, New York: Doubleday, 208 pp.

A brief section provides the historical background of such vehicles, though the major thrust of the work is current vehicles and their design. Secondary sources.

967. Ogorkiewicz, Richard M. (1970). *Armoured Forces: A History of Armoured Forces and their Vehicles.* New York: Arco, 475 pp.

There are sections on developments, in the 1920s and 1930s, of American tanks and their organizational structure. In addition there is information on different kinds of equipment and its problems. Bibliography of secondary sources.

968. Rothenberg, Gunther E. (1986). "The 1919 U. S. Army Transcontinental Motor Convoy." *Indiana Military History Journal, 11, No. 2,* 9-21.

Based upon wartime experiences with motor transportation and a feeling that conflict with Japan was possible, the Army decided to try to move equipment to the West Coast by motor vehicles. Those pushing a highway building program also supported the effort. Two documents included. Primary sources.

969. Swain, Donald C. (1967). "Organization of Military Research." In Melvin Kranzberg and Carroll W. Pursell, Jr., (ed.), *Technology in Western Civilization, Volume II: Technology in the Twentieth Century.* New York: Oxford University Press, 535-48.

Developments in military research began to slow down after World War I, but were reenergized in the late 1930s. A new level was reached in 1940 with the creation of the National Defense Research Committee. No sources cited.

970. Terrett, Dulany. (1956). *The Signal Corps: The Emergency (To December 1941) (United States Army in World War II, The Technical Services)*. Washington, D.C.: Office of the Chief of Military History, Department of the Army, 383 pp. SD D114.7:Si2/v.1.

An account of the development of the Signal Corps in the interwar period, especially in 1940-41. Among the topics considered is the development of radar and portable radios as well as the role of the Corps in relation to the ground forces and the Air Forces. Primary sources.

971. Wik, Reynold M. (1980). "The American Farm Tractor as Father of the Military Tank." *Agricultural History, 54,* 126-33.

A description of two military developments coming out of the early Caterpillar tractors: their use to pull large artillery pieces and the inspiration they gave to the developers in England of the tank. The author also makes clear how reluctant the Army was to mechanize. Primary sources.

INDEX

About the Author

MARVIN FLETCHER is Professor of History at Ohio University and author of *The Black Soldier and Officer in the United States Army, 1891-1917.*